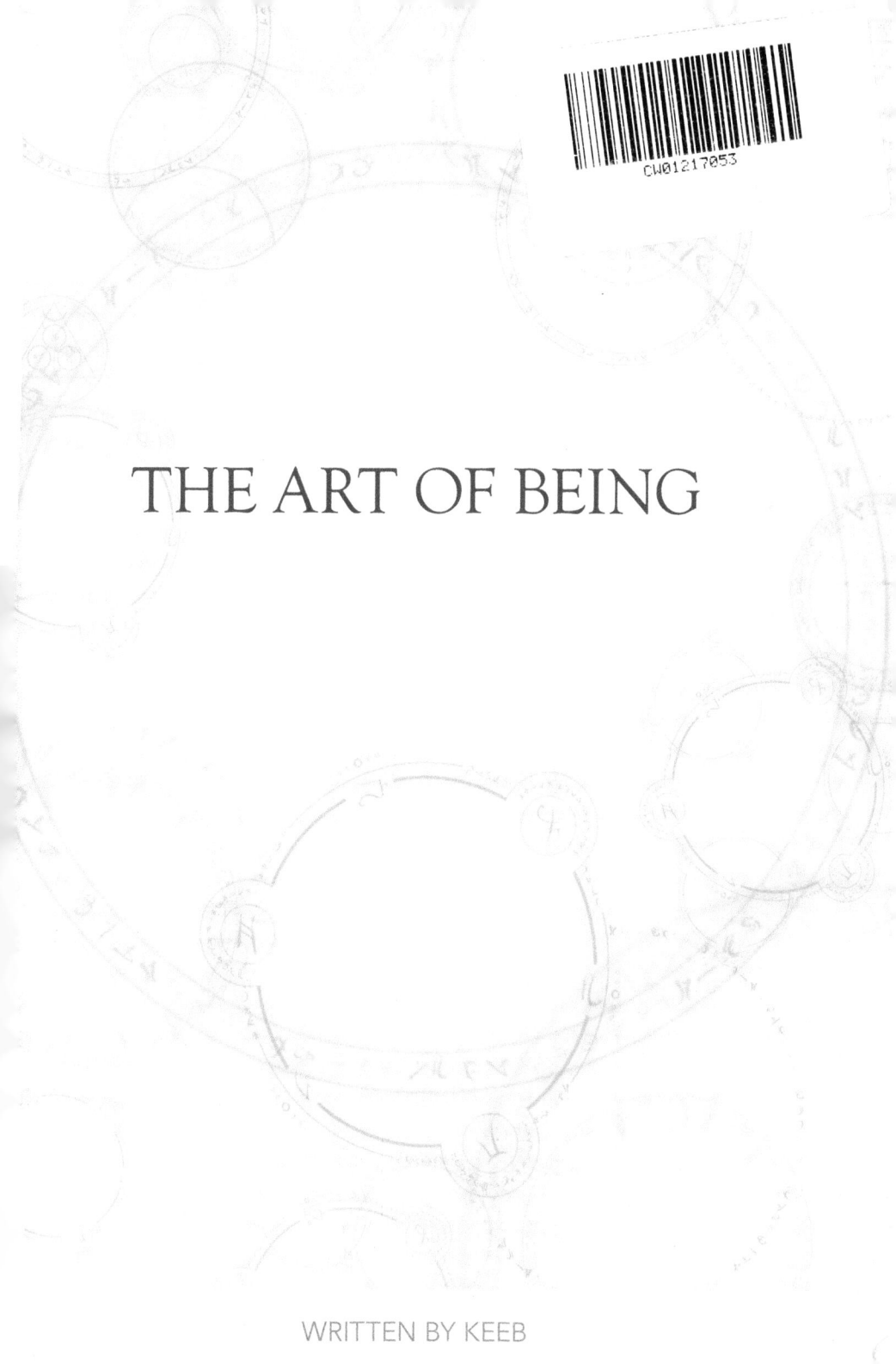

THE ART OF BEING

WRITTEN BY KEEB

The Art Of Being

First Published in the United Kingdom in 2012 by Keeb Publishing Ltd.

Copyright © Keeb 2012. All rights reserved.

Keeb has asserted his right under the Copyright, Designs and Patent Act 1988 to be identified as the author of this work.

ISBN 978-0-9572654-0-0

No part of this book may be used or reproduced in any manner whatsoever without written permission except in the case of brief quotations embodied in critical articles and reviews. For information contact Keeb Publishing Ltd. via the contact page on www.keeb.co.uk

Edited by T.F.K. St Clair-Ford

Layout by Catie:Lou catielou.design@gmail.com

Printed in the United Kingdom by MPG Biddles Limited

Contents

Preface		*v*
Introduction		1
1	Can Thought Ever be Free?	9
2	Dependency vs. Intelligence	33
3	The Way of the Buddha	63
4	Buddha's Message	85
5	Your True Nature	117
6	Only Love Dispels Hate	149
7	Good & Evil	175
8	Fundamental AMness	195
9	Sensation	215
10	Desire	235
11	Desire: A Deeper Look	263
12	Meekness is Most Powerful	285
13	Love & Forgiveness	305
14	Quality of Stillness	349

Preface

Q. *Tell us a bit about yourself?*

A. 'Should I? I don't mean to be terse, brutal or unkind with my response here but why is this question so important? Is it so that you can have a relationship with the image that I (or others) present of myself? Are you assessing me to see if we share the same values – the left, the right or political centre? Am I a communist, a socialist, a free market man? Perhaps you want to know if I follow a system like Hinduism, Buddhism, Judaism or Christianity ... or whether I proffer a particular philosophical school of thought? My answer to these questions is very simple: can a man of understanding ever follow a system? Should he identify with a certain point of view, assert and tender it as so many have done across the centuries? The answer is really rather obvious. Institutions have destroyed human minds, disrupted their very pattern of survival; it is intrinsic to the information an institution will generate. Systems have destroyed human minds; to obey is the greatest of mistakes. If I answer your question, and we disagree, conflict becomes inevitable. That is an obvious fact. To see and see clearly one must be free of conflict and contradiction altogether. One must be free of the endless chitter chatter and bondage of the mind. One must be able to put the views of oneself, and those of humanity, aside for a moment so that there is deep stillness and clarity. If I propose an 'ism' – religious, philosophical or otherwise – surely in doing this I am denying the very nature of Truth?

Am I an educated man, am I qualified? How have I been trained in my work? These questions are all rather superficial, aren't they? Does education, as we understand it today, bring about freedom? Can a guru bring you to freedom, or does freedom come to you only once there is self-knowledge? What is freedom and do we understand it? Now that would be a better question. A consciousness that asserts itself as free, or is even aware of its own freedom, is not free. There is no such thing as freedom *from* something. Please, think this out for yourself.

Perhaps if we share the same values you will then examine my work to see if it fits with your existing evaluations. Can there be understanding when the mind is comparing and evaluating according like or dislike? To make Truth a matter of personal opinion, the result of choice, is to turn it into a means of gratification. What you find may be satisfying, pleasing to you, but please do not call it Truth. You cannot choose Truth. It is 'what is' irrespective of your choice or preference. Comparison between what this philosopher or that guru said, according to like or dislike, according to opinion and therefore pleasure, must be dropped if Truth is to be. Is Truth the Word, a theory, a dogma, an 'ism'? If you try to find out about a teacher before listening to his or her words, you are simply looking to reinforce your existing identifications. If you and he (or she) don't share the same values you naturally hold an aversion to that person. Perhaps they have no values whatsoever. What then? Remember that the key to Right Action is action that is free from idea; this brings you to love (as we explained in detail in the book *Question Mark*).

Most of us cultivate a reader-author relationship based upon pleasure. We read for pleasure, and there's nothing wrong with that. But a book of integrity is not about pleasure or my fancy or your fancy, it is about our relationship to Truth. Relationship based upon like or dislike is what we do all the time in our friendships, in our interpersonal relationships but it is of no use here. A relationship based on sharing, on looking and investigating together is what is required. Then together we are practicing the art of investigation.

Most of us have relationship with images of each other. These images are how we each like to present ourselves to the world. We also have relationship with ourselves merely self-projected onto others – like, *I have my view and I wish to convince you of that. If we agree I like you and if we don't I hate you.* Ask yourself if it's really any different to this. Do we observe and share time with others without the distorting interpretations of the 'me', interpretations that are satisfying to the self? What a different world it would be if this was the case. Do we look without judgement or comparison? Can we be free of all measurement with each other and thus avoid conflict with one another? A person of understanding must ask these questions. The sad truth of the human condition is that we like some but not others. The question which we began with is a familiar reflection of this process. Our love or affection is conditional and we make it a product of thought, attaching various and binding criteria to our time and attention. We read to get something out of it, a reward or some kind of incentive. Is Truth a reward?

We are selective, we choose (either in person or as a reader) to be with those who reinforce our identity and thus give us satisfaction. We steer clear of those who disturb us. We refuse to grow because we do not like to be disturbed. Our aversion causes us to avoid 'what is', what is taking place in and around us, and then we fear 'what might be'. Our desire not to be disturbed is even translated into our search for Truth, our preferred guru, philosopher or scientist if you like. This is why the New Age movement is so terribly toxic. We like those teachers who make us feel better, each superficially seeking more, without ever addressing the foul and foolish within. An authentic teacher will encourage investigation into all aspects of life but many will shy away because they feel deeply shaken. Can the attention of love ever be this divisive, this selective? Can it be exclusive and based on usage in this way or is love non-exclusive, free, non-binding, unconditional, indivisible? If I tell you 'who I am', you will no doubt evaluate me according to your preferences and ideas. Surely it is because we live through images of each other that there is no authentic relationship in this world. And without relationship, with others and within ourselves, Truth cannot be. So please, don't worry about who I am – focus on who you are.'

introduction
Beware of the Master

Beware of the Master

IF YOU LOOK AT THE teachings of genuine masters more closely, all relate to self-knowledge. In this approach, they point to the development of one's own understanding rather than adherence to a set of rules. They encourage you to look into your aloneness, to look into your ideas about death, to look into your feelings of insufficiency and to understand these fears and their consequences. An investigation into attachment to a person, to an ideal, to a system, to a reward or to an idea of 'what should be' rather than 'what is' will show that such attachments are always rooted in fear. It is only because of our fears that we form attachments. See that your attachment gives you comfort, for without that comfort you are lost; you form attachment so that you do not feel lost. All activity of this kind is rooted in the fear of loneliness, of insufficiency and of death – which is all, at heart, the same kind of fear. To understand our selves, we must understand our fears. All derive from our sense of separation from existence.

In response to this fear, you take on a direction of thought in the form of a clinging, a craving or a motive because you feel isolated from existence and you wish to alleviate this inward fear. In response to your fear you seek permanence in a universe that is impermanent. It does not matter what you are attached to – God, enlightenment or the leaving of a legacy – it is all a search for permanence. You may be attached to your name, your wife, your family or your current consciousness; whatever it is, know that behind it will be this quest for continuity. You then put your trust in thought or in systems of thought to try to overcome the problem. Thought strives, thought prays, thought gets caught up in various systems and all the time it is moving in these directions it is forever building a wall around itself. Thus, thought becomes increasingly isolated. Thought is limited and divisive; its action is separating but it never realises this. Thought comes from memory, from language, from the past and what is past can only ever be limited. It is our failure to recognise the limitation of thought that drives all human fear, indeed all human behaviour, including attachment. Understand that if you are attached to Jesus, to Buddha, to your guru or to your belief system then there is only one area to start your investigation: fear.

Remember that masters are not gods, they are our equals. A genuine master will stimulate your own realisations; he walks you through the processes of your own mind to bring forward latent wisdom and goodness within. His wisdom will resonate deep within your heart, penetrating you so that you form your own understanding rather than take on his – or any other – understanding. If he is teaching you his idea of virtue or of truth, then these will be borrowed ideas. There is no need to teach virtue; you can only uncover the inherent virtue and goodness that is already within you. This is how you know if someone's teachings are true. It is not something that you need to intellectually analyse; you will know intuitively. There will be no doubt.

The sign of a genuine master is one who warns you against becoming attached to his teachings. A genuine master would never invite followers or devotees to become attached to his system, knowing that as soon as we do we cling to his every word in a dangerously literal sense; we become attached to his methods and these methods start to take over. His method becomes law, his method soon possesses us, and all method is a movement in a particular pre-set direction. When you are moving in a pre-set direction you are moving towards a fixed goal and there is always the danger of becoming attached to that goal. If you are attached to a goal you are no longer free. Even your motivation to become free prevents you from being free. Your motive is the striving for a goal and any striving for a goal is attachment. We wish to escape attachment because we can see that attachment brings suffering, but if we are operating within just another field of attachment – that being the reward we seek, offered in exchange for obedience, offered in the name of enlightenment – then what, fundamentally, has changed? We want to be just like the master, we ache for the reward that the master speaks of but whilst we depend upon him there is fear. You are no longer investigating for yourself and until your thinking and your exploring is yours, you cannot come to Truth. You have to be a light unto yourself, as they say. Buddha says, use his methods if you want to get started but once up and running, drop them. It is like using a canoe to get across the river, once you are over you needn't carry the canoe with you, it is heavy and it will drag you down, so abandon it! No matter how effective the methods were to get you across, they become a distraction and the distraction can soon turn into a burden. You are not free if you are burdened. You will never be free if you think you have to get across to the other shore; in reality there is no other shore, it is simply a creation of your own mind. Start here, start near and then you will go far.

In strict method arises authority and in authority there is no love. You may look up to the master, but by doing so you are creating a comparison between yourself and the master. Your admiration clouds your ability to grow. In comparing yourself to others there is a lack of love for the self, for love has no hierarchy. And comparison is a distraction. If the mind is occupied it is not still. Without stillness there is no direct perception.

This love for the master, this love for the guru encouraged by so many cults and religions, is not love at all; it is nothing more than a relationship built upon ideas of gain. It is like a business arrangement and the profit from this arrangement is your idea of reward. You are dependent because you want the reward and fear that you might not achieve it. How can you be free if you do not see that your dependency arises because of fear? Can you not see that your feelings of insufficiency are strengthened when you worship and adore another? If you are looking up to one, are you not looking down upon another? Ask yourself this question and be truly honest with your answer. Take time to examine the motivations behind your attachment to spiritual groups or to a certain set of teachings. Perhaps you would like to belong, be part of the group, perhaps you are looking to create meaning, perhaps you believe that a certain teacher is a divine being and you are not. No one person (or thing) is any less or more a part of the whole than anyone else (or anything else). Every human that has ever lived – slave, maid, farmer, machinist, servant or king – is as much a divine being as our so-called prophets, messiahs and saints. Fundamentally all humans are the incarnation of every other human that has ever lived. You, like everyone else, have the memory of Buddha, Jesus and Mohammed somewhere deep inside your mind. Any person who claims to be some sort of unique avatar, chosen one, messenger, prophet or the current incarnation of Buddha clearly does not understand the critical characteristic which binds the entire universe, that the whole exists in every part. The centre is everywhere. No one person is divine where you are not. Equally, you cannot be divine unless each single thing can also be. As we will come to realise, your dustbin is just as divine as you are! Like you, at its deepest level, it contains the whole universe within its information structure.

If you love only your partner, your guru or your messiah but not a stranger then it is not love, it is self-interest. It is love that is designed by thought, but love designed by thought is not love, it is a form of gratification. Love is not thought. Love for a selected few rather than for all is not love. Love is equal; it is never separate or selective. It is neither deserved nor conditional. Love is not of the mind, it is of Being. This Being is love, and at root our fear is the fear of not Being. You want the reward of freedom that the guru offers, but then you become attached to the reward. You become attached to the idea of freedom and you desire the idea of freedom, but together this can never be freedom. Your motive to be free of attachment turns into a form of attachment. You are striving for a goal, you are attached to the goal and all this time you are suppressing one form of attachment by replacing it with another. The goal is to be free of the self and free of all attachment but the ego cannot ever release the ego, which is why there is no such thing as freedom *from* something. And the only reason you seek this freedom is because you exist in fear. So it is these fears that must be addressed and the only way to address them fully is on your own. A genuine master is wary of his own methods and his own assertions, recognising their potential to reinforce dependency and fear.

Buddha said it. Zarathustra said it. All the great Chinese Sages have said it: *'Beware of the master!'*

As we ascertained in the book *Question Mark*, you have to stand on your own two feet. If you want to discover the 'why's of the universe, the 'Big Questions', by all means look to the masters but then look to yourself. You have to self-parent, you have to not rely on others, you have to master your growth on your own. A master is not serving you if he allows himself to be a pillar to lean on; at the beginning this may be appropriate as guidance for your journey, but after a while you have to venture out alone if you are to really grow. What is freedom if you are relying on a master or the system of a master, or are comparing what is being said with what another has said? Your pursuit of their ideal, their goal, is a transfigured and subtle form of ambition and therefore self-perpetuating in nature. Their ideal is now your goal. You may dress that up in humble pursuit, with the appearance of sincerity and earnestness, but you are still giving significance to the identifications of the 'me'. You are still striving for your idea of a reward. How can there be humility when the mind is diligently or even subtlety striving, choosing, comparing, calculating, acquiring? Ambition disguises itself in many forms and one must be constantly aware of this process, for it distorts and conditions the mind. There must be humility otherwise what you seek is mere gratification, a form of pleasure, which does nothing but tether one's own investigation. Truth is beyond choice, beyond self-orientated discernment. There is no humility without the ending of comparison, nor is there humility when we follow another.

The setting up and following of authority is the denial of one's own discovery, one's insight, openness and therefore understanding. Vicarious understanding is no understanding at all. If you seek in order to find, you may indeed find what you are looking for. How do you know that what you discover is Truth? What you create as the ideal can only be self-projected; a glorified version of the 'self'. Can the mind, the known, understand the unknown? Can the mind really discover Truth or is Truth beyond mind, beyond all measure? It is important to ask these questions otherwise the mind will inevitably engage in its own illusions.

If the mind is diligently comparing what each philosopher is saying, busy with everybody else's arguments, calculating who is making the strongest assertions, then it is distracted from self-discovery? If the mind is occupied in this way it is not still and without stillness there can be no clear and direct perception. Without direct perception, how do we know what is true and what is not? Humility is necessary for Truth to be. The mind must be free of all comparison, evaluation, choice, judgement and censorship. The mind must be innocent.

chapter one

Can Thought Ever be Free?

Can Thought Ever be Free?

WHAT IS THE FIELD IN which human thought operates? Thought requires knowledge, thought requires language, for in the absence of verbalisation, how is the process of thinking to take place? Without words, or more correctly language, it is not possible to think. There is of course instinct that is mental activity and thus a form of thought; we call it primitive thought because it is clear that instinct has a different, more primal quality than reasoned thought. Instinct is neither reasoning nor contemplation – both of which require words – instinct is more like instruction or adaptive learning, carried in an instructive language of its own. It must still be a language, otherwise instruction or experience writing neural networks would be impossible.[1] How can there be instruction in the absence of language? How can neural networks be written if there is no information in the writing? This language from our innate nature – from our genes, our DNA, fields of consciousness or some other source – derives from a base language human scientists have yet to understand. All thought requires a language of some form, and reasoned thought requires the language of the word. If we are trying to ascertain whether thought can be free, then we can immediately eliminate instinctual thought as not free, because instruction[2] and adaptive learning clearly are not free. So we need to be discussing thought that we perceive to be beyond such a lack of freedom, and that would be thought in the shape of contemplation, logic and reason.

The nature of this more advanced quality of thought is the organisation of concepts through the use of language, namely 'the word'. Instinctual thought is also the organisation of concepts but through a separate language; after all instinct requires no word-based vocabulary, although a vocabulary of some form is still required. What

---

[1] For simplification we are ignoring the emission of electromagnetic fields from living organisms, which carry information specific to each organism.
[2] This provides a clue into the nature of instinct for our discussion in the book *Time is Thought* regarding 'Fields of Consciousness'.

seems clear is that the type of language thought uses is what differentiates types of thought, in a way similar to how the computations of a computer (its thinking) can use a variety of languages. 'The word' is the language of human logic, contemplation and reason; something beyond the word is the language of instinct. However, since we are discussing the type of thought that can be free, we do not here need to understand the base language or mechanism of instinct – not yet at least. Instead, we are discussing thought in the shape of contemplation, logic and reason because we are trying to ascertain whether such a quality of thought can be free. Our gut feeling is that reason and contemplation must be free, but are they? To answer this question we must understand what they are. Reason, contemplation and logic are the organisation of concepts arising out of our understanding through the use of word-based language[3]. These organised concepts form the thoughts of the conscious mind and add to our overall consciousness mix.

What is this 'consciousness mix'? It is its content – conscious thought, sub-conscious thought, primal thought and so forth. This content clearly could not exist without the existence of language. Thoughts are the content of consciousness and all content – whether of a computer or of a human mind – requires some form of language to define one piece of information from the next. So to understand conscious thought and find out whether it can be free, we must understand the nature of its intrinsic relationship to the language of the word. We understand this language because we have learnt it, consciously, from scratch. Conscious thought (hereafter referred to simply as 'thought') is learnt in much the same way as we learn language, over time; this is because naturally language is a component of thought. Words represent concepts which, when organised in our understanding, become our thoughts[4]. Equally, thought is the holding mechanism

---

[3] Mathematical symbols are also included in this definition. We will discuss the distinction between a priori and a posteriori reasoning later in the book.
[4] There is something universal about the recognition of a triangle before our labelling of it using the word 'triangle' or our drawing of it as a triangle, when we take it down from what Plato calls the universal into the particular. The word is not the thing; it merely represents the thing.

of language. Without thought there would be no words, for how can the word exist without thought? Do look into this for yourself rather than just trust what you are reading. Examine the nature of your own thoughts. Clearly, we cannot build a wall of stones without stones. Language and thought are like this; you can't build thought without language or language without thought. It is difficult to ascertain which came first, or to distinguish the true difference between language and thought. Can we differentiate them at all?

Thought is Time

LET US CONSIDER THE RELATIONSHIP between thought and time, beginning with memory. If there is limited thinking due to limited language, what is the effect of this on one's capacity to remember facts, events and impressions – what we call memory? Without thinking, what then is memory; is memory at all possible? Conversely without memory, what is thinking? It is clear that thinking draws from memory and memory is the accumulation of thought. There must be a quality of memory that is proportional to thought and a quality of thought that is proportional to memory. Think of relatively simple animals such as fish, then progressively complex species – lizards, elephants, humans. Humans have a large prefrontal cortex, more neurons and thus a greater capacity to exercise broader mental activity than other animals. Given the strength and depth of human memory, clearly memory capacity is in proportion to the capacity to think beyond instinct; conscious thought. Given the strength and depth of human thinking, our thinking capacity must be in proportion to memory capacity. This is straight forward.

If you examine your own thinking processes you will recognise a quality of memory that is seemingly independent of reasoned thinking and almost instinctive, like stored visual images, symbols, people or places, as well as the remembering of sounds, smells, tastes and so forth. Memory forms from a variety of sources and does not rest entirely in conscious thought (in the reasoned thinking of 'the organised word'). Other forms of thinking in the formation of memory require the use of some form of base language to differentiate and organise information so that the memory of, say, a particular place – a certain tree, the shape of a hill, the colour of the grass from a certain scene in your life – can be remembered in a structured form to create the memory. For without the ability to structure elements at least symbolically, the memory would simply collapse into chaos. Reasoned thinking does appear to help this process, adding to memory capacity. It gives coherence to thought structure and further ability for it to organise, expand and make links. Certainly, memory and thought are deeply intertwined.

Our hypothesis, then, is that there is a quality of thinking that is proportional to memory.

Thought over time – our instinctual thoughts from the processing of our basic sensory awareness, our early logical reasoning, to our historical thoughts up until right now – is all memory. Or is it? Can we remember early basic instincts or people and places we visited as an infant in the pram without a link to a more contemplative thought or anchor point? Think back to when you were a child, most of us cannot remember much of what took place before the age of four years, or perhaps three if we are lucky. Why is this? Before and up to three years old, your language was limited, the brain's structure was simple[5] and so too was your knowledge, therefore your thinking and your conscious memory of this time is scarce. This scarcity of memory creates today your sense of 'no time' in relation to this period. In the absence of contemplative thinking back then, there was little or no formation of conscious memory[6] and thus there is little or no perceived history of this period for you today. That is why the moment between when you were born and your first memory is time that you have experienced but you cannot remember, and so to you today it remains largely unknown, as though it never actually took place. For you there is missing psychological time, or perceived history, even though time did actually pass.[7]

---

[5] Despite the greater abundance of neurons.
[6] We will discuss the subconscious memory later.
[7] Babies are actually closer, in this sense, to pure awareness and natural empathy – which, to quote Cornelius Crowley, *"is the ability to 'read' the signals that*

A comprehensive memory requires a mechanism to store experiences. Such a mechanism requires a process of thinking – the language of the conscious mind, sub-conscious mind and so forth. Although there may be the perception of an experience – the cognition of a certain event or object – the recognition and storage of that experience requires a system or mechanism for holding information, such as association, which in turn requires knowledge. Thus with limited knowledge, conscious recognition is also limited. There may be awareness of a physical experience, but if this experience cannot be described, thought through or at least structured in some way at the time of experiencing, then our conscious memory of it will be poor. Hence our infant memories are difficult to recall. Of course it would be absurd to say that our infant experiences did not occur or that we are unaffected by them because we know the subconscious mind remembers everything, especially trauma.[8] It is simply that the infant

---

(7 continued) *come from the environment accurately and to be able to utilise that information appropriately.*" Babies are conscious without thought in the shape of contemplation, logic or reason, and consciousness without such thinking is awareness. Psychological time is thought, thus the sense of the era before conscious thought as being without time. What is also intriguing is that this is the most open, susceptible and therefore important period in one's life for the building and writing of neural networks; leaving limbic imprints that go on to shape our adult behaviour.

[8] "*Limbic imprint is the term used to describe the processes of experience 'writing' the neural networks, the connections within our brain, heart and body during our time in the womb, and in particular during birth, and often in the immediate aftermath of birth.*" (C. Crowley)

The subconscious operates on a different level to conscious thought because its language of construction is more susceptible to limbic imprinting. Rather than being based on reasoned evaluation (logic), the sub-conscious is based on conceptual interpretation at the point of experience and language formation. For many, our early childhood experiences are distorted and unnatural. Empathy is a biological imperative and so a child comes into the world expecting to receive and give love. When this is denied, its nervous system is imprinted negatively and distortions at this level become embedded deep in the psyche. The mind writes and builds neural nets of mistaken understanding in relation to, for example, its rightness of being. These can make even the most seemingly sane adults behave in an irrational manner in response to certain triggers because their subconscious thoughts around certain issues – like a lack of care or parental devotion, or abandonment – were formed at a time when the mind was unable to dissect and logically understand what

brain finds it difficult to process these experiences consciously, thus limiting the extent to which the adult brain can then return to them.

Thought cannot exist without memory because only memory stores concepts as language. Thought is constructed language and language is structured thought. The relationship between thought and language and thought and memory can be condensed into a relationship between thought and that which encompasses memory and language: our knowledge. So to return to the opening of this chapter: without knowledge, what is thinking? Can thinking exist without knowledge? It is not possible to think about the unknown; you can only think about the known, which is your knowledge. You may think about new combinations of the known, for example '*Pink hippos smoking Havana cigars in Moscow*' may sound new, but really it is the re-chewing of words that we already know and have chewed before, only in other contexts. You cannot think about what you do not know; try it now and you will find that thinking requires knowledge.

Thought Requires Knowledge

THINKING REQUIRES LANGUAGE AND THE information that it knows (memory) in order for it to be organised as thought. Thinking operates within what it knows which is its knowledge. What it knows can expand – of course knowledge can expand – but thinking outside of that knowledge, thinking from the realm of the unknown, is not possible. To think from the unknown would mean that thinking is operating from what is outside language or memory and clearly this is impossible since thinking is understanding, organised as language and memory. A dog

---

(8 continued) was happening. This is particularly acute when we are very young, which is why psychologists always probe into early childhood. Babies are very sensitive to the external environment, in the womb and at birth. If these early understandings are not cleared, balanced and ordered, they go on to create distorted thought constructions and thus problematic patterns. Distortions of understanding become deeply embedded into the thought structure of that person and this is how troublesome behavioural patterns and life scripts begin. If we are unaware of these patterns and scripts, then clearly these sub-conscious thoughts are not free. (See the movie 'What Babies Want'.)

thinking about quantum physics is not possible unless it learns the language of physics at university (after passing the entrance exams, of course!) and remembers what is learnt; its field of the known must expand. Clearly thought requires knowledge and dogs have no knowledge of physics which is why they don't think about quantum physics. Knowledge is memory, knowledge is what we know and our thinking derives from what we know. We can go into the neuroscience of all this but at present it is sufficiently clear that thinking derives from what we know, from our knowledge.

As our knowledge base increases, so increases our capacity for thought. If there was no knowledge, no memory, no experience, there would be no thinking; that is obvious. So if thought operates out of the field of knowledge and knowledge derives from our life experiences and deductions – from our learning at school, the playground, teenage kicks, jobs, relationships and all that goes on in the memories of our lives – then thought is operating out of the past, out of its conclusions. Even our ideas about the future – our hopes, dreams and ambitions – are formulated in the present using knowledge from the past. So knowledge is past, knowledge is conclusion. We may increase that knowledge by learning something new, usually from an external source such as an academic paper, or we may go through our own process of logic and thinking to understand the new idea, but as soon as we attain new knowledge we then use it from memory, which is past. What is learnt from memory becomes further knowledge, the field of the known increases and so do our conclusions. But Truth is not found in conclusion; it is found in the ending of conclusion, in our innocence from conclusion. Only in innocence lies the mystery and wonder of existence, where both Truth and the perceptual unknown reside. But we like to operate within conclusion because there is safety in knowledge, security in the known. The paradigm in which we operate is constructed in experience, memory, knowledge, thought and action; this is what, in accordance to one's interpretation (which is itself influenced by knowledge), determines the nature of the next experience. Can you not see that if thought is operating only as a response from the past, it is to some extent limited and if it is limited then surely thought is in a prison? It is not free; to be free is to be unlimited.

What about new ideas, new creative moments of insight? If we look closely at these moments, does not all new creativity stem from a mind that is quiet? You may go through a logical process to understand a problem, you may think about it, chew over it, ponder, question, but doesn't inspiration derive from a mind that is quiet? *'Aha!'* moments of new understanding that we seem to pluck out of nowhere – the ether, the empty state or whatever you wish to call it – aren't these moments when the self is not? If you are deeply honest with yourself, you will realise that these moments happen when the mind is open, innocent, at rest and quiet. So new understanding, new creativity derives from a mind that is quiet, from a mind that is not busy thinking, that is free of thought. Therefore understanding and thought do not always go together. What is going on? Is not all thought defined understanding? Is not all understanding thought that is incorporated in itself? Which of these two statements is true? The best way of approaching this is to go through it ourselves.

Understanding

OUR THOUGHTS ARE CONCEPTS AS words. Concepts are defined understanding in the form of words. But our understanding seems to be beyond thought at times, beyond intellectualisation. Understanding is larger than thought that is incorporated in itself. There is this understanding that is beyond conventional, verbalised human thought, understanding of the quality or suchness of a thing without the word, understanding which belongs to a consciousness that is truly awake.

The intellectual is just the mind. If you live through just the mind you live a dry, arid life. You can learn how to dance, you can learn the waltz or the samba step by step and you can be technically perfect in your dancing, but if you do not feel that dance in your heart, if you are unable to let go of yourself and melt into the joy of it completely so that your forget yourself, then you are not really dancing. You are like a robot completing steps; there is no beauty, no mystery, magic or aliveness, it is just arid and dead with no feeling. The intellect is arid; intellectualisation is not true understanding because true understanding carries unknown yet recognisable qualities; true understanding carries feelings. True understanding is not describing the dance or analysing the dance, it is living the dance, being the dance. The heart and the intellect must combine for there to be movement away from textbook dancing into the unknown, and thus the awakening of intelligence.

Thought is the known. Thought can describe a picturesque view with words and language that it knows, but it will never understand or convey the quality or suchness of that view. Thought and true understanding are not the same. The experiencing of a picturesque view is never based on its description or definition by thinking; it is based on the suchness or quality of the experiencing of that view. A different, more primary mechanism is at work for the experiencer; when the experiencer is 'not', (his) understanding changes – it becomes truly real. There is a whole new dimension of Being now. Quiddity is found in Being, not in intellectual knowledge.

Thought over time, from our first thought up until right now, is memory and memory is past and so thought derives from the past. All thought is old, all thought is concepts as language chewed over and over again creating this conclusion or that conclusion. One cannot come to Truth or freedom through conclusion. Conclusion must be dropped because reality is dynamic, alive, vast and never past. The moment you map the dynamic, it has changed; to map what is changing and form a conclusion is impossible. This is what thought is trying to do, this is what knowledge is trying to do. In this reality, only change remains unchanged; so if all thought is old, if thought is conclusion then thought will always operate out of what J. Krishnamurti calls 'the field of the known' and can therefore never be free. Because thought is never free, there will always be conflict in the human mind; especially if one is seeking freedom through a system or a religious method which is thought, which is the field of the known. We are discussing this in order to highlight the imprisoning nature of the human dependency on thought, on method which is knowledge, to achieve spiritual liberation.

There are different types of understanding. For example in our daily lives there is understanding from memory – where the post office is, how to add up your shopping, how to boil an egg – and this constitutes our daily knowledge. There is understanding that is beyond memory, beyond knowledge, beyond the word; these are perceptions of quality like that of a mountain, flower or tree when the observer is not, or they may be creative moments of understanding that often convert to art, which likewise occur when the self is not, when the thinking mind is quiet. Art provokes fresh understanding which is undefined yet still possesses a recognisable quality. That quality is a form of understanding even though we cannot define it with our current system of language. They say that art that can be described is not art; this is because art is beyond knowledge and knowledge is the describer. The described is the word but the word is never the actual quality of a thing. The described operates in a prison; the actual quality of a thing, its unnamed understanding, is free of that prison. Such understanding is beauty. See how beauty IS when the 'me', the self, is not.

There is this understanding that is again beyond memory, beyond knowledge, beyond the word, but which expands the field of the known, like in breakthrough scientific research. Post understanding, thought comes into operation creating new language to describe new concepts. Because it comes into operation quickly, we think the new understanding is verbalised thought from the very beginning rather than understanding that is separate from thought, rather than a recognisable quality that IS prior to our intellectualisation of it. (For example, our insight into a scientific problem prior to our explanation of it.) Thought may verbalise its new understandings into words and memory, but it is never more than a description of a recognisable quality that IS. So thought itself is not new; it is merely describing understanding that is new and this is how new language forms. Where there is new language there are more tools for thought to describe understanding, but it is vital we differentiate between the understanding and the thought (the conscious thought). It is the understanding that is new; the thought – that being the word – only comes after. So thought, even new thought, is always operating from the past. New thought operates post understanding, so it is past. It is awareness and understanding that are present; all thought and knowledge are past.

Thought appears to be new because it is describing new understanding but understanding, which rests within what here is a currently undefined conscious awareness[9], has a different dimension which it is hard for us to comprehend (unless of course you work at the edge of neuroscience and artificial intelligence research in areas such as symbolic processing). Human thought is derived from our limited perception as separate individuals, while true understanding operates from a deeper dimension, and appears to be beyond our limited perception since it can exist when thought is not.

Thought may describe the concept of freedom, but it can only operate from the prison of the past, and is thus never free. Even in practical life, you make decisions about tomorrow based on the past; based on experience, memory, knowledge, thought, action. Such decisions are never free; they are rooted in knowledge and memory. There is no freedom if we only operate out of a paradigm such as this. It is vital that we operate not strictly from thought and knowledge but openly, from understanding and awareness. As Buddha always asserted, only awareness is needed if we are to be free.

The Pleasure/Pain Prison

THOUGHT IN DAILY LIFE IS concerned with pleasure and pain. The pleasures of life and the pains of life have been much the same for most of history and very little, if anything, is new. We operate towards pleasure and away from pain and these parameters define the space in which daily thought operates. If we are operating inside a defined space then we are operating inside a limited field. If things don't go our way – pleasure is denied or we face pain – we may react aggressively. If our behaviour is so predictable, can we say that we are truly free? If a mind cannot see this, then such a mind is operating from a prison. It may like that prison, it may put flowers on the iron bars of that prison, but in essence thought is still operating within a limited field, a field defined by the pursuit of pleasure and the avoidance of pain. Such a space is secure for the mind because the parameters are known, safe, comforting and predictable, however if there is never any movement into the unknown such a life will feel dull, petty and narrow.

---

[9] Some speculate this to be Plato's Forms.

An alternative to such a predictable existence is to live dangerously, to break out of our belief systems and thought structures and step into the unknown. Masters have advocated that we live on the edge of life and face each of our fears head on. In breaking out, there is wonder and freedom within the uncertainty and insecurity of the unknown; there is beauty in such uncertainty because if everything was predictable and safe, life would be dreary, mechanical and boring. So embrace insecurity for the wonder, surprise and freedom that it brings. If you cling to security and what is known you might as well be dead, you are operating out of a limited field which is never new. You will be nothing more than an imitation of others, a robot like everyone else – conforming, copying and never shining and sparkling as an individual who is free. You are freedom, you will always be freedom. You need courage to step out of the known into the unknown, only then will you grow.

But the great majority of humanity fails to do this. We like the known. We like our habits and our daily routines. This can continue for years and years until the rot and indifference sets in. If daily thought is only ever operating out of the field of the known then meaning becomes extraordinarily important. Life does have meaning but to construct that meaning as the activity of one's own thought is a form of vanity. A mind of humility does not need to construct a definition of meaning. We form habits and daily routines because they are satisfying, which means we lack humility. Because we lack humility we start to want something new, unaware that even that which seems new remains little changed from what has gone before. Very little of what we do or what we say is ever new; we merely repeat the activities of those before us. It may be the illusion of leaving a legacy, or an experience of God (we want euphoria, we want a transcendental experience), but we define these states with what we have learnt from the past, projecting what these experiences 'should be' from an idea that we have already formed, and so we limit our awareness of the unknown. Even looking towards 'unknown' experiences we are operating from the field of the known. Our search for meaning follows structure, method, prayer or strict meditation techniques. Because we are so conditioned to only ever operate out of the field of the known (the safety of experience, memory, knowledge, thought and action), we cannot learn to let go of these and thus there is no awareness or understanding of the unknown. There is no stepping into the beyond. Occasionally we may experience something that is uniquely new, but most of what we do operates out of ideas (or interpretations) from the past. Few of us break free and follow our own path. Thus thought continues to operate within what it knows, namely the pleasure/pain paradigm, whether seeking gratification or pleasure through God or by following the teachings of others. Can thought operate anywhere else, outside of what it knows? It seems clear that thought can only operate in areas that it knows, because if there is a field about which thought does not know, then how can it operate? To re-iterate one last time, thought and knowledge are intrinsically linked together, and if knowledge is past then thought too is past; thought itself is limited. Why cling to what is limited?

The objective of this analysis is to emphasise our unnecessary dependency on thought. When the mind can see the limitations of thought, what it can and cannot do, then a different kind of intelligence comes into operation. What masters call innocence or chastity is characteristic of a mind that can empty itself of the past, of memory; a mind reborn with absolute clarity, a mind that recognises the limitation of its own thinking and thus its own conventional limitations to reaching new understanding. This intelligence can reach beyond the field of the known into the field of the unknown. This unknown is defined by the very presence of our limited perception, which exists by default of selfhood. This unknown is the rest of existence; it is that which underwrites reality. To live is to exist without bondage, it is to connect with existence. This connection is joy, it is life, it is our aliveness. Such a mind can move beyond itself, it can move beyond the duality of observer / observed into pure observation and into freedom from the known.

Meditation begins when there is freedom from the known, from our mind and our projections. The self is the known and the self can never release the self. The known cannot be free of the known if it is using the activity of the known. 'You' are the known; you are your knowledge. You cannot be free of yourself, which is your knowledge, by using more knowledge; hence the previous assertion about this nonsensical idea of freedom *from* something. Freedom *from* something is a reaction to a person, thing or incident that disturbs. As we explained in the book *Question Mark*, this disturbance is not separate from you. *You* are the disturbance. It is the disturbance that must be understood, not how to break free of the disturbance.

When there is freedom from ideas of God or enlightenment that we have learnt in the past and are now projecting into the future, meditation can become something that is not a projection of our desires or an escape from ourselves and our fears, but something that is new and fresh – a living, breathing thing rather than a mechanical process. Traditional religion has distracted humanity for centuries because we have found it difficult to move away from the past, because we have placed too great an emphasis on thinking and knowledge and thus method. We have been more interested in escaping, pre-occupied with this idea of freedom *from* something, rather than understanding the true nature of disturbance. Our pre-occupation is a form of greed. And because we want something greater, because we are caught up in the idea of spiritual achievement, we are caught up in the idea that we need help from another or help from some form of structure. The result is that we are unable to stand alone and be free from the conditioning of others; our minds are never innocent of the past, never free from ideals of 'what should be'. This leaves us open to deception and we have been deceived for a mighty long time. Deception can only rage when you want something, but if you are happy just to be curious, if you are free from any burning desires like the demand for something transcendental, then your investigation will be free and clear. Then you can enquire into the nature of Truth with clarity not distracted or inhibited by the structure of religious method or the notion of achievement. When your clarity is crystal clear, you don't need courage to stand alone, you will do so automatically. You can see clearly that the known is old, past and dead and that the unknown is fresh, new and alive. Only awareness is needed. This clarity is awareness, and with such awareness you become impossible to deceive. You cannot find liberation in the known. The known is thought in movement, the known is the process of what creates time; only the unknown is the ending of time and the stepping into Truth.

Strict methods of meditation belong in the field of the known. You cannot force the ending of thought with thought, as they teach you in meditation class. Order cannot be enforced because order is freedom, where the enforcer is not. Remember the enforcer is himself a fragment of thought and thus operating from the known. Even his action to end thought is action from the known. When you enforce you get locked into a pattern; there is suppression, control and conformity which together make the mind dull, mechanical and imitative of others. You turn into a clone. You put yourself into control, into an army boot camp of the mind, into a prison which moves away from 'what is' towards 'what should be' and thus there is conflict, which is disorder. You are imitating others. What is imitation? It is rooted in the fear of 'what is'; it is the denial of your absolute correctness, which is 'what is'. Can a system of fear bring order into being, when order is freedom? Obviously not. Order comes into being when there is the understanding of the disorder within oneself, the lack of freedom within oneself. True religion is freedom from belief, requiring no faith and no following of imposed systems. True religion is most maverick and anarchic in nature because it is beyond the structure of society. True religion is freedom and freedom is in the first step, not the last step; a truth that is contrary to what many religious systems or gurus dictate. If you start by being imprisoned at the beginning, you cannot come to freedom at the end; if you are imprisoned at the beginning your mind will never be sensitive, truthful or courageous enough to look at your fears and face them head on. You will remain dependent on others or on their systems. To be free you must not rely on another, but embrace the uncertainty of going your own way. Then you will be able to see your fear and be free of your fear, which is freedom and beauty.

Integrity

A MIND THAT IS HONEST cannot be deceived. This is not a contrived honesty in accordance with some lofty ideal, this is a total and complete honesty in oneself because one has learnt and understood that it is only when there is total honesty in oneself that there is true possibility of growth. Growth is not possible in self deception, and deception creates vanity where we think we know when clearly we do not. This is worse than knowing nothing at all. It is better to approach this investigation with the admission that *'I really don't know, I really don't know anything at all!'* so that one is able to die to the past each second, be open now, ready to transform, ready for the future uncorrupted by the knowledge and expectation which distort our clarity. This is what innocence means, this is a chaste mind, this is the awakening of intelligence because for the first time you see 'what is' as it is, not what you think it should be according to your conditioning. If you can examine something without having an agenda, a goal or a craving, then you are not open to deception.

Explore knowledge, explore memory, but be finished with it so that it does not burden you. If you continue to crave a certain experience or desire a certain goal, then whatever it is that you view or investigate will be in some way distorted, and thus deception is not just a possibility for you, but an inevitability.

Beauty is the absence of the distorting 'me', when we can watch without the judging, thinking observer. When the nature of the observer being the observed is truly understood, this is the beginning of inner beauty. When you say, for example, *'I am jealous,'* there is only jealousy; there is no 'I' separate from the jealousy. When we look at jealousy as it is without trying to move away from it, suppress it or correct it – all of which distort it – then there is clarity that the observer is the observed, that the 'I' is no different from the observed. The 'I' is jealousy, not different from it; they are the same, there is a principle of sameness. The disturbance which we call jealousy is not separate from you, it is you. When this is understood, there can be pure observation of jealousy as a psychological disturbance that exists and lives only within the conflict of the self.

When we give ourselves over to anger, jealousy, guilt, or whatever and do so completely – such that there is no conflict to change – we soak up their very essence and understand the emotion in question, totally and utterly. When we do this and do this completely, we can move beyond them immediately, in a flash. In such awareness – that jealousy cannot be anything but itself, anything but the living concept of a jealous disturbance that exists with us as a vehicle for Truth – then there is the deep realisation that jealousy only exists in our misunderstanding; the observer is the observed, we are jealousy and not separate from it. We are not separate from our misunderstanding. Any idea of separation is merely an illusion of thought, a defence mechanism of the ego. In this awareness, there is clarity of the nature of jealousy, the understanding that jealousy can only continue to exist in the conflict we create around it. This conflict is its continuity, it exists in our movement, our suppression, our escape, our attachment or whatever it is that we have been conditioned to do when we feel jealous. There is the continuity of jealousy only within the conflict around it, when the 'I' separates itself and then tries to correct jealousy as though it were an independent, distinct and discrete entity. But once the nature of conflict – the pattern created by the ego – is understood, there is no movement, no conflict to constitute 'jealousy' (or anger or whatever) and so it ends. There can be freedom from sorrow, in an instant.

We are not operating from thought and knowledge which create the direction of 'what should be' when we are jealous, instead there is simply awareness and understanding of 'what is' and this is without direction. There is love for jealousy, the embracing and comprehension of the 'what is' of jealousy and thus our understanding of it. That which understands can see beyond. In the understanding of jealousy there is no longer conflict around it, there is the seeing beyond it by not taking a direction. The mind is free of the idea of psychological progress.

The experiencing, the totality of cognition of what jealousy is, is freeing. We can then move beyond jealousy. We have gone through jealousy to the very end of it, and this is what it means to truly experience. This is life. This is love. We must love that which we wish to understand; we must embrace it and comprehend it, not deny it. This includes our darkness. Remember embracing is not the acting out and hurting of others, it is to soak up and understand the essence of a concept, to get to the very end of it. Denial only brews trouble

– look at the suppression of life in practices such as Catholic guilt or Hindu asceticism. Freedom is the experience of concepts without getting caught up in psychological time whereas asceticism and guilt are psychological time. Such time is our judgement upon ourselves and others, precisely what Jesus warned against with his teaching, 'Judge Ye Not'. Such time is our trying to escape or move away from the jealousy that we have been discussing. Freedom is to experience it and then be finished with it completely, to be able to wipe the slate clean. Such a mind is once again empty of the past, open, innocent and chaste, free of jealousy having moved beyond it by understanding it. Only understanding is needed and this understanding is not the language of thought – the word – it is an understanding beyond definition by the word. When a mind is this honest, this capable of seeing what it can and cannot do in relation to the living concepts of life, then there is beauty. There is the abandonment of the 'me' when and where necessary in order to experience the true suchness of life. This is the door to true freedom.

Method

MOST OF US, HOWEVER, CANNOT abandon the 'me' when it comes to spiritual curiosity. We hear stories of Buddha, stories of Jesus, and of course stories turn to myth and legend and they become more distorted and divine over time. They seem far removed from and alien to the world that we know, and so we create lofty ideals of what we think we 'should be' so that we can be just like them. In such imitation we leave ourselves open to deception, blinded by our own desire. If you are at all serious about finding out what it is to be free, which is what enlightenment means, then maybe it would be worth asking the question '*Why am I so serious about all this?*' You are serious because you are seeking, you seek because you fear, and because you are fearful you end up following a system. If you are following a system then you are not free, no matter how free the system claims to be. You get drawn into a system because the option of going your own way entails that you stand alone and standing alone is scary, instead you have to face your fears on your own. Naturally we confuse this standing alone with being lonely on our path, lonely in the sense of being unable to relate to others; becoming a recluse, a repressed monk in a cave obsessed with God, guilt and sex, feeling totally and utterly isolated and therefore miserable. To overcome this loneliness, we prefer to join a system; 'there is safety in the system'.

The true master will always appear to be a rebel and to be alone, but this aloneness is something completely different to what we usually conceive. Aloneness is not isolation, aloneness is when we are no longer influenced or conditioned by others, where there is no such thing as psychological reaction. This is not aloofness – that being the creation of an isolating wall around ourselves – it is being in complete relationship with everything and everyone. This aloneness is to be sensitive, empathic and vulnerable, yet invincible because there has been a total surrender of the 'me'. You are invincible because you are already defeated, already surrendered; there is nowhere left to go. No conflict, no resistance, just awareness. This is beyond reaction. A mind that is alone is not dependent on others; such a person can stand on their own two feet and is capable of reading their own content or the content of others. Theirs is an empathic awareness that is free from conformity or fear, and without conflict or disorder. Then there is healing, recovery and transformation without the conflict of guilt, shame or blame. Such a mind is swift, subtle, sensitive, vulnerable and yet unshakeable like a mountain. Such a person is not just his own best friend but is nature, and replenishes himself from nature.

The bearer of such a mind can see the nature of religious or social suppression, they can see that conformity and comparison are all rooted in fear and, in this understanding, see the conflict in the mind. Simply the understanding of conflict brings order to that conflict. Such order does not follow a pattern or structure, it arises from understanding the disorder. Order is a living thing, order is understanding, order is part of life. Since there is no pattern to understanding, order cannot adhere to systems, structure or method. We cannot import order from method or from religious texts for in doing so we only create more disorder in the shape of conformity and suppression. Remember, understanding is beyond human thought. Of course human thought can describe understanding and turn it into knowledge, but it will never be free, it will never be able to adapt to reality's constant state of flux. There is understanding that is beyond human knowledge and that is the order and awareness that underpins existence.

Unless order exists within a human mind, then it is pointless to start following a system or a method; it will only add to the confusion within the mind. There is already disorder in the human mind, yet we seek systems and methods in order to cultivate order within ourselves. What happens? By following a system we are conditioned to change 'what is' into 'what should be', but love is the acceptance of 'what is' not the striving for 'what should be'. Actually that is not quite right. Who is accepting? In accepting there is an entity applying this idea in order to gain and so the conflict of duality is still there. 'Non-duality' here is meant in the context of all conflict ceasing; a surrender that is without direction. There is no need to strive for anything. If the goal is to Be – and to Be is not a goal but is instead simply 'what is' – then how can there be striving if there is to be love? It is when there is striving that there is no love. In a system like those professed by our main religions, we do this, we follow that, we practice X and repeat Y; in all of this activity we become more dull, more stupid and more easily deceived by promises of freedom because the system we are operating within is nothing but mechanical and repetitive. Freedom is in the first step not the last step, and so a system that promises freedom only in the last step is bound to be false. For this reason, all the major religious systems are false.

Can Thought Ever be Free?

IF THOUGHT DERIVES FROM MEMORY and memory is the past, is there anything that thought can do that is inherently free? We know thought can discuss freedom, make a space in an interval between its thoughts and then call that freedom (when it is not); we know thought can result in books written about freedom and songs sung about freedom, but do any of these activities really succeed in putting aside the 'me' and moving beyond thought? Are not all of these activities rooted in knowledge, memory and experience – the field of the known – activities of the self which simply describe art and freedom where there is the ending of the 'me'; simply describe the putting aside of the mind and the embracing of existence? These are interesting questions.

It is in the very moment of a painter painting that there is the ending of the 'me', when the mind is truly quiet and there is the embracing of existence. Freedom for the painter is in the actual painting of the picture there and then as he paints, when the 'me' is not, rather than when the painter has finished his painting and is talking about it. Post this moment of creation, the result – the song, the book, the canvas – only describes freedom. Of course when we melt into another's creativity, inspired to do so by the freedom and art of their painting, song or poem in its creation, then that art can elicit a state of freedom for our awareness.

You will discover that thought is not freedom, it only describes freedom. Freedom is embraced not discussed. True freedom is the freedom of the absence of thought, which is love, which is the stillness of mind, peace and serenity that we try to define with words but where the words are not and can never be the actual. Love is not of the mind because as soon as we state that love is a defined thought, then we are introducing criteria in our thought, and that is not love. Love is free from condition and criteria and it is not selective; love is not of the mind but of awareness. Love is to never ask anything in return, to never attach conditions, to never impose one's fears on another. Love is not thought. Freedom is freedom from the field of the known and the field of the known is knowledge and memory, both being thought. If love is not thought and freedom is not thought, are love and freedom together? Free flowing meditation is the ending of knowledge. So if you are meditating according to a method then you are still operating inside the field of the known, still inside the past, still operating from memory, and if this is so then there is no freedom and thus no love. When the mind is free from knowledge, which is freedom from the field of the known, then there is the stepping into the unknown and thus the awakening of a deeper intelligence. This is real meditation, which is love.

In the book *Question Mark*, we explained the 'why' of meditation in relation to limited perception and how limited perception creates the possibility of unknown Truth. Here we are saying that meditation is awareness of the unknown, the dimension outside of our field of the known, the same unknown which – in different terms – can be thought of as that dimension of intelligence beyond conventional perception. This is not the explanation one sees on posters at Yoga centres, many of which instead deal with the question of 'how to end thought' using various methods. 'How' implies a system, control, subjugation and concentration; it implies effort and tension and thus a great deal of conflict. In conflict there is no beauty, no order, no freedom from a pattern. In 'how', we have just another escape for someone trying to seek a quiet mind, not realising that the effort itself is the conflict. Thought, method, system – all that activity can never end thought because activity is thought. Beauty is the absence of that activity. In that beauty there is freedom, there is love and there is Truth.

chapter two

Dependency vs. Intelligence

FOR CENTURIES HUMANITY HAS SEARCHED for a Truth that is abiding. What is the motivation behind this search, and what is the nature of this search? We feel that there is something missing; we suffer and find life arduous and so we seek answers to these problems by searching for a Truth that is beyond the conventional mind. The human mind is confused, in a conflict of fear. In order to overcome our suffering, we seek answers in an external God, or in an equation, or in enlightenment through meditation. Wherever we look, the search is still the same; it is the search for inner peace. Why is there something missing inside? Why are we not at peace?

Our problems arise because the mind is a battle; a raging conflict of control, suppression, conformity, guilt and comparison between 'what is' and 'what should be'. We have failed to address the fundamental disorder of desire and fear within, and this has been going on since records began. As long as the human mind remains disordered, dual and disarrayed, we will always need to import ideas of goodness from an external other. People are conditioned by external patterns, whether from a church, the law or society's morals – and in this state our problems will continue. When it comes to virtue, we generally move in one of two ways; we either follow a system that has been laid down by another, laid down by tradition, or we go our own way, learning exactly why the mind and our actions follow certain movements. Let us consider this tendency to follow, not just the following of external systems, but the nature of following itself. We are not saying that it is a mistake to follow, not yet; we are simply questioning the implications of following.

Why Follow?

WE SEEK ADVICE FROM A religion, a master or a guru; we follow a system (which may be religious or it may be some other form of society, club or identity marker) in order to uncover who we really are, what within us is true and what is false, to 'find ourselves' and end our search. We see that the image we have of ourselves may be a lie and to expose this lie, we seek the company of a wise teacher, whether dead – Jesus, Buddha, Mohammed – or a living guru. We hope that this system or teacher will present us with a way of living that cultivates understanding, greater clarity and goodness within; and so we immediately become dependent upon this system and its projected authority. In order for us to see ourselves with clarity, we need the guru or the messiah and his system; we need his presence in some way because without this the clarity of our idea of our own fallibility is lost. In order to attain any sense of clarity we now need the master, we need the comparison. What value is there in clarity gained through comparing ourselves with another? What are we really saying about ourselves? Do look into this for yourself, rather than wait for an answer.

So we compare ourselves to others, to ideals, in order to see things clearly. But any clarity that is rooted in comparison has no value whatsoever. In fact, when based upon comparison and measurement it is not clarity at all; it is the worst kind of disorder. There is no freedom and no acceptance of what you already are. Instead, comparison builds up pressure, moving you away from your Being towards an image that you have formed in your mind as to what you 'should be'. All activity of comparison and measurement is a prison, and in this prison there is no love. Not only is there a lack of love for oneself but when I, for example, compare myself to you – by judging you or finding weaknesses in you – I no longer honour you.

You show another love and dignity only when you look at them without comparing, which is to move beyond the resistance of the self. Comparison is not needed for clarity. With clarity, you see that comparison is an escape from what you are. Such an escape breeds illusion and only adds to your conflict and confusion. Comparison is the conflict between 'what is' and 'what should be'. True clarity arises only when one is able to see the conflict within one's mind, able to see why this conflict continues. In true clarity, one is able to see the disorder of comparison and the lack of love for oneself in comparison. Clarity is the seeing of 'what is' that comes with the total acceptance of 'what is', without the distorting comparison with 'what should be'. Any notion of 'what should be' is an ideal, an escape, and such self-projections prevent understanding. Comparison is a way of avoiding oneself, and in this there can be no clarity.

Nor is there clarity in dependence. You chase the guru, the messiah or the master for answers but when you chase, when you really want something, you leave yourself open to deception; not necessarily deception by the guru (although many so-called gurus deceive) but self-deception driven by desire. As we saw in the previous chapter, deception is only possible when you want something. When there is no wanting and no needing – when there is humility and freedom – then deception is impossible. If you have allowed a messiah or a master to become a crutch for you, then you are deceiving yourself because you are operating under the influence of another. Freedom cannot flourish from dependency on another and goodness cannot flourish from the following of authority, whether external or internal. Freedom and goodness only flourish from one's reason and one's capacity to work things out on one's own. Then you don't depend on the rabbi, the priest, the guru or the messiah; you don't depend on anybody at all and that is when intelligence comes into operation. You face your own disorder alone, you learn why you conform, why you imitate, why you control, sublimate and suppress, why you submit to your fears and why you are easily led by your desires. As you learn about these 'why's, your self-understanding deepens, and with it come order and a virtue that is your own. This is authentic virtue. It is only through self-understanding that humanity will ever be good.

The Nature of Seeking

WE ASSUME THAT THE RELIGIOUS search for Truth is a 'good thing', but we rarely question this. Is Truth something that can be found? How do we know what we are looking for? Can we find the unknowable? Isn't most of our seeking based upon a basic fear of not achieving a long-term goal? We have heard about heaven, enlightenment or nirvana, we like the sound of it and so we desire it. We have heard about reincarnation, karma and the repayment of karmic debt and so we desire to overcome the implications of these too. However well-disguised, these activities are some form of preservation of self in an after-life or a future life; motivated by the 'me'. We are motivated by a reward or a gain of some form and so we put aside an hour a week to go to church or to a meditation class, snatching a brief moment for reflection and tranquillity within. Our lives are disordered all week and we hope to solve this disorder in these short moments of calm and reflection. Is such activity religious or is it completely superficial?

If one hour per week is dedicated to understanding, what about the remaining 167? There must be a total commitment to the process of understanding one's confused and disorderly mind, a commitment that is 24/7. Only then can one ever find that which is truly sacred – not the church, cathedral or mosque, not our holy books or the man-made objects that we have decreed sacred, but a mind that is free of its own disorder, a mind that is free of the 'me'. We call this mind an innocent mind, a mind that is chaste. Only this mind is truly sacred. Attending a weekly church service or meditation class is the activity of an immature mind, a mind that is wishing to gain and striving for reward. A mature mind can operate in the absence of 'me', without the need to acquire anything or conform to any conditioning. But this is not the mind operating in today's society. Much of the world today operates with the mind of the 'me.' This immature 'me' does not love and until it understands the nature of 'me' and the freedom of the absence of 'me', there cannot be love. There is no point even looking into freedom when the objective itself has already been dictated by 'me'. Then you are operating from what you already know; from the field of the known, from your conditioning. Where is the freedom in this? Examine the motivation of today's religious mind and you will find that the self, with its desires and fears, is at the root of most religious activity. Can this ever be good? Seeking out of desire or fear, can this ever be good?

You submit to the influence of another because for you this influence promises a reward. You are open to deception because you want something and this is the beginning of 'the follower and the followed': the main problem of religion. By following a religious system – or any system at all – we become dependent because we want to receive the system's reward. If you look into this a little deeper, you will see that at its root is fear. There is always fear driving your desire – your desire to preserve the self, to attain something – and there is always a nagging fear that you will not achieve the system's reward. So in all your action you are operating with this reward in your mind. This reward, or more precisely the fear that comes with not achieving it, is itself a prison. All wanting, all striving for 'what should be' (that being your idea of a reward) is rooted in the fear of not Being. All fear exists in the relationship between what one is and what one would like to be. Fear is born in the contradiction of opposites – between being good and not being good; between pleasure and pain; between desire for success and fear of failure. There is fear wherever there is the search for reward or gratification, because searching is by its nature isolating.

Most of the world today is deceived, as much by ourselves as we are by others. There is a direct relationship between dependency and deception. You are dependent because you want to receive, you leave yourself open to deception when you want to receive and you only want to receive because you think 'what is' is not good enough. It is this thinking that is the actual problem. You are distracted from seeing the beauty and suchness of reality because there is always this reward, this objective of yours, hanging over you. Any objective will always be a distorting factor between you and Truth. The distortion lies in your dependency and you are only dependent because you seek the reward of a system. You only want the reward of a system because you do not know who you are – why you fear, why you desire – and you do not know who you are because you are following a system. See the trap! By following a system, your mind is distracted away from the essence of your Being. Any movement away from your Being is a movement by the self, a movement that will always be isolating and self-enclosing. Everything that the self does is for the pleasure of the self in some way, be that your security, some form of escapism or psychological comfort. This movement, which is always directed towards something ultimately satisfying, keeps you immature and therefore more capable of self-deception. We want 'what should be'; we always want more because we have been conditioned to want more. We are ignorant of the bliss of the present moment; a state of being that is beyond mind and beyond thinking. It is this constant striving for more that is the prime cause of most of our afflictions. Dependency arises from our drive to change and this dependency makes us easy to deceive. It is in the relationship between deception and dependency that authority and the imprisonment of humanity are able to rise and take hold. This has been going on throughout recorded history.

Freedom & Authority

IT IS IMPORTANT TO BE able to investigate religious questions, and what it means to be truly religious, without some authority hanging over you. As soon as we accept the authority of a system or a guru, what happens? We are presented with a method that promises a reward, one that promises to alleviate our fears and help us break free of our inner pain and sorrow. We seek this reward because we are unhappy in ourselves, we feel insufficient, lonely, small and limited and so we are persuaded to run away from these fears by exchanging them with the search for something more, something abiding, something that promises freedom. Freedom is to not be dependent. If we are depending on a system that promises to end our dependency and give us freedom, does that system not simply become another form of dependence? What has changed?

When presented with a system to overcome dependency, what happens to our own capacity to understand dependency? In a system or a religious structure where there is a predetermined path that effectively does your thinking for you, your capacity to solve your own problems moves into the background. Your own intelligence lies dormant as you become dependent on the structure (or the guru) to show you the way. Would it not be better for you to find your own way? Isn't true freedom having the capacity to solve your own problems rather than look outwards to have these problems solved for you? If we no longer have the capacity to solve our own problems, then we lose our potential to realise freedom. Freedom itself requires freedom from dependence. Does not freedom from dependence lie in one's capacity to understand the nature of dependence? If such capacity is denied, so too is one's insight and fortitude; freedom is then simply not possible.

Attachment is the product of dependency. As soon as you rely on a certain thing, you become attached to that certain thing. It is clearly absurd to attempt to overcome our attachments, any attachment at all, by becoming attached to a system that promises freedom. Our motivation to overcome our attachment locks us into another movement, another pattern; a new direction that shapes our freedom, or lack of it. Our attempt to overcome attachment has simply become another attachment; we have done no more than exchange one attachment with another. There are many systems of meditation existing today that promise freedom from attachment if you follow what the guru says. And so you start following his system because his system promises a reward at the end of his boot camp. There is meditation discipline, mind control technique, chanting, the 6am cold showers; you are aware of these so-called spiritual activities that go on. You want to be free but now you are craving the reward; see that it is this very craving for freedom which limits your freedom. You are attached to the reward. Your attachment has a different name, albeit a nobler and more socially acceptable name, but now your attachment runs far deeper than the attachment for mere worldly possessions. This is the great poverty of spiritual elitism and the lesson that lies in waiting for every devotee.

If we are dependent upon a certain activity to achieve happiness – whether religious or some other form of system – then there will always be anxiety and fear; the opposites of happiness. If the goal of this activity is not forthcoming – be that enlightenment, heaven or nirvana, the sensation that is desired or whatever it is we think will make us happy – then there is the anxiety of not achieving the goal or the ideal. There is the fear of not becoming what we think we should become or achieving what we think we should achieve. We fail to realise that the goal is in Being, and that Being is not in the becoming but in simply Being, and thus cannot be a goal. Our fear and anxiety about becoming and achieving will never end. When taken to the extreme, this fear can breed aggressive behaviour as we strive to reach our objective, and this takes place under the deluded shroud of 'what should be'. This in itself explains much religious violence across history, from the Crusades to today's fundamentalists. The Koran states *'Be and It is'*. These four words are a statement of love. Again, this is the truth that *'Being is not in the becoming but in simply Being and thus cannot be a goal'*. Buddha stated this, so did Jesus; so have all masters across history, yet this message seems to have been lost by many of our religious systems.

A Mechanical Mind

YOU MAY THINK THAT IF an individual submits to a certain religious system voluntarily, then that individual is still free in making his or her choice. However, remember that where there is conformity there is fear, and where there is fear there is not true freedom. You may accept a religion or a teacher voluntarily, but by conforming to the dictates of that religion or teacher you are conforming out of fear. You can dress this up however you like, you are still being conditioned and with this come imitation and compliance; the ending of your alertness and the beginning of a mind that is mechanical. Any form of voluntary submission is rooted in fear. If you submit yourself to rules and fixed patterns of conduct so that you are free to learn and observe yourself, what are you really learning? Conditioning, that is what you are learning. Those who are conditioned are not free.

The routine of compliance with a system – following rules of practice and methods laid down by others, day in day out – only makes your mind more mechanical, more repetitive and thus rigid, narrow and limited. In your quest for security, your mind loses its sensitivity, its aliveness and spontaneity as it numbly follows a repetitive pattern.[1] But reality does not follow a pattern; reality is always new, always changing. If your mind is locked into a pattern, rather than being sensitive and swift, it becomes lifeless, dull, mechanical and rigid as it operates only from conclusions. If you operate only this way then you miss Truth. You can hold a map of reality in your hands but as soon as the map is complete, it is already old; reality has moved on. Innocence is to not operate from conclusion. It is to understand the role of knowledge and learn when to be free of all that is known. It is to die to all that is past – your expectations, memory, dependencies, attachments, knowledge, practices, everything – and instead be ready, open, courageous, empty and clear to what is new. When you

---

[1] A by-product of such a mechanical mind is, of course, greater insecurity.

die psychologically to everything that you have known, then you can enter the only time that is real. This is the time of Now – the only true time, which is eternal and which is not found in routine. Repetition of patterns and the methods of others are not real; they are imitative and cannot lead to Truth.

When there is control and suppression in meditation systems, when you ask *'How am I to end my thoughts?'*, there is automatically a method and thus effort, tension, conflict and conformity. In such method there is a thinking mind, operating out of what is past and therefore not free. Such a mind will continue practicing for years and years under the heavy weight of suppression and control, getting nowhere, and this will continue unless there is understanding of this whole process. Motives are a form of desire, no matter how noble they are. The motive to end the activity of the self may be a noble one, but as a desire it only serves to reinforce the self even further. Understand that thought can never free itself of thought. It is impossible to prevent thought using thought, using control – that being a controller, because the enforcer is the enforced. The thinking mind cannot end thought without creating conflict between the controller and the controlled, the enforcer and the enforced, and cannot therefore be used to stop itself. It is impossible to prevent thought by following a method because the moment you follow a method there must be a pilot and thus a centre. Any space that you create is space that is derived from the will of a centre, meditating in an attempt to empty its own thoughts. Where there is a centre there is an observer and an observed; accompanying the centre is a periphery, therefore a boundary and thus a confined space. This is not the immense space of freedom that has no centre or boundary.

You may say that you are going into a method from a state of freedom, but under the system of a religion or guru you will always be influenced by that system. You are following another's path, and not your own. Remember that vicarious wisdom is never authentic. Rather than dance through the woods, enjoying the birds and the trees, you are too busy watching your feet, so concerned about getting the dance steps right that you miss the beauty of your surroundings. You are distracted from your own investigation, busy chanting a mantra, perhaps, or stubbornly trying to stretch the gap between your thoughts longer and longer as you strive for a quiet mind. These techniques fail to open up a space that is vast, as anything created by thought is necessarily narrow and limited.

In following another, there is no standing on one's own two feet, there is no sharp, investigating mind; instead we become gullible and easily deceived. Practicing method only makes the mind dull and dry of life; it prevents the mind from learning its own way. Life is the great teacher. There is already a system in place within reality to bring about one's own maturity, to bring about greater awareness and understanding. This system is called life. The great teacher is the human experience and it is vast. It is a system that has been devised by a mind that is far greater than any single teacher. Who is a teacher to teach others? A person's freedom is their own business. Life itself will provide leverage for us to find our own understanding. This we already know through our own life experience to date (and the science of this can be found in the comprehensive study of astrology). If a teacher claims to all have the answers then be wary of him. He is not privy to the lessons that you need to learn at this very moment, his system will be general and the particular cannot be solved with the general. Your life is the particular, and cannot be generalised to fit into his life or his system.

In experimentation, one may find stimulation and inspiration in various existing systems and teachings. External sources may raise questions in your mind, helping to stimulate your investigation. This is the extent of the master's role. Just as he cannot go to the toilet on your behalf, nor can he solve your conflict for you. Only you can solve it. It is down to you to be free, not the master, not the guru. It is not his business to interfere with your freedom. By devising a system and then advertising that system as the answer, a guru denies those with minds that are still seeking, still immature, from going their own way, from learning their own life lessons, their own mistakes as well as their own insights. There is of course one lesson lying in waiting for every devotee of a guru, this being that to follow is not the way.

Look at the practice of the guru and the devotee, how many devotees ever reach a state of true freedom? Always there is hankering after the master and whilst there is hankering for the master, enlightenment is simply not possible. Only you, standing alone, looking at your life, can see the cause, the 'why', of your own sorrow and only you can face this sorrow directly and be free of it. Like learning to ride a bike, you must do it you own way. A guru's system prevents you from seeing reality as it is without distortion, because always there is the shadow of 'what should be' hanging over you. *'Should I do this or that?'*

> "All instruction is but a finger pointing to the moon; and those whose gaze is fixed upon the pointer will never see beyond. Even let him catch sight of the moon, and still he cannot see its beauty."
>
> *Buddha*

The Great Escape

A SYSTEM PROVIDES A MEANS of escape, and if you are caught in a system as a means of escape then you have not understood the nature of the problem. The problem is YOU; the conflict and the disorder are within. Until that conflict has been resolved through your own understanding, rather than through the repetition of the understanding of others, you will not be free. You can go to lectures and you can listen to advice, but it is outside knowledge that is not yours; it belongs to another. If you have a problem and a master explains how to solve that problem, then you still have the problem. For example, a master can explain why you feel insufficient, why your deep fear of loneliness drives all your activity and that all of your activity only reinforces your sense of isolation even further; he can explain the difference between aloneness and loneliness and that only through understanding loneliness will you ever know the freedom of aloneness, the freedom of standing up on your own two feet. And so you listen and you nod, but it is meaningless unless these insights are yours. Your problem only ceases when you have understood it deeply for yourself; another cannot understand it for you and then explain so that you can adopt it. Such a strategy has no value; your understanding is bound to be incomplete. This takes us back to the difference between knowing something intellectually, and understanding it in the very essence of your Being. Knowing something intellectually does not necessarily prevent you from erring. If someone continues to err, it is because their understanding is incomplete. Unless you are grown up about all this, unless you examine your own mind – the source of your own thoughts, your desires and fears and all that goes on – unless you undertake your own meditation and not that of another, then you will never be anything other than a parrot, repeating knowledge while holding no authentic wisdom of your own. Where there is authentic wisdom there is goodness and there is virtue – not virtue cultivated out of a textbook, but virtue that is a living thing, a happening that is uncaused. Then there is no dependency, there is freedom. But very few of us are truly free.

We are unhappy and we seek to become happy. We seek through religion because we believe that by following such a system we will escape our inner sorrow, drive away all pain and find something abiding, solid and lasting. So we are seeking in order to escape from ourselves, but the seeking itself is an escape; it prevents us from seeing ourselves as we truly are. We think of freedom, heaven and enlightenment as 'over there' whilst 'I' am 'here'. I may walk towards that goal on the horizon, but the cause of the sorrow is me and it has always been me. If I am walking over there – to the mirage on the horizon – in order to overcome my suffering, then I am just avoiding the problems of the me. The religious search becomes one big distraction. Any system followed is no more than an escape, a distraction from the problems that already exist inside the me. Would it not be better to turn all attention into myself and find out why I am suffering, find out why I am searching, rather than just be pre-occupied with the search? Is it not better to examine the cause of one's unhappiness rather than look for an escape? We must ask ourselves what we are escaping from. The problem will follow us to wherever we escape because the problem is us. (This reminds me of a cartoon by Charles M. Shultz, where his lead character is trying to escape from a rain cloud that is directly over his head. Wherever he goes, the rain cloud follows and so the protagonist never escapes getting wet. It is the same with the escape into the religious search; you will always get wet because you can't escape from the rain cloud which you are carrying around with you.)

You cannot escape the problems of the me without realising that it is you that is the problem. Freedom is only possible when there is the understanding of what is not freedom. For example, if you desire freedom, the moment you desire freedom you are no longer free. Equally, fear is not freedom, nor will it ever *be* freedom. We get distracted into systems to gain freedom, but one's freedom is not to be found in the overcoming of one's fear through a system; fear is never overcome, eliminated or conquered by a system. Fear can only ever be understood, and once it is thoroughly understood it can be transmuted. We can never understand fear if we are running away from it through the use of systems. We may escape from the me temporarily in prayer or mantra, but this is completely superficial because the me is both the cause and the manifestation of the problem. The me is where all of the fear, conflict and disorder lie and it is because of this conflict that we conform, imitate and accept the authority of others as we try to import solutions of order to overcome our own disorder. Order – and thus virtue – cannot be imported, they only come into being when the mind can see or begin to see the disorder within itself. Why do you conform? Why do you imitate? Why do you fear X, Y and Z? Why do you desire A, B and C? The enquiry into these 'why's and other conflicts within you help to establish order. You will learn to see the disorder within, and see that at its root there is and always has been fear. We battle with ourselves only because of fear, but there is no battle when one's understanding is complete and one's own. Then you do not need to import virtue or goodness from the outside, you can recognise that the only true authority, goodness and virtue is your own.

This investigation, this self-understanding, is not searching; it is surgery. It is not a pill that temporarily masks the pain of the symptoms, it cuts to the root of the problem and removes it. The religious 'pill' may make you feel better for a while, but it is escapism, masking the inner sickness without curing it. You continue to carry the sickness within, in the misunderstanding, fear and disorder of your mind. Would it not be better to go to the root of your suffering and be free of suffering altogether? Such activity is not searching, instead you are finding the root of your disease at its source and you are removing it, like a surgeon. A master is a surgeon to himself. The only medicine that humanity truly needs is Truth; not god or prophets or pills. Truth nourishes like raw food and just like food it is cancerous when processed. Truth is found in the light of awareness, which uncovers and understands the causes of suffering. When you overcome your suffering you are truly free; what else is freedom if not this?

Searching for enlightenment is just another means of escape, a means of overcoming one's feelings of insufficiency and loneliness. If reaching enlightenment becomes an ambition, this is not love. Such an ambitious mind is caught up in 'what should be' rather than embracing 'what is', and Being. 'What is' is not enough because we don't understand the gift of 'what is'; instead we want more because we are accustomed to wanting more. We strive for more – whether for heaven, for enlightenment, to be saved or to be someone special – and the more we strive, the more we desire and the more we leave ourselves open to fear, dependence and deception. It is our striving for more that is the very cause of our grief. We run after the messiah, the guru or the saint asking, *'Show me the way.'* In so doing we are denying ourselves the opportunity for our own investigation. We deny our capacity to solve our own problems. This is what every master has done for himself and this is what you too can do. A master can show you the door, and perhaps introduce you to techniques which you will find initially helpful, but ultimately you must drop the master and drop the techniques. If you need his presence in order to see the mistakes you are making, then you are still hankering after him, still dependent upon him. You are operating from fear. If you remain dependent on the master or on the technique, you cannot grow. Authentic goodness cannot blossom since goodness and growth come together. Goodness can never be imported because growth can never be imported; goodness like growth is its own living thing. It comes into being when you have understood your fear. You must learn for yourself and not be dependent.

Only by understanding our fears will we ever be free; never will we be free if we are running away from our fears on paths to enlightenment or caught up in the systems of gurus and religions. How can there be love when a person is using his life as a passage to an idea his mind has created, like heaven, nirvana, enlightenment or even something as simple as social ambition? If you think life is a waiting room (like they do in India) or a testing ground (like they do in Italy) or a social competition (like they do all over the world), then you do not know what it means to love. The total and complete acceptance of 'what you are' is love, not 'what should be' at the end of a journey. If we are caught up in a system striving for A or B, even if one of these is the striving for 'what is' or 'what you are', then there is no love. We cannot love if there is any striving, no matter what we strive for; striving goes against the nature of what it means to love. Can we be happy without being dependent upon anything? It is really important that we ask this question because we cannot be happy until we have understood the ache of attachment – to our assets, our reputation, to our perception of 'what should be', to our goals, to our systems, to whatever we strive for. Love arises when we are not dependent upon anything, when our dependency upon everything has dissolved.

For example, you may see that attachment is inhibiting because your thoughts are being dictated by an inward fear and so you want to take action to eliminate this. You may realise that there is no freedom if you are possessed by your own possessions, that there is no freedom if you worry about your worldly goods. If you try to eradicate such attachment with action or a 'solution' like the practice of detachment, you only create another form of attachment. Beware of the trap of replacing one form of attachment with another. Your attachment to possessions may now be replaced by an unhealthy attachment to a spiritual path; attachment to detachment! If you give away all your possessions and then announce this to the world, then you are clearly still operating within the field of attachment. That which you can give away freely does not possess you, but if you need to announce this to the world, then you are still possessed by the act of giving away your possessions. You are running away from attachment, but nothing has really changed. Genuine understanding of attachment is vital if we are to be free from dependencies and achieve a happiness that is free from any dependency at all. This is achieved not by escaping from, but by addressing and understanding our problems.

Our Perception of Dependency

WE FOLLOW SYSTEMS AND METHODS because we do not understand the nature of dependency. We have spoken of its roots in fear, we have discussed its relationship with deception and we have seen how freedom and goodness cannot arise within the field of dependency. Now if you look again into dependency, you will notice that we usually only move away from dependencies that cause us pain, rather than away from those which provide us with a sense of comfort. But any comfort or happiness gained from dependency is just as much an illusion as any pain or conflict. It is illusion; an image we have created psychologically about a person or a system in order to make ourselves feel better. A man is dependent upon his method to find God as long as that method provides him with comfort and security. His religion may be comforting, it may make him happy, but he is only happy on the surface. Deep down there is fear and anxiety that if he does not conform in the way set out by his religion then he will not arrive at the religion's promised goal. This is the true nature of our dependency.

In most cases, humans are happy as long as they are not disturbed. As long as our presumptions and the images we have formed – about our religion or our identity – are not shaken or questioned, all is well. We think we are happy when worshipping man-made 'sacred' objects, referring to holy books, conforming to our chosen system and never deviating from our centre, but really we are locked into dependency. Rather than enjoy a relationship with the true essence of religion – which is the absence of the distorting 'me' – we form an image about our chosen systems in order to feel an illusion of fulfilment. Such happiness is sought through something external, such as a religious structure, and can therefore only ever be transitory and unstable. Is there such a thing as authentic fulfilment that is a result of thinking? We are asking whether it is possible to be happy and not be dependent upon anything for this happiness, to step beyond achieving happiness through something – a person, a system, an ideal or a situation – and overcome the problem of dependency altogether. Can our happiness be uncaused?

When we depend on external sources for our happiness, such as seeking happiness through the following of a system, can there be authentic happiness? By following a system we are stating that our happiness requires a cause. By following a system we are laying down criteria for our happiness; our happiness is conditional upon us undertaking certain activities and dependent upon us reaching certain goals, like enlightenment. It is dependent upon the existence of external objects such as systems, individuals or holy books. If our happiness is conditional then it cannot derive from love, it cannot be authentic. Remember that there is no such thing as 'conditional love', it is a contradiction in terms. Love and condition do not sit together. Love is not of the mind, love is not a product of thought; love is your very Being and the embracing of 'what is' in the absence of thought and in the absence of the distorting 'me'. Whenever there are criteria for love, created by the distorting 'me' – such as condition, control, conformity and dependency – then there is no love. A religiously ambitious man cannot love; his activity drives the momentum of the self, he is ambitious for the self, he has set conditions for the self and is comparing himself and others with projected ideals. In this ambition there is a lack of love. If our happiness is conditional upon a certain activity, then really it is no more than an illusion of fulfilment that our mind has created around that activity; it is this illusion, this image, this false idol, that drives our ambitious activity – religious, economic, social or otherwise. Authentic happiness derives from love. Love is not caused; nor is authentic happiness. What use is following a system if that system and its goal act as a cause for your happiness? The happiness derived from following a system will never be genuine because true and authentic happiness is uncaused. Please see this clearly; it will be of enormous benefit if you can appreciate what is being said.

We can only be truly free when our happiness is uncaused and authentic. If we need a cause, we surely become dependent on that cause for our happiness and when dependent, we are not free. The nature of dependency is to lock people into a pattern of thinking and action; thereby creating a limitation of view, a distortion of clarity and thus limited intelligence. Dependency is not love, co-dependency is not love; all dependency is fear. Dependency and fear feed each other. Uncaused happiness, on the other hand, implies no dependency on anything. Without dependency, where is fear? And without fear, there is freedom. Where there is freedom from any cause, there is joy; the joy of Being, which is love. Uncaused happiness only comes with understanding important truths and concepts such as love, freedom and dependency. Only in such understanding is there the ending of all dependency and the birth of freedom. We tend only to understand dependencies that cause us pain and not dependencies that provide an idea of comfort, like our religions and systems. As such, this prevents a deep understanding of dependency as a concept in itself. This is why religions and other systems have dominated the spiritual landscape for the last 2000 years.

Understanding Freedom

WE FOLLOW BECAUSE WE DO not understand the true nature of freedom, that being the embracing and comprehension of 'what is' rather than 'what should be'. To be present to what is alive within, observing without attraction or aversion. We do not understand the relationship between freedom and love; we do not understand the binding nature of thought itself and the very significant implications of that realisation. If we misunderstand freedom, then how can we ever possibly *be* free? The foundations of freedom have been laid down by various masters across history and these foundations can provide us with templates of understanding. However none of these are useful to the seeker if the seeker does not understand his or her own motivation for seeking; we do not wish to become dependent on the teachings of another. If the seeker continues to look elsewhere for an imported solution, then the search will be in vain, regardless of how many masters are consulted. It is the mind that is the actual cause and source of suffering, and it is the mind which must be the subject of inquiry.

Until we have understood the nature of freedom and what it means to be free, discontent and dissatisfaction will remain. Freedom is to be free of fear. To follow the system of another is not to be free because you are neither free from yourself (you are escaping), nor from your fear of failure. Where is the freedom in that? Freedom is not something bestowed upon you by an external other such as God, nor is it something that you stumble across by accident; freedom is what you are already inside. You will only realise this when you uncover what it is that prevents you from being free. These are the many layers of thought such as ideals, dependencies and projections that the mind creates around love, fear and freedom. What we desire as ideals cannot be truth but only self-projected, a method of self-perpetuation. To desire truth is to deny it; for Truth to Be you must cease. You have to understand the nature of freedom by understanding what freedom is not, you have to understand the nature of thought and understand 'what is' when thought is not (this is what much of the last chapter was warming us up to), you have to understand your fears and face these fears head on – on your own, alone, maturely and intelligently. Most importantly you have to understand what love is by understanding what love is not. Only such a capacity of understanding will bring freedom, not the regimented following of the system of another.

Alertness & Meditation

THE PURPOSE OF MEDITATION IS to be aware, alert, alive, vital and sharp. Now, can these things be taught or are they inherent? Your mind is busy and full of noise, and this noise blurs, distorts and pollutes the clarity of your mind. We can all appreciate this and thus see the value of a quiet mind, but we err when we try to enforce such silence upon ourselves through systems and methods. Silence can never be enforced, it comes only from understanding the nature of thought and awareness. Your awareness is always alive, alert, sharp and fundamentally clear like a bright blue sky; this is the nature of pure awareness. Thought, on the other hand, is a distorting factor. Outputs of thought, such as belief, block the clarity of our awareness and can induce rigidity, dullness, indolence and a lack of vitality. The only precondition for greater alertness is a body that is healthy, balanced, rested, watered and oxygenated; something most of us can easily achieve[2]. As soon as the clouds of distortion – the endless mental chit chat and the activity of

---

[2] Yoga and raw food are helpful in this respect.

the 'me' – dissipate, alertness and sharpness will arise. They arise naturally because they are inherent to awareness itself.

Now when you follow some kind of externally imposed system, you are following a method and with method comes routine. As we discussed above, routine flows against the clarity of awareness, like a dampening fog across the sky of your mind. Routines carried out in the name of sharpness or alertness only make the mind dull, mechanical and narrow and thus go against that which they are trying to cultivate. In routine there is repetition, tension, subjugation and conformity. Do these make the mind sharp, or dull? Alertness cannot be imported, learnt or cultivated because it is not thought. You cannot cultivate that which you already are, you can only clear that which blocks this fundamental essence. The clearer your awareness, the more evident becomes your alertness. Alertness arises when your mind can see the possibility of change – change from the burden of thought, from the heavy fog into the clear blue sky of awareness. When you see this possibility of change you open yourself up to great energy; the energy to connect to 'that which is indescribable'.

If the mind is to be alert then it must be clear. If it is busy talking to itself, if it is busy controlling itself, saying to itself, *'I must do this'*, *'I must do that'*, then there is conflict and constant movement inside. A mind cannot be alert if it is not clear and it cannot be clear if it is not still. You need not be physically still for this stillness to be – a mountain climber has a quiet mind and yet his body moves – it is the mind which must be still. Think of the alert poise of the predator; there is perfect stillness in such alertness. All psychological movement and activity must cease if there is to be alert clarity; what mountain climbers and daredevils call 'hyper awareness'. Any distracting chitter chatter creates movement in the mind. If you are rushing around in response to this chatter, following one train of thought one way and then another train of thought the other, then how can you see clearly? You are not free from thought. We all see the value of a quiet, undisturbed mind but when we try to create this state ourselves, the very act of creating – the control, the concentration and the limiting nature of that concentration – instead leads to disturbance and disorder in the mind.

What we tend to do is try to enforce stillness within. This tendency has given rise to systems of meditation which give us techniques to concentrate our minds and control our thoughts. In these strict techniques there is control, and where there is control there is no freedom. There is effort and where there is effort there is conflict. What we are doing in effect is putting our thoughts in a prison, where the jailer is the controller and the enforcer; an aspect of thought. The idea of attaining freedom through that which is in itself not free is absurd. It is bound to create conflict. How much freedom do you see in suppression, concentration, control, restraint or containment? Remember that if meditation is concentration then it is not meditation; concentration is narrow, inhibiting and rigid. Only when meditation is effortless and open is it authentic.

If you are not free at the beginning, how then can you hope to be free by the end? If there is no freedom in your first move, then you will always be operating inside a prison. We may decorate the bars to make ourselves feel at home, but we're still in a prison. Freedom is not achieved through subjugation to method, through suppression, conquering or distraction; freedom is understanding the nature of that which binds you – your desires, your fears and your dependencies. Freedom is understanding; then there is no dependency. You are dependent when you do not understand. Understand that freedom is freedom, that it does not incorporate control or dependency otherwise it could not be freedom. Authentic meditation requires understanding, not control or dependency; where there is dependency there cannot be freedom, and where there is control there will only be conflict.

This conflict is in the duality between the observer and observed, the controller and controlled, and like all conflict and all subjugation it is rooted in fear. Again, it is the drive towards 'what should be' due to a lack of openness to 'what is'. Inevitably, there follows tension and disorder. It is very important to understand that you cannot quieten the mind using control. Techniques are just tricks which may temporarily quieten the mind, but the only long term solution is in understanding. There is no 'how' to stop thought; as soon as there is a 'how' there is a system and thus conflict. Instead, we must understand the nature of thought, what thought is, how it arises, why it arises;

only in the understanding of this – which is true intelligence – can the mind become quiet of its own accord. This silence is effortless, fun and joyful rather than the heavy 'must be' silence of control, suppression or subjugation. To be free is to have no direction, and all method is direction. Instead in freedom there is the choiceless awareness of 'what is', there is the attention of all senses without boundary or frontier, there is the stepping into your suchness and your Being-ness, and this Being-ness has no centre.

If there is control then there must be a centre. If there is a centre then there is a boundary around that centre and thus limited space, and if it is limited then it is not free. If there is a method, then the 'I' is directing that method and so immediately there is a centre. Please appreciate that all method is self-centred activity and thus binding. On the other hand, a mind that is not pre-occupied with achieving a goal, but which is simply enjoying its own essence or suchness, is without direction. There is no direction in meditation; if there is, it means you are meditating not out of joy but out of purpose. Any effort is a source of conflict; order is to have understood this conflict. Without the foundation of order within the mind, meditation is no different to prayer; just another form of religious escapism. This is what most of us are doing, praying and meditating out of a sense of purpose. In authentic meditation there is no purpose, there is no goal; instead there is the savouring of the suchness of existence and its many nuances at every moment, where the 'me' is not. A quiet mind comes only from understanding; you cannot seek it and you cannot enforce it, and this has been the problem of meditation.

Intelligence, Not Thought

INTELLIGENCE IS TO UNDERSTAND THE nature of thought and the nature of knowledge. In this understanding, there is no *'How am I to end thought?'* As soon as we start asking, *'How?'* there is a method. The nature of any method is that of procedure and structure and if we are following procedure and structure then there is the introduction of effort; there is conflict to change 'what is' into 'what should be'. This conflict is driven by a desire to achieve a certain goal or a fear of not achieving that goal, but there is no freedom in desire and fear. Genuine, inner freedom is to be beyond one's own desires, fears and inner disciplines. It is to have sufficient understanding such that internal discipline is no longer necessary. It is to understand that even the ambition to end thought is itself a distraction from your inner existence. You will discover that your inner existence is the same existence as all existence; what therefore is the point of ambition?

Rather than the 'how', we have to understand the 'why' of thought. What is the source of thought? To enhance our understanding we must consider ourselves to be the content of our consciousness, and consider how this content moves in certain directions, such as the desire to be enlightened. If we do not understand the shape of this content, which we call 'I', then we will only ever be able to operate inside the field of the known, for the 'I' only exists in the field of the known, that being the subconscious or conscious. The 'I' is the past, the 'I' is memory, the accumulated history, experiences, happenings, knowledge of certain things and ideas we have about the future, all formed from the past. The thinking of the 'I' will always be a prison because it is derived from language, memory, knowledge; all past. Such parameters limit understanding. Remember that creativity and moments of insight arise when thinking is not. Understanding is not necessarily verbalised thought.

Intelligence is to understand the function of knowledge, to know when it is appropriate and when it is not. It is to understand the limitations of what knowledge can bring and what it cannot. Knowledge cannot bring freedom because knowledge is derived from the past, from the known. If your meditation practice is based upon knowledge, a continuation of methods and techniques from the past, then how is it free? Truth is always new, always free, and cannot therefore be drawn from the past, from knowledge. If we are to be free, to understand Truth, then we must understand the function of knowledge. We have already investigated learning and seen that knowledge derives from education and life experiences, and these go on to form memory. All such knowledge and memory is constituted of thought.

Throughout the centuries, humanity has been preoccupied with thought, seeking freedom through thought and its many mechanisms.

In the last chapter we investigated the nature of thought and saw that it is drawn from what is old, what is the field of the known. Total freedom is not possible if we are operating from thought because thought draws only from memory and knowledge. It is vital we understand that to be free from the field of the known requires the ending of knowledge, because knowledge is the known and the known, the human mind, is polluted with ideas of heaven, hell, enlightenment or 'what should be.' Any continuation of knowledge – whether through meditation method, rigid spiritual practice or the many popular systems that humanity has devised – only serves to lock us into what we already know. The continuation of conditioning reinforces further conditioning, thus limiting our freedom. All forms of religious method hinder our realisation of freedom, as is evident in human history. Method, passed down in our varied traditions, has conditioned us, and it is this conditioning that prevents our freedom.

Freedom does not exist within thought, or a space that thought has created, it only exists within your very Being, which is not thought. There is no freedom if you are following only the mind and not the heart. Your Being is the energy of the whole of your life; it is the very foundation of what you are, never a fragment of it. Freedom is not achieved in an hourly assignment of time that the mind puts aside each week in search of freedom, but in a commitment of your very Being to freedom, when freedom can be unlocked through your very Being-ness. This commitment is not an obligation, for how much freedom exists in obligation? Instead it is the commitment of intelligence, the union of the intellect and the heart to understand the nature of thought so that the heart and awareness can operate freely from thought. The way to Truth is not through the mind alone. Remember that if you follow method and system like a parrot, then you are using only mind, only thought. Only when you look inwards to the heart, when the heart and mind speak as one, is there intelligence and thus freedom from your conflict and disorder. If you seek freedom through only the mind and its thinking – through systems and methods – then the task ahead of you will be long and arduous. If you look inwards to your heart and your own nature, you will clearly see the door to freedom.

Order arises when the mind sees the disorder within itself, when the mind and the heart start speaking as one. The heart can see and the mind is blind, the mind can move quickly and because it moves quickly it stumbles at every turn. When there is a communion with the heart, then and only then can the mind see clearly. The mind can see that its very striving is the cause of its own sorrow; that ambition is the activity of a mind that is blind. Ambition is a mind in motion but really a life on hold. A mind that is clear can see that there is nothing to become that you are not already, that there is nothing to achieve that you are not already. You are perfect already, your essence is absolutely correct. When this is understood deeply, then there is freedom, there is the joy of one's Being, there is love. When we look inwards to our inner space, a space without boundary, we not only see the essence of our Being but realise we are not – nor have we ever been – separate from it. This essence of Being is the essence of existence itself, the same essence that underwrites the entire universe. It is the ultimate freedom.

But first we must be free of all the images that we create, all the knowledge we rely upon, all our desires, our dependencies, our fears, our attachments, absolutely everything; to let them go and leave all of them behind without argument, without trying to settle them. The mind that moves beyond itself can leave all this behind, recognise its own limitations and look within for answers. Such a mind is moving beyond its image of the self, beyond the field of the known, beyond the prison of thought. This psychological death is genuine meditation; it is to wipe everything away by surrendering completely and absolutely to one's Being. It is a surrender that is yielding, abandoning and effortless. This Being is timeless, it is now and it has always been now. It is the eternal instant, the same instant of Being-ness, the instant of existence. This Being-ness and the embracing of it is love. The true revolution is love, and it is only reached through one's psychological death. To die daily to desire and fear is freedom and the foundation of love; it arises from a mind that is innocent of 'what should be'.

The Foundations of Meditation

IN THIS AND THE PREVIOUS chapter we have been looking towards a realm or space that is beyond the limited boundary of what is known; a realm of the unknown, a space for the immeasurable, a door to Truth inside 'the house of many rooms' which is somewhere deep inside this process called 'me'; a door underneath the layers of the 'me' which leads to the vast meadow beyond (as described in Chapter 12 of the book *Question Mark*). This door is the heart. The way is the heart. When the heart and the intellect come together there is intelligence, wisdom and understanding. But what do we mean by 'the heart'?

The heart is love, it is freedom, it is compassion, and it is reached by understanding what love is through understanding what love is not. Love is not jealousy, love is not dependency, love is not condition, love is not control and love is not a product of thought. If love is a product of thought then there would be criteria to it, which is not love. Love is your very Being and the Being of all things; free from criteria or condition. So we must be free from thought and free from what thought is, from the known, in order to unlock the door of our hearts and enter the freedom of the vast meadow. This requires full understanding – of the nature of thought, the nature of knowledge and the nature of freedom. This understanding is the groundwork for authentic meditation.

Authentic meditation is freedom; freedom from the past, freedom from knowledge, freedom from method. Method is a choice and, like any choice, it is a movement and a direction. Freedom has no direction; it is not a choice. True freedom is freedom from the movement and direction of the choosing mind. Our awareness must be choiceless and without direction. A clear mind sees the danger of direction, the conflict that is involved. It does not choose. There is no entity engaged in the act of choosing. That is why there is no centre, no 'I' driving forward with an objective or goal. There must be space but not the space that thought creates and then thinks is infinite space, like the extended interval between thoughts, but the immense space when the 'I' is not, when there is no direction, no method, no choosing, no needing and no wanting. This is true freedom and there is immensity in such total and utter abandon. It is the immensity of soaking up the very essence and suchness of every moment in the absence of the 'me'. It is like stumbling across a view so breathtaking that the 'me' is forgotten, abandoned for a moment; but now this is true of all moments, not just the rare few. The freedom of choiceless awareness is available in every step, in every mouthful, in every contact with another, in every sensation as the breeze whistles past; not just in those few moments when you're sitting in lotus position. You can be aware whilst weeding the garden, you can be aware whilst walking to the railway station, you can be aware anywhere. Such awareness at every moment, in the suchness of both the pleasant and even the unpleasant, is true meditation and true freedom. This emptiness, this quietness, this stillness of freedom is what is holy, divine and beautiful.

It is only in such space, such freedom, that we can see that which is truly sacred, that which is of a different dimension. Awareness moves freely into all senses; then there is contact with existence, a contact which is beyond the described. This contact, this relationship with existence is what is truly divine – not a system devised by a guru or a holy book or a cathedral that humans have made and decreed 'sacred'. The relationship between you and existence, the communion of observer and observed in pure observation, this is what is sacred. The communion of the self and existence comes about when the strength of the self surrenders absolutely to the utter magnitude and immensity of existence. In the total surrender and utter abandonment of the self there is freedom and invincibility. It is freedom from thought and thus freedom from time and, ultimately, freedom from space-time. This is the meekness both Jesus and Buddha talk of.

"Meekness is most powerful."

Buddha

Your search for inner peace will eventually lead, full circle, back to you. Why? Because you are already here. The freedom, peace and communion that you seek are the love which is your fundamental nature, your Being-ness. In this Being-ness there is no striving, no ambition, no comparison or measurement. Here, your mind is clear, still and free to love. To realise this you have to nurture understanding, which lays the groundwork of Truth. And you have to do this alone, not by following the methods of another. As soon as you see the Truth of this, when the grounding of understanding has been laid, then authentic meditation can begin.

chapter three
The Way of the Buddha

THANKS TO HIS TENDENCY TO look up to the stars and the sky for inspiration, man has always looked outwards for answers about his origins and purpose. What distinguished Buddha was that he was one of the first to stand up and say that the search for Truth (the religious or scientific search) is not external, but internal. Buddha does not negate the external, but he made it clear that to understand the external one must first look inward. In doing this, Buddha turned the religious and scientific search into one of practical psychology and meditation. Rather than look at the causes of the universe as aspects that are separate from us (which exist out there in the stars, or somewhere in the past), rather than look at the scientific factors involved in the creation of the human form, Buddha recognised that existence is an ongoing process which is fundamentally related to all life forms, and that all life co-exists within existence in the present moment. Buddha recognised that human life is conscious and that all life is energy; this led him to question the relationship between consciousness, existence and energy. He asked *'Who or what is creating this life force, this consciousness, this energy that is my Being? Is this existence that I am, fundamentally related to all existence?'* Rather than look outwards for a creator or creative force, Buddha turned the search onto the searcher. This has been a masterstroke.

Buddha presents a religion that perplexes theologians. It is a religion – for want of a better word to describe Buddha's approach – with no God, no structure and no belief system; where what is taught is not the acquisition of new virtues, but the uncovering of layers of falsehood to reveal abiding Truths that are already within. It is a religion where the final objective is not to have an objective, where 'God' is recognised as merely an idea that humans have formed because of our primitive, fear-orientated minds. It is a religion where its primary teacher denies the existence of the soul and one that informs humanity that the world is merely a dream and that one day, on the day of your death, that dream will end. Buddha says that all of your relationships, your possessions and your attachments are part of that dream and therefore ultimately not real. Buddha says don't have attachments because the nature of reality is impermanent. He says don't cling to that which you think is permanent because your thinking is misguided; nothing is permanent, not even your sense of self. He says all relationships are transitory and ultimately you are on your own. Buddha takes away everything from you: your home, your possessions, your relationships, your reality, every aspect of 'you' down to the last remnant of 'I'. He says everything that you think you are, you are NOT, not one bit at all! In death nothing of you will remain; absolutely everything you have ever known about yourself – your body, your mind, your idea of a soul – will dissolve, and that which remains is something you know nothing about. Every element you would deem recognisable about yourself will be gone when you die; absolutely nothing of 'you' will remain.

'Why should we put ourselves through this search for Nirvana? If my life is a dream, if my relationships are to cease and I am not who I think I am, at least let me pretend that it is all real otherwise what is the point of anything?'

According to Buddha such an attitude will not help you because any type of pretending is false. If you live a life that is false, then you are not free and whatever is not free can only ever suffer. Because we do not know any different, we may think we are not suffering but Buddha says this is illusion; the very nature of selfhood, the very nature of feeling cut off from existence, is to suffer.

'But my life is the only real thing that I know, to negate this is to negate everything!'

Buddha is not suggesting that you negate your life, your relationships or your life history as many ascetics have done, far from it. He is simply suggesting that you recognise that you are part of a greater process that is happening now and that one day, the process that is you will end and another will arise. You will die and all that will remain is something that you cannot understand right now. Buddha is immovable on this point. *'Absolutely nothing of me'* is hard to comprehend, it feels very much like a total death, a total non-existence, but this does not automatically mean there is nothing at all; what Buddha means is there is nothing of 'you' – the difference is monumental. Since we do not understand, since we cannot comprehend a 'no self' existence which is not total annihilation, we think 'that which remains' must be our soul. But as Buddha explains, the self disappears completely, there is no 'I', there is nothing of you that remains, yet there is something that you cannot understand that will remain. We grasp onto this and think, *'Buddha says nothing of me is to remain yet something will continue. This something must be life continuance of me in some way, surely then it is a form of soul?'* But Buddha couldn't be more resolute in his denial of the existence of the soul – one of his deepest offerings to humanity. This something you think is your soul is not your soul. A soul remains a subtle form of ego 'I'. You need to understand that the ego 'I' with all of its subtleties will be gone; the soul is part of the 'I' and the 'I' will die completely. Every idea you have had about yourself will die completely. Buddha says you are nothing other than pure, empty space; you are nothing but pure, empty awareness. He does not say more about this, he does not say what comes after death. On this he stays silent.

To Buddha the circumstances were clear, and his instruction was appropriate for the time in which he lived. He did not want to distract others from their own enquiry by revealing his experience in detail, giving clues about God or no God or saying something that could be misinterpreted. He knew that if he said there was God, people would latch onto this and then they would never feel free – *'God is always watching, is he not?'* He knew that if he denied that there is something else, people would feel completely lost, that life would hold little or no meaning and so Buddha chose to say nothing. It is easier that way. Today 'emptiness' scares people; people are put off Buddha's message because it is a message that strips everything away. Other religions add layers on to us and we like that, we feel that we are gaining something and we find this comforting. But when we listen to Buddha, there is nothing but negation, negation and more negation. Everything is being stripped away and there seems little to gain apart from the prospect of being completely empty. To be frank, it isn't very appealing at all. In a way it takes deep courage and tremendous commitment to see, by account of your own 'experiencing', whether what Buddha is saying brings liberation. Buddha never asks for your trust; his advice is that you trust only yourself. When you have explored your own understanding and experiences, you will know when something is right. When the experience of contact with existence becomes very real for you, then a new kind of trust with existence emerges. This is not faith, faith is the product of belief; this is trust, the product of knowing. You will be able to trust yourself, knowing that you will be able to experience all that you need to by yourself without guidance from another. Now you can be on your own and happy alone. Now you are embracing and understanding the freedom of your aloneness, which is to be free from all influence. You have understood that thought created your idea of loneliness, your fears and your dependencies. Your intelligence begins to work for itself, and you grow. Buddha removes every layer of not just your limiting beliefs and who you think you are, but every aspect of <u>all</u> thought within until there is nothing left but pure, empty awareness; nothing but pure space. It is the greatest liberation.

Buddha's Truth

BUDDHIST TEACHINGS ARE OFTEN REFERRED to as a philosophy rather than a religion, but any categorisation is inadequate. What such labels suggest is a doctrine or an 'ism', as soon as anything becomes organised into an 'ism' it is no longer Buddha's way. Buddha says Truth cannot be organised nor is it consistent. New evidence from the Dead Sea Scrolls is uncovering evidence that Jesus had a similar message; religion cannot be organised, for as soon as it is organised it is dead. It is dead because strict methods do not reflect the freedom of existence, and they are enslaving rather than joyous. And it is dead because a religion only becomes successful when it compromises itself to suit the demands of the masses. The religions of the world today are more interested in you than they are in Truth. They are more interested in providing you with comfort and a false sense of security than they are in exposing you to Truth so that you can grow. Under the guise of growth, the church is a business geared towards numbing down our inner fears in this life and satisfying our desire for fulfilment in the next; it is the greatest ever trick played upon humanity.

To the man who feels incomplete, who is not yet mature, who is operating purely for the self, what happens when a religious system is offered to him? He will only listen if you promise him a reward.

He hopes that the system will bring him completion – heaven, God, Moshka – and we can see this the world over. What value lies in a system that is reliant only upon reward? Is this not bribery? Is this not how we incentivise our children? Our religions feed off the immature human mind, a mind that is searching for something external and looking to gain from following a system. Such a mind is easy to deceive. Remember that deception is only possible when we want something and we only want something when we feel incomplete. While Buddha suggests looking inward to discover that your completion already IS, much of the rest of the world is busy looking outward. When fulfilment is sought from external sources – whether in religious systems, money, fame or some other illusion – it is short lived because it is caused rather than uncaused and thus fundamentally pseudo. All over the world the 'I', the 'me', seeks completion and because we are collectively looking to gain, because we are collectively looking to become this or that, we are collectively caught up in the trap of striving and so we leave ourselves open to all kinds of disappointments and deceptions.

We are deceived not only by others but also by ourselves, because we apply the 'I' when listening to others, rather than listening with complete and total attention. Even those who claim to walk the spiritual path are not immune to such deception. Many listen to the words of masters via interpretations of the 'I' – *'What can I learn so that I can be enlightened?'* This is not the art of listening; the art of listening is to listen with pure and open attention. It is to soak up the essence of what is being said without the 'I' trying to mould or coerce the information according to a preferred pattern. It is to listen to what is being said without any resistance at all; it is to listen to all internal reactions that are going on and have an understanding as to why you are reacting the way that you are; it is to be aware of all of these things simultaneously with complete attention to everything. Your attention must be everywhere in this whole process; not isolated in one corner and thus resistant to the other corners, not concentrating on just one element, but instead attentive to all elements; the speaker, your reactions and the reasons behind your reactions. In this listening process you begin to understand the nature of the self. You recognise that the self will always impose itself and consequently distract attention away from what is really being said. It is well known that people only hear what they want to hear. If you listen with the 'I' and the 'I' holds this belief or that belief, you listen to an interpretation of what is being said that fits with your view; a translation that meets with your belief and thus gives you a form of pleasure. For example, if you believe in life after death and then someone comes along and says there is no life after death, then of course it is going to be very difficult for you to listen to the essence of what they are saying without your view distorting your interpretation of their words in some way. To be free of deception, your attention must not be locked up inside such boundaries of belief, view or judgement. Instead, see the nature of the self for what it is. Find out if it is a process composed of belief, view and judgement. When the self is understood as a process, it drops of its own accord and then attention can be without boundary. The art of listening begins.

If a spiritual search is motivated by a desire or goal, this motivation distorts attention, placing a filter in front of what is being said. Where there is distortion, deception follows. There are countless examples of groups who have been deceived by false gurus and cults because they are desperately seeking something. Instead, one must understand the causes of deception and see clearly what it is that distorts one's view. One must understand the nature and shape of the 'I'; why it is so disorderly inside, so confused, why one conforms, imitates and follows the procedures and methods of others blindly. By careful, attentive listening and heart-led understanding, and with the application of intelligence, your vision can be free from distortion. Then your curiosity for Truth is sharp and open, rather than over zealous and distorted.

Much of human behaviour around the world is neither heart-led nor intelligent. It is driven by the human search for comfort and our aversion to anything that shakes the foundations of already held beliefs and views. This is why the pure teachings of Buddha, the essence of his teachings, have been so distorted into the many forms of Buddhism that exist around the world today. These forms of Buddhism do not reflect Buddha, in fact by giving his teaching rigid structure, mechanical method and compromise they fail to express what Buddha was saying. There is no path to wisdom, no formula. If wisdom is formulaic then it becomes knowledge, a pattern, something to be repeated; a product of the known. Wisdom is not something that we accumulate according to a pattern. Whatever exists in a pattern must be binding and so there is insufficient freedom to discover and comprehend the new. Discovery only exists in seeing and meeting the challenges of life as they are in the present moment, not according to the rigid framework of self-projected patterns and conclusions. To follow any form of pattern is to escape, it is to deny 'what is' and this can only lead to pain and self-deception. Wisdom is the understanding of oneself from moment to moment; to see 'what is' as it is; free from the past, free from knowledge, free from the field of the known. Buddha's teachings cannot therefore be defined, structured or made mechanical. Truth is only discoverable when you discover yourself as you are, never according a blueprint or plan. Buddha is nearly always misunderstood, that is why there is Buddhism. Buddhism exists because Buddha's truth shatters and it shatters because many of us do not practice the art of listening. Buddha's truth exposes lies that humans have built up over time and this is why his original teachings were ejected from India many centuries ago; they were deeply unpopular because Ganges valley incumbents could not handle the ruthlessness of Buddha's truth. They could not cope because they were unable to listen without the 'I' projecting itself, without their own ego-based desires and fears distorting and filtering what they heard. In the presence of such distortion, of course misinterpretation and self-deception will arise and of course the teachings will be misunderstood and thus abandoned. After being ejected from India, the teachings of Buddha were compromised and doctored in order to win popularity, and what resulted was the spread of Buddhism elsewhere throughout Asia and the world. Buddhism was created in order for what happened in India never to be repeated; so began the watered down version of Buddha that we call *Buddhism* today.

The Way of the Heart

"The way is not in the sky. The way is in the heart."

Buddha

DO YOU HESITATE BEFORE AN act of kindness? Do you walk past someone who is cold and homeless on your way home from work? If you hesitate, if you walk past, know that it is your mind interfering. It is thinking, *'Why should I help right now? I have to get home, I have my family reception to get to. Besides when I have enough money, then I will help, then I will donate.'* This mind is your ego and ego is inherently selfish. When we listen to our heart we automatically do good, when the mind says, *'I'll do good next week'*, know where those words come from. The way of freedom is in the heart, not the mind. The way of the heart is the way of embracing what you are, freed from the distortions of ego. This is the way of joy and of freedom.

The secret of all joy is feeling 'what you are' because 'what you are' is unbounded. Your boundless Being is larger than you, and naturally when you are your Being you feel more than you were before. It is a strange feeling, and sounds paradoxical. Rather than evaluating this in your mind, explore and feel it in your heart, where you will know it to be true. The sensation of falling in love gives us a glimpse of this expanded sense of Being. For a while you are walking on the clouds, you are all starry-eyed, your love is unbounded. You feel that you are somehow more than yourself, that you are expanded in a way that you cannot define. This is a glimpse of the feeling of boundlessness that comes with understanding existence and reconnecting with our Being. The way of Buddha is known as the way of the heart; when it has been understood existentially, you don't fall in love with just one person or a few people, you fall in love with all existence; you feel that you are existence and existence is you and so begins your outpouring of bliss.

When you penetrate into the heart of what is true, you realise that you are and yet you are not. It is difficult to put into words, it cannot be described. You can only understand your essence when the

'I' is fully known and recognised for what it is. This is the process of liberation from the self. As we discussed in the chapters on Ego in the book *Question Mark*, this essence is hidden by the layers of ego and personality. Think of a bright lamp that is covered by layers of thick black cloth. As we peel away the layers, we begin to see the light shining through. Flickers of light appear through gaps in the heavy cloth. This light represents you, masked for much of your life by your personas and your identifications such as fear, tension, attachment and desire. What is true and authentic and what is your fundamental essence has been masked by what is false; all ego personality is false. You cannot destroy what is true, it can only be masked.[1] The ego is a suit of personality that you have been wearing, and we each have a lot of different outfits. When you truly know yourself, when you see your essence as it truly is, you will know what existence is because you will have found that they are one and the same. You are existence, only you have been wearing too many clothes and you have been thinking that you are separate, individual and made of form.

The idea of independent existence generates the illusion of the ego boundary and belief in the self. It is this idea of self that is the most fundamental cause of human delusion. You exist but you are not separate. You are not a 'self', you are a 'non-self'. Ultimately there are no boundaries between you and the chair you are sitting on. Physicists today tell us that the universe is a system of information and that we are all made up of and constructed from this same fundamental information. We think of reality as something solid, tangible and real, but it is just information. Boundaries exist only in your perception and of course since they are perceived they are therefore valid, but the truth is that nothing is separate. Information contained within information is still information. You will see that you and existence are not separate at all; you are simply different aspects of the same fundamental system. Interdependent existence is the fabric of the universe and we are all a part of the same fundamental something.

---

[1] You may be interested to know that the Mayan word *Apokolypto*, as referenced in their prophecies regarding the end of the Long Count, is thought by some scholars to mean *the unveiling of the leather mask*.

Our fundamental essence is the nothingness, the emptiness that is left behind when all the layers of ego have been peeled away. This is our true nature. Think of Russian nesting dolls (also known as Matryoshka or Babushka dolls), which each contain another smaller doll inside, and another smaller doll inside that, continuing in smaller scales until there is only one tiny doll left. Each doll is like a layer of ego; as one layer is removed the next layer is revealed inside. This continues until one day all that is left is the last layer – the final, smallest doll – and when that is removed all that is left inside is nothing but pure, empty space. Your essence is not a thing that is tangible; it is an emptiness, a nothingness. It is only 'you' the self that seems tangible; you are the layers, but nothing more. The essence of you is nothingness, it is an emptiness that is free, that is nowhere and everywhere. The essence of man is empty and yet at the same time he is all of existence at once. This essence is without boundary, limit or frontier.

Buddha says there is freedom when all layers of the self are removed. It is the layers of the self, the layers of what is false that inhibits what is fundamentally true. That which bounds and confines you only creates misery because it goes against your true nature, a fundamental essence that is freedom. When you are limited – whether by belief, attachment or fear in the mind – you feel trapped and confined, you do not feel free and so you suffer. This suffering can cease. Rather than fight suffering with forceful resistance, Buddha suggested that the best way to neutralise suffering is to understand it. Understand its cause and then it can be eliminated. If the roots of our problems are not identified, then what hope do we have of eliminating those problems? As any gardener will tell you, there is no point weeding if one does not dig up the roots. So to be free of suffering we must understand the nature of our suffering, and in doing this there is freedom. So much of our suffering arises from our thoughts; authentic freedom is freedom from thought. There is no need to go out and actively search for joy or bliss, all that is needed is to understand the nature of thought, and from this understanding joy and bliss emerge of their own accord. This happens not in your action, but in your inaction. Freedom does not arise from method, it arises from the ability to see and see with absolute clarity what is blocking your joy and your bliss from being and blossoming of its own accord. These obstacles to joy are your thoughts in the form of beliefs, ideals, attachments, cravings, identifications and fears. Your intelligence must come into operation in order to understand the nature of these thoughts, the nature of the self and how these filter your clarity. This is Buddha's method for the cessation of suffering. It is very simple.

For example, Buddha sees the search for God, for enlightenment or for spiritual fulfilment as an expression of fear. This fear distorts your mind, leading you into constricting methods and practices. Life is free flowing and open; it cannot be mapped and turned into mechanics because life is always changing, always making itself anew. Methods that are fixed and mechanical will trap you and make you miserable; this is so because systems and methods by their nature enslave. Instead, Buddha teaches understanding to get in touch with your Being, understanding bliss, understandings which can guide but which are ultimately your own. Understanding is free flowing, open; method on the other hand is fixed and mechanical. A method is a map for life, but life cannot be mapped for life is always changing. Life incorporates the new. How can you map the new? You don't know the new, so mapping the new it is nothing but impossible.

Cruel to be Kind

BUDDHA LIKES TO TALK IN terms of absolutes and for those of us who do not understand, his words can seem ruthless, cold and frightening. When Buddha says there is no soul all we can think of is annihilation, but Buddha is concerned with the Truth, no matter how it makes you feel. Belief in the soul is a subtle form of ego 'I', and as long as this subtle layer remains, your communion with Truth cannot take place. You can only have an experiencing of Truth by Being, by Being existence, and existence is a non-ego state. It is possible to exist in a non-ego state; this is meditation. All ego states, no matter how subtle, must be gone if there is to be this great contact, this great communion between you and that which is fundamentally real. And so Buddha is cutting all ties with whatsoever can form an ego state; hence he denies the soul. Buddha chose to speak Truth that will aid this process and this Truth just so happens to be packaged in absolute terms. Fundamentally he is correct; at the deepest level of existence, at the heart of the intelligence underwriting the entire universe, there is only ONE intelligence, there is only ONE 'oversoul', and this is what Buddha is referring to when he denies the existence of the soul.

Buddha also likes to use negative terms in his descriptions and he does this in order to help us. For example, Buddha describes Nirvana as nowhere, yet it can also be said that Nirvana means everywhere. How can something be nowhere and everywhere? We cannot see this clearly because our minds are locked up in limited thought patterns, such as our tendency – in this case – to think in terms of space and volume. Buddha chose to describe Nirvana as 'nowhere' for a reason; he chose nowhere in order to prepare you, so that you have nothing to grasp onto because it is the grasping that is the problem, the grasping is a form of ego. 'Everywhere' creates the illusion that you can grasp onto it, even though you cannot; 'nowhere', on the other hand, is final when it comes to the idea of grasping and so this is why Buddha describes Nirvana in this way. He is always thinking in terms of what is helpful for preparation for complete liberation.

In death you will be gone, in death everything about you will disappear; Buddha says this in order to leave you with nothing to cling to because it is the clinging that is the problem, not what happens at death. Buddha is ruthless because he has such deep compassion for you; his Truth cuts through the lies of the human mind like a hot knife through butter. This may seem cruel but that is only your perception; Buddha's teachings are there to help your growth, not to make you feel better. Our lies and all of the beliefs that we have put in place in order to make ourselves feel better don't help us. If we are to grow, we need to overcome the lies and distortions between us and Truth. We need to step out of our illusions and break away from all the falsities that we cling to so that we ARE Truth, so that there are no distortions between us and what is real. Buddha is preparing you so that you are ready to unravel your own deepest Truths. His concern is for your preparation, and that is all. Buddha says the relationships you treasure so much, the relationships you dream will last forever – your closest companion, your soul mate, your partner, your best friend, those you cherish so deeply – will all dissolve when you die. It is a bitter pill that is very hard to swallow, which is why Buddha is not the most popular of teachers. Buddha leaves nowhere for you to hide, he takes everything away from you so that you are freed of your self-imposed slavery. Remember: that to which you are attached will imprison you. So don't be imprisoned, don't cling, don't crave, otherwise you will continue to suffer. Whatsoever you cling to you lose because clinging is impossible, reality is impermanent and death will always separate. And then here comes the great paradox – whatsoever you can let go of is forever present. Naturally, we find this very difficult to understand.

Talk of death frightens people because it is the great unknown; death is the most misunderstood part of life. Many of us assume that no-one has experienced death and lived to tell the tale, but this is not true. Masters and Shaman navigate into the realm of what we call Consciousness Totality regularly. They explore the death experience through meditation. As their experiences attest, there is nothing to fear. Death is very much a transition of consciousness between realms of consciousness. Rather than fear this transition we should prepare for it so that we do not enter death terrified of annihilation. Yes, the self will not exist, the 'I' will cease, but your essence, that which is empty awareness, that which is sentient, is eternal. What is empty cannot be destroyed and what remains is beyond your conception. It is like nothing you could have ever imagined, and this is why you either deny or fear it. It is our fear and our misunderstanding that have led to belief in heaven and hell. You believe because you do not understand.

'You too shall pass away. Knowing this, how can you quarrel?'
Buddha

If you remain identified with the self, if you bind yourself to persona, you bind yourself to a life of conflict and regret. Life is far too precious to waste it fighting or quarrelling; life is too beautiful and too short for such regrets. Imagine yourself on your deathbed – will you regret not being powerful enough, not finishing your work, or do you regret not having enjoyed time with other human beings? The true master dies with no regrets, he lives presently until his last moment not worrying about what is to happen. His attention is on what he sees, what he feels and what he senses even in this, his moment of death.

We are not able to thoroughly understand what remains in death, as our limited language cannot describe this non-self existence. It is not a 'state', a state implies a subject having an experience; in death there is no subject there to have an experience. There is only experiencing, no experiencer and no experience. There is simply nothingness, an emptiness, yet out of this nothingness there is everything. This everything is all of existence; it is the ocean of all life, every bit, every byte, every part, every element. What you were in this life still exists in a way, only now it is somewhere in distant memory. What you were before you are no longer; now you are something else, now you are something altogether different. So vast is this something else, so altogether different, that Buddha is right to say *'You are no longer.'* The self will be gone, nothing recognisable as 'you' will remain. You are now all things, there is no 'old you' there to recognise it but what is left is absolutely familiar. You are home and this ISness has always been home. It is so far beyond words that any description would be futile and whatever can be said would be completely inadequate. Buddha's suggestion that we leave it well alone is for our own benefit; any enquiries we make about this realm whilst holding a conventional view will lead to misunderstanding and this can distract us away from the undertaking of practical steps of self-discovery such that we can have this realisation for ourselves. On this point, the withholding of information assists our development. Nothing is stated in absolute terms and that is part of the magic of Buddha. He prepares us for the realisation that we are nothing but pure, empty space. We are made of emptiness, yet out of this emptiness exists all that has arisen.

That which remains is both nothing and yet at the same time everything, and as such it cannot be destroyed. That which remains is eternal; it was before you were born and it will be after you die. It rests in the only true time, the time of Now. Eternity is an endless sequence of moments of now. Time exists only in thought, and did not exist prior to being conceived, but the moment of NOW has always existed.

In the face of these hard-to-understand truths, only existence is real. Only existence always is, has been and will be. Only your existence, my existence, the existence of your family, friends, enemies and neighbours is what is real. In the absence of all limited perception, there is only existence, one existence. Ultimately we are alone, but we are together in our aloneness.

Love Your Aloneness

WE ARE CONDITIONED TO SEE loneliness in a negative light, but the aloneness of your exploration is something to be embraced and, when you embrace it, you will find that it is something altogether different. Learn to be alone and enjoy that aloneness. Learn to feel fulfilled within your own Being by simply Being. Learn to be comfortable, calm, complete, joyful and blissful in your own company, to be a light unto yourself. In aloneness your joy is uncaused, your happiness is without reason; you are your own source now, you do not need another person, situation or object for your fulfilment. You can simply Be and enjoy Being, not worried about what others think, not worried about what you think you must do and what you think you must become; you already know that any idea of becoming distracts you from your fundamental Being, you already know that it distracts you from your true essence and thus your inner Truth. Happiness is being one's inner Truth. Buddha says drop your idea of God and learn how to stand up on your own two feet, learn how to be happy within; without any props, without becoming dependent, without needing to run away from your deepest fears.

Buddha advises us to embrace rather than fear the freedom of our aloneness. This is how to grow, mature and become wise. It is a growth that happens from within your deepest core. But we are so scared of our own freedom that we don't know what to do with it when we have it, so we willingly hand it over to those who claim to know. In this state we are easily fooled by the cunning and the clever: *'Better give responsibility to someone else rather than face Truth on my own!'* To be awake, to face Truth engenders pain, it requires attention and this attention bubbles up inner tension. Collectively – and individually

– we prefer to avoid 'what is'; our inner tension. We are lazy and frightened so we opt for the easy route and this is the route of dependence; it is much easier to shift responsibility onto someone else. We give ourselves over to authority – the church, the state, the guru, even the party – and where there is authority there is power and centralisation, and thus the inevitable problem of corruption. All exploitation breeds dependency for both the exploiter and the exploited, and it raises this absurd notion of a hierarchical structure in the pursuit of Truth. A master or leader cannot bridge the gap between you and 'what is' because the gap is *you*, it is within you.

There is no authority. There is no leader. There are no distinctions in love. What blocks you from love is your craving for security and certainty, which breeds inner conflict. (You may wish to escape this conflict but all escape is illusion, the very nature of escape is self-projected.) Anyone who claims to know clearly does not know; in fact, their lack of understanding is demonstrated by reason of their claim. But we don't see this, we choose to follow, we choose to obey, we choose to co-operate because we are lazy when it comes to our growth. If we are not chasing gurus or getting caught up in religious entertainment, we are instead watching the television or reading gossip magazines; anything that will distract us from asking the right questions for ourselves. It is far easier to follow another than it is to be intelligent for oneself. We obey because we do not know who we are; we obey because we are ignorant. Ignorance is not knowing what IS, it is the ignoring of what IS because everything that there is to be known already exists within you. This is very important to understand. Buddha shows us a way to break down our ignorance so that we can no longer ignore 'what IS'. You have to understand that his approach is existential, and that you are ultimately alone in your experiencing of it. But Buddha helps us along the way, showing us to an experiencing of this unnameable that is so deeply existential that it cannot be ignored. His way is the way of inner freedom and it is only possible through self-knowledge and self-understanding. So your idea of God for example is certainly not helping, it is providing you with a crutch, keeping your mind immature, preventing you from seeing and knowing who you really are. Only when such lies are cut can we move beyond ourselves.

You already are that which you seek, but you cannot see because you hold too many layers. All that is needed is the uncovering of the unnecessary layers that are preventing you from seeing Truth within. The self is striving to be *that which already is* and this is the paradox of the self. The self strives to be happy, not realising that happiness and freedom ARE when the self is not. It is the self that is the problem; the self is the barrier between you and existence, between you and freedom. Meditation is to have an ego death; that is why meditation is so blissful. In deep meditation the barriers between you and existence come down and so begins the euphoria of existence; you become deathless, you know what is going to die and what is going to remain. That which is going to die is all that is part of this dream we call reality, including your perspective, your personality, your history and your memory. That which is to remain is the awareness you detect when you look into the mirror; the awareness that is not your personality, the awareness that has remained the same ever since you were a young child. This awareness is the same awareness that pervades all life and all existence. You are that which never dies and that which is never born, you are eternal awareness. You are simply pure, empty space.

Intelligent Awareness

THE KEY TO HAPPINESS IS growth and growth is the emergence of intelligence. Intelligence is the ability to see what is true and what is not, free from all judgement, all dependency, all memory, all that is past because what is past distorts what is now. Understanding is achieved through the art of listening and the art of observation; the complete and full attention of consciousness to understand the nature of a fact (or the falseness of a fact) without the listener distorting what is heard or the observer distorting what is seen. It is to observe without the distorting 'me' with all of its baggage and accumulations interfering, disturbing or clouding essential clarity. To see with clarity is Buddha's central message. This he called Vipassana and this, he said, is all that is needed. It cannot be taught, sought or caught, it is what you already are; you simply need to uncover the layers of falsehood that distort your perception of the real. The distortion is 'you' – not the essence of 'you' but what you think is 'you'. So you must understand what of you is real and what is not. To find the real, you must be real, honest and integral. There cannot be denial, or the craving for achievement or experience, otherwise you are immediately projecting yourself onto what is real. You cover what is real with a layer of projection and so what you see is a distortion, an illusion of your own making. So there must be humility otherwise the result will be illusion and where there is illusion there can only be self-deception

To know the essence of you, to know what is real, you must understand your attachments, your desires and your fears. You must understand the nature of the self and how your thoughts shape your identifications and thus your motivations. When listening and observation are skilful, such that there is only listening and no listener and only observation and no observer, then you will see all aspects of ego for what they really are. The way to the real is the way of awareness and from this awareness comes understanding; not just the understanding of the mind but also the existential wisdom of the heart. This is the wisdom of seeing with the clarity of no mind and only Being, when your knowing of 'what is' and 'what is not' is automatic. Free from attachments, desires and fears the heart is intuitive and wise. This is the meaning of 'intelligence'; it is a union of the intellect and the heart. There is no learning how to create this union because it is already in place. You cannot learn what already is, what is part of your nature, you can only learn what prevents you from this nature and this is done by understanding what distorts. You can only learn what divides and separates and this is the activity of the ego. When we talk of understanding, it is only through the heart, through the existential, that there is ever any authentic understanding. The intellect is clever, but what is clever is not always clear; in fact what is clever can often distort and delude.[2]

For clarity one must unlearn all that is past, all that is knowledge, all that has gone before; not through action because action distorts,

---

[2] This reminds me of the Hindu story of Purusha and Prakriti. Intellect / Matter (Prakriti) is blind and able to move: Heart / Spirit (Purusha) can see but is paralysed. Only when Prakriti carries Purusha on his back can they both see and move.

but through understanding the nature of thought, why it arises, why it distorts, why it is old. Unlearning is another process of understanding. Only awareness can understand the nature of thought, only awareness can see that which is thought. Only awareness can cut through thought without distortion because only awareness is not thought. Awareness is the tool Buddha brings. Then you can know the nature of love, the nature of loneliness, aloneness, impermanence, dependency, attachment, distraction. When there is understanding of the nature of these concepts, which together constitute an understanding of the nature of thought itself and thus meditation, then one comes to joy and to freedom without even thinking about how to do this. One day you will see how life has been a game created by a greater aspect of your own intelligence and how the intelligence of the human mind is limited when measured against the intelligence of the heart, which you experience as intuition. As we shall come to understand, your intelligence has been busy making and exploring concepts and all this time you have been operating under the illusion of separation and isolation; an illusion that demands ego-based perception.

All of these things must be understood otherwise meditation becomes not a tool for insight and understanding as the Buddha intended, but just another escape for the mind from our confused and disordered lives. When we look around at the world today this is what seems to have happened. People might find an hour a week for a quiet mind, and then spend the rest of the week in turmoil.

We hear about enlightenment, we like what we think it is and then we desire it. Now we are seeking to achieve, we are seeking out of fear; we seek out of motivation. There is no humility and so begins the confusion, the illusion and the self-deception. In freedom there is no seeking and no desiring, there is only Being. All method is a distraction from our fundamental Being and if Being is not in the becoming but in simply Being, then all systems and all methods can be disposed of. It is not really a question of following this or following that, it is a question of not following and this is a question of intelligence. Rather than seeking and searching and following methods, the way of freedom requires intelligence and intelligence is the ability to see, not to follow. So intelligence is not to follow – not through suppression since suppression involves arduous effort, but rather not to follow the rules of your mind or the rules of your god or your guru. It is to be of such understanding that you are not following rules at all. In Buddhist Dzogchen, they call this the awareness of a truly intelligent mind. Out of awareness arises order, clarity and with these follow freedom and joy of their own accord. You need not concern yourself about how to cultivate joy or freedom, they cannot be cultivated for they already are; they are already present, they are lying in wait behind the falsities and distortions of the ego. Use your intelligence and awareness to understand the distortions of the ego self, and behind these distortions rest boundless joy and freedom. This is the way of clarity. Clarity is to die each second to all that is past and all that is distorted; you are then ready and open for the new, free from all falsities and distortions. This we also call innocence, chastity, intelligence, maturity; all aspects of Vipassana, which is the ability to see 'what is' with absolute clarity.

chapter four
Buddha's Message

WHILST EACH OF OUR UNDERSTANDING of Truth is individual and unique, religion is organised and structured for the masses. That which is organised and structured is intrinsically not free, nor is it intrinsically able to see the particular of 'what is'; it is therefore ultimately flawed as a mechanism to uncover Truth. In fact, no mechanism can uncover Truth because Truth belongs to no path and no doctrine. Only if something is not organised, only if something is fully accepting of others without trying to change these others, only if something is free-flowing and is freedom itself can it be love and thus truly 'religious'.

True religion can only be freedom, and is thus a little chaotic and without form or structure. Religion has to be individual because each of us is only ready for a religious life in our own time. We cannot be forced into it, you cannot impose freedom; freedom can only be embraced and welcomed. Of course you can enforce a system and history demonstrates many fine examples of such impositions, particularly when we look at the history of the world's religions. Systems, by their nature, are either imposed, adopted or ignored. The key point however is that try as you may, you cannot impose freedom; its very nature is beyond imposition. If true religion is freedom, then anything that has been enforced or structured cannot be religious, in the truest sense. Religion can therefore only exist at the level of the individual. A person is ready for freedom when he is fed up with being enslaved, fed up with his conflicting beliefs, his conflicting values, his deep fears or his many other enslaving thought patterns. We each come to freedom in our own time; it cannot be enforced or imposed. As soon as you say, *'I follow this religion or that religion,'* you are no longer religious, for freedom has no dependency.

How can that which is deemed suitable for the collective solve the problems of the individual? To solve the problems of the individual by imposing what is designed for the collective will surely only lead to solutions that are concrete and unchanging – from the perspective of the individual, that is. In this there is no freedom. This is what organised systems – whether religious, political or otherwise – have done, and the effects are clear to see. Utopian political systems, which are imposed on societies from above, lead to oppression and imprisonment. Any form of imposition goes against freedom. Once an individual has understood that as soon as a method or a system becomes organised its fundamental freedom is lost, then it becomes possible for that individual to explore teachings that are in place without becoming attached to them.

We are a diverse and complex species, each of us unique and different. Truth belongs to no tribe, no sect, no cult, no single system. Truth is, as J. Krishnamurti puts it, *"a pathless land"*. Truth must be pathless for it to be free. If this was not true and Truth belonged to a single path, then of course that path would be fixed. This would imply attachment to that path and the whole notion of 'what should be'; this can only ever foster imposition to walk that path and whatsoever is imposed is never free. A path suggests the idea of changing 'what is' into 'what should be', and in this way systems and methods are most destructive. Love is always free; love is not, nor will it ever be, 'what should be' or attachment to 'what should be'. You cannot proclaim love and then try to change another into 'what should be'; your proclamation would be false, like the proclamations of the church. 'What should be' is imposed, 'what should be' is intrinsically against freedom. 'What should be' is not 'what is' nor is it the acceptance of 'what is'; how then can 'what should be' ever be love? One cannot come to Truth without love. One cannot come to Truth following 'what should be'. You are already here. Truth is here, it is 'what is'; it is not something there at the end of the path. Enlightenment is to understand that you are already here. Here is enough, here is more than enough, here is wonderful! The searching may cease but the growing never does; we are all growing, even Buddhas grow. Understand there is no finish line, there is no destination, there is no true enlightenment; there is only the way, the way towards greater freedom and that way is the way of 'what is'.

How is one to awaken the minds of those who are asleep or fearful? Is it the business of the church or the mosque or the guru, or is it better that people are left to get on with their own business? In which of these two options is there freedom? If you interfere, like the church, then you are creating 'what should be' which is not love. If you leave them alone, then is that love? If someone is suffering, where is the greatest compassion? Do you make them feel better by imposing your views or beliefs or is it better that they come to understanding in their own time? What alleviates suffering is understanding and understanding is only authentic if it is yours, rather than imported. What brings one to awareness? Life. Life teaches you because life is the greatest teacher. This is what the theatre of life has been designed to do, with its forces of grace and its numerous strange attractors. Each of us will realise in our own time that we are suffering and that the way to overcome this suffering is self-understanding, not dependency. This is Buddha's message. No master, no teacher, can be a greater teacher than life, than existence itself. This is the function of your life experience, this is why you have made mistakes and learnt lessons from those mistakes. Mistakes teach and when humanity breaks away from guilt and 'what should be' and instead sees mistakes as opportunities to learn, then there is potential for a quantum leap in human consciousness. What is it that we are all doing? We are all learning from different perspectives, we are generating further understanding and feeding the growth of Truth; this is what we are doing.

There are tendencies already in place inside life and existence which bring about understanding. These tendencies are far greater than you or any organised human system. The most we can hope to do is to try to understand the nature of these tendencies and how they may uniquely manifest within various transitions or progressions throughout our own lives. In order to do this effectively, it is vital that you know yourself and know yourself deeply. It is this self awareness which Buddha is helping you to achieve. An individual's freedom is their own business, not the business of a business like the church; we are each ready only when we are ready. Some of us may need to go looking into every corner of the Earth and search and search until there is no more searching left to do. If you find nothing in India or Tibet or Jerusalem or wherever it is that spiritual seekers go, when you find nothing and give up searching, then perhaps you will realise that you were looking for fire when already holding a candle in your hands.

We each have to see for ourselves how our life is disordered, and recognise that our suffering is not alleviated by conforming to strategies or rigid systems. When you realise that freedom has no dependency and that to be dependent is not the way, then and only then does the mind look inward to its own disorder. Rather than get caught up in a system, make enquiries for yourself. This is the way of freedom. Without freedom there is no order and without order there is no virtue. Without virtue how can there be goodness or wisdom? Joy arises only from wisdom and wisdom – just like goodness, virtue, freedom and joy – has no dependency.

In your own investigations, you will come to recognise the intrinsic connection between freedom, joy, order, virtue, goodness and wisdom. They are all facets of the same understanding of what it means to love. Then your jumping out of conformity is natural; it happens of its own accord, it is not forced or compelled but free flowing and harmonious. You have to see how your striving and your ambition distort and prevent a genuine acceptance – and thus authentic awareness – of 'what is'. When you see all this for yourself, you see the potential for change. Now you are ripe, now there is the energy to look inward and bring about radical transformation. Now you are ready to walk alone, but you must come to this in your own time. Only then does meditation become worthwhile and not just another escape from another disordered life.

Joy & Freedom

BUDDHA'S MESSAGE IS A MESSAGE OF FREEDOM. He says that when you are free, there is joy. Joy is not caused by freedom, joy happens *in* freedom; it is a happening that is automatic because there is an integral relationship between the two. That which is free is joyful and that which is joyful will always be free. You cannot be joyful if you are not free, it simply cannot happen, but when you are free your joy happens of its own accord, spontaneously. Freedom and joy are two faces of the same Truth, and are so deeply intertwined that they cannot be separated. As with all of Buddha's teachings, you can discover this for yourself by looking carefully into your own life experience. When you felt miserable you felt miserable because you felt trapped; there was no way out, the situation felt like a prison, it felt like it would never end. The situation may vary but the root of the situation is always the same;

that which makes you miserable is a form of slavery, always. Just as freedom and joy are interrelated, so too are misery and slavery. Understanding the nature of freedom is central to Buddha's teachings.

Think of a simple example from your own life experience. Remember the last day of school: you are walking out of the school gates and the summer holiday is about to begin, you are stepping out into the big wide world, you are joyous now because for once, even though the holiday will not last forever, even though you may be returning to college in a few months or you may want to get a job, in this moment you feel unbounded and free. It is how you feel in this moment that is real to you. When you felt free, even though in purely practical terms that freedom was not total, even if it was just a partial freedom like the long summer break, you were still joyous because you perceived that freedom to be boundless. What matters to you is how you perceive freedom and if you perceive it to be without end, then for you it is real.[1] Equally, the slavery that makes you miserable exists within your perception. All slavery is misery and that slavery can take many forms; physical, political, economic, psychological, emotional, spiritual, even our perception of what is existential. You fight for political freedom and then there is the problem of economic freedom, you fight for economic freedom and then there is the problem of psychological or emotional freedom, and so it continues with a new layer of slavery always lying in wait for you. You are always fighting, always struggling; it never seems to cease. In the face of such a struggle, when we are always looking for an escape, how can there be freedom? So our perception of existential freedom is vital if we are to understand freedom. Understand this freedom, the deepest and only authentic freedom, and the rest will follow without you having to think about it. You feel joy in this, the ultimate freedom.

Freedom is without end, without boundary or frontier. Wherever there is the sensation of being beyond boundary, any boundary at all, you are certain to feel a form of joy. Joy happens, it is not caused; your joy is not caused *by* freedom, it comes *with* freedom. It just IS when

---

[1] Technically this is an incorrect assumption. We are too early in the discussion to explain the nature of this illusion.

freedom IS; it is in the very nature of things. Understand that freedom and joy are not separate, they are together and they are the same. This is central to Buddha's message.

'Joy' is not to be confused with the conditional and transient happiness which so many of us conceive. That happiness is rooted in ideas formulated by the ego, leading to desire and our quest to satisfy that desire. That happiness is a product of thought, a conditional satisfaction that we perceive will be when certain criteria have been met. That happiness is transient and passing, a fleeting feeling that lasts for just a few moments before we return to our regular, dissatisfied state. That happiness comes with condition, it is a happiness that is caused and this is what most of us are chasing. What we refer to here as 'joy' is uncaused; it happens not through your action but within your inaction, where there is no will, no motive and no agenda driving forward. Joy happens when you forget yourself, it happens when you feel you are outside of the body, when your attention is without a centre; when it is nowhere or everywhere. For example, you lose yourself in a song, you lose your sense of self on a mountain top gazing out; you feel joy because in these moments you do not feel limited – there is only the music, there is only the wonderful view and that is all that matters! You have forgotten the body for a moment, you have forgotten the chatter of the mind and for a glimpse you feel unbounded. In this moment of clarity, in this moment of freedom that is happening right now, you feel like you have literally melted away into the music (you are nowhere) or you feel so unbounded like you are all of existence (you are everywhere). When lost in music there is only listening, there is no listener or listened; in watching the mountains there is only observing, there is no observer or observed. You are experiencing 'what is' and you have dissolved completely into that experiencing. The self is not, all boundaries have dissolved, your attention is out of the body, your attention is not localised at all; you feel free and unbounded as though you have dissolved into existence. That is what the term 'Nirvana' means, *'dissolved into existence'*; completely and utterly dissolved into existence, where you are nowhere and everywhere at the same moment and where this moment is a moment of overwhelming freedom and joy.

Freedom and joy are the very nature of existence, but for many of us this existence is unknown and unsuspected. We seek happiness through various activities because we do not know this relationship with existence. We seek completion through another person, through reaching an ideal or through various actions that we have decided must be so; we are always seeking fulfilment through something, and as long as this search continues we will always attach great importance to the object of our attention. We become dependent upon this object, we become attached to it and so begins our self-imprisonment. In this dependence and clinging we lose touch with the true nature of existence, and become further removed from freedom and joy.

Bliss

WHATSOEVER IS TRUE OF JOY and freedom is also true of kinaesthetic bliss. Joy, freedom and bliss are together; there is an integral relationship between all three. In sexual orgasm you forget yourself for a moment, you abandon yourself briefly and the focused attention of the self melts away. The boundaries between you and existence have dissolved for a few seconds and so, in your mind-body, you glimpse the orgasm of existence. You feel free because the self is not, you feel free because your attention is nowhere and everywhere. In this moment of freedom you experience bliss. Whenever freedom is, bliss is. The human obsession with sex can be explained in this way. People who are constantly striving to lose themselves in the sexual act are trying to get back to the bliss of existence, trying to re-connect and plug back into the orgasm of existence by abandoning the self in sex. Behind sexual desire is a sub-conscious attempt to re-establish the relationship with existence.[2] Bliss is what existence is built upon. As we can learn from Buddha, freedom, joy and bliss are the nature of existence.

The relationship between the bliss of sexual orgasm and the bliss of existence is explored in Tantric practices. The rushes and tingles

---

[2] The root meaning of the word 'desire' is 'reach for / fall from... the stars' (*de sidere* = *from the stars*). It refers to our separation, in terms of relationship, from the cosmos.

experienced when one loses oneself in pure orgasm afford glimpses of the primordial truth of existence. Tantra opens this relationship with existence, re-opening your relationship with joy and bliss by re-engaging the throbbing heart of reality that exists within you. There is a ceaseless and continuous flow of energy that vibrates through every cell of your body. You first feel it dripping down through your head and as a buzzing in your fingertips, then it enters your arms, your legs, your tummy and your torso. The boundary between you and existence dissolves, and where there is no boundary there is freedom, joy and bliss. This is a happening which begins in freedom. It cannot be grabbed or taken, you can only open yourself to it and as you open and surrender to its utter magnitude, so begins your connection with your true essence. You are joy, you are bliss, you are freedom; you have simply forgotten, that is all. The understanding set out by Buddha and the masters who have followed help you remember what you fundamentally are.

This bliss of existence is not to be confused with God. As we have seen, God is simply an idea that we have invented out of our fears, desires and our search for fulfilment. Buddha's technique is scientific in that it explores and reveals existence by presenting and advancing our relationship with existence. We have forgotten relationship with existence, with the universe, and in our ignorance of its nature we suffer. This suffering derives from our feeling of isolation and separation from existence. And so in our forgetfulness and the ensuing sense of incompletion, we have created the idea of God to fill the gap that we subconsciously and universally perceive between us and the universe. We feel incomplete and so we create God in an attempt to extinguish our suffering, a suffering which is intrinsic to selfhood. Until we understand that we are not the self, we will continue to suffer. All suffering exists in the self, in barriers that are constructed and dictated by the self; in the barrier between us and existence. When there is no barrier there is joy, freedom and unfathomable bliss. What care do you have for God when you are already in bliss, when there is total, complete and utter fulfilment?

> "Your pain is but the breaking of the shell that encloses your understanding."
>
> *Kahlil Gibran*

The understanding propounded by Buddha helps to remove the layers that inhibit your relationship with existence. As these layers of ego are peeled away, the joy and bliss of existence are revealed. As humans we are vast, far bigger than we can ever comprehend. Every human is the entire cosmos, but the barriers between humans and the cosmos must be removed before we can fully realise this. Buddha says that you are all of existence and that all of existence exists within you. He says that what is outside of you actually exists within you, but because we are all caught up in fixed patterns of thinking we find this difficult to comprehend. Our reference points within space-time are limited, and too often we have misunderstood the role of perception and the nature of consciousness. So poor is our understanding of consciousness, that even in the 21st century and with all of the science in the world, we still do not know where the mind is or where 'we' are inside our bodies; we cannot isolate our sense of self. If we cannot even establish this, then how can we be expected to accept the assertions of Buddha? Buddha's message is one of understanding. We are not called upon to accept anything blindly, but rather to explore and understand our own experiencing, thus peeling away the layers that exist between us and the bliss of existence; the same layers that exist between us and Truth.

Enlightenment is Freedom

ENLIGHTENMENT IS JOY BECAUSE ENLIGHTENMENT is freedom. That is what enlightenment means: *freedom*. We have said that freedom is to be free of fear and we have said that freedom is to be free of thought, but Buddha goes further than this. Buddha says that your freedom can be absolute. This is not the partial freedom of when some boundaries fall – like when you lose yourself on a mountain top – but the freedom that IS when all boundaries have dissolved, the freedom that IS when the body and the mind are not; the freedom of death. Boundaries start with the body and the mind. The physical body presents clear demarcations, such as the skin, distinguishing where 'you' end and outside existence begins. The mind with its various levels of thought, primal, conscious and subconscious distinguishes where the self ends and where existence begins. Breaking down these boundaries is the technique of the Buddha. All barriers must dissolve; otherwise you are bound to feel limited, confined, imprisoned and therefore miserable.

According to Buddha, these boundaries exist because you think that you are your body, and you have become attached to it. As it is with all things, that to which you are attached will imprison you. To be released from this attachment to the body, one must understand one's relationship with it. The endless search for sensations in the form of pleasure or the avoidance of pain is an enslaving feature of our attachment to the physical body. When you understand the true nature of the body, you need not worry about how to detach yourself from it because once you understand the misery of its confinement you will be able to step out of it without even thinking about it. Of course it sounds strange to think that our consciousness can exist outside of the body, but thought and awareness require no space or volume. We may not know where we are within the body, but we do feel embodied and so begins our sense of restriction. We are restricted because we are attached to the mind and the body.

The Truth is, you are pure attention and by its very nature that attention is vast. We do not appreciate quite how vast this attention can be, for so often it is focused solely within the physical boundaries of the body. The duality of the observer and the observed is the extent of our comprehension, but the truth is that this perception of what we call *ordinary appearances* is in fact limited, very limited. Restricting attention into a body is like trying to pour an entire ocean into a china teacup. Imagine walking around all day long in a pair of shoes that are too tight, there is great relief when you finally get home and take them off. Just imagine the relief that lies in wait for an ocean that is released from a teacup! When our attention is freed from the boundaries of the body it becomes boundless, it is everywhere and nowhere, and in this state there is great energy. This is true of both sleeping and meditating; your attention is everywhere and nowhere, and so there is great energy. There is a relationship between attention and energy. Have you ever wondered why deep sleep is so blissful?

The body is a form of confinement for consciousness, and there is joy and bliss when your consciousness is finally free. Within the body you are bound to feel misery because you feel confined and so you are constantly pushing to break out. You therefore seek freedom; everything that you do without exception is a subconscious expression of your search for freedom. Behind every activity that you are undertaking, freedom is your goal. Freedom – and our struggle to attain freedom – is a basic human need. When you break down one layer of freedom, there will always be a new and more subtle layer of imprisonment behind; there is always another type of slavery lying in wait. You may have moments of joy when freedom has been attained in one area, but inevitably you will move onto the next layer of slavery and so your struggle for freedom begins once again. Your whole life is spent struggling to escape slavery; Buddha teaches a way of ending that struggle.

Buddha recognised the simple truth that all freedom is joyous and all slavery is misery. In freedom you feel joy because freedom is what you already are. Always you feel joy when you are what you are, when you live out your true Being; it is only when you deny what you are (or are denied what you are by another) that you feel misery. Any kind of imprisonment is misery. Buddha is helping you to the ultimate freedom; freedom beyond all political or economic slavery, freedom beyond all psychological fear, freedom beyond all emotional pain, freedom beyond even the physical body or your idea of spiritual self-continuance. Buddha is helping you to the ultimate freedom: existential freedom.

It is the freedom of what is the essence of you, of what is your very ISness; it is the freedom to simply BE your inner Being, both in life and in death. It is the freedom not just of your own Being but the freedom of all that IS Being – the trees, the animals and the stars up in the sky. This freedom of all Being is vast, for it is the freedom of existence itself; it is the freedom of 'all that IS'. What Buddha is saying is that within you rests the freedom of the entire universe in motion and that the freedom of your Being – as a human being – is no different at all in principle to the freedom of all that IS existence. Because all within the universe is fully interdependent, there is the same potential freedom for all aspects of itself, including you. This is the freedom of 'ISness', not just your own ISness but the ISness of everything! Are you following this? We are not just playing cheap word games here; we are, with the terms available to us in English, describing the interrelationship between the essence of humanity and the essence of existence. Of course the description can never be the actual, but we include these descriptions here in order to highlight the fact that Truth exists, and is structured, in terms of concepts and how they interrelate to one another. Buddha is saying that authentic freedom can only be total, never partial, and as such there is absolute, unblocked freedom; there is access to (and merger with) everything. Whatever you wish to call it – existence, the universe, the source, the ocean, God, Allah, the Tao, Dharma, Truth, that which is unnameable or Fred Flintstone – it does not change the truth that you are this by nature and that you come to it through the freedom of Being; by being your true nature, a nature which is freedom.

It is superbly elegant: please give this your full attention. You are all existence and existence IS. There is only ONE fundamental existence and this existence cannot do anything other than BE its own ISness. So ultimately there is only ISness, there is only 'that which is'. Existence is 'that which is', it is the ISness and exactness of everything. Surrendering to ISness is love; or rather, an aspect of what love is. Existence surrenders completely to its own ISness; existence is love.

If you don't quite understand, contemplate the following: There is only one fundamental existence as a concept within Truth. Existence need only BE, just once, and it IS. As the Koran reads, '*BE and IT IS.*' How can there be Truth without existence?[3] Impossible. Buddha says when all barriers have dissolved, existential freedom is the freedom of the entire cosmos because whatever is purely existential is always free and existence is existential. Existence is freedom, existence IS and

---

[3] Truth can only be conceived or perceived; what else could Truth be? Conception or perception is only possible within intelligence and any intelligence can only be intelligent if it actually exists.

whatever is being its own ISness will always be free. That is what freedom is, the freedom to BE. This is what love is, the freedom to BE. This is what the universe is built upon.

Buddha helps you to discover freedom. That is all; nothing else is needed. That freedom is the freedom of Being, what masters call *'freedom of the heart'*. What is this freedom of Being? It is the total acceptance, forgiveness, communion and imbibing of your Being, or the Being of another. Is this not love? Whatever love is, surely it must encompass this? The way of Being is the way of love; your true Being is love and this is what Buddha shows. The closer you are to your Being – to your fundamental nature, which is love – the greater your joy, your freedom and your bliss. The freedom of Being is a freedom whereupon there is no further slavery and misery lying in waiting, there is only joy and bliss. Joy needs no description but you can gather a sense of this bliss from moments in your life; the euphoria when you are lost in music, lost in the view, lost in orgasm. The euphoria when you are nowhere and everywhere; when you are not, but the euphoria is! This is how it is, how it has always been. This euphoria is a non-ego state, you are nowhere and yet everywhere. You are like a flame that has been blown out into existence, where has the flame gone? Attention is nowhere and everywhere, but the bliss still IS; it comes from no direction or centre, you are without boundary or frontier. Even to say 'you' is misleading because 'you' implies a centre; there is no centre. The non-ego state is nirvana; it is freedom. We can say absolute freedom, for freedom can only ever be freedom; it must be total, never partial. It is indivisible. Existence is a non-ego state, but your daily perception of existence draws from an ego-state. Understand that your daily experience, your ego state, rests within the concept of limited perception. The reason why you suffer is because you do not know your inner nature, you do not know the limited nature of the perception of self and that once the self is gone, only existence IS. You are not and existence is. This is what Buddha, and then Jesus, called meekness.

All freedom is joyous and all slavery is misery, this is Buddha's message; it is a very simple message, there is nothing else to it. Yet it is its simplicity that makes it so poignant and so absolute. Of course you can debate whether or not you are existence and it is to be expected that some people will consider this absurd. Buddha would want you to doubt it; he doesn't care what you believe, he cares only about what you know in your heart. Belief is irrelevant; Truth is only Truth when it is known[4] and so Buddha deals at first with what is known. He starts at the beginning, he starts with the most basic truth. You cannot debate that freedom and joy are not together; you know in your heart that this is so. Whatever your argument is about other aspects that you have heard, you have no argument when it comes to this.

This first step of Buddha is also the last step. When there is freedom, there cannot be more. Freedom is an absolute: whatsoever is free cannot be more free than free; whatsoever is limitless cannot be more limitless than before otherwise it was not limitless in the first place.[5] If freedom can never not be free, the first step of freedom and the last step of freedom can only ever *be* freedom; this is why system and doctrine are so dangerous. Strict systems never lead to freedom as they oppose freedom in their very structure. If your first step to freedom feels like imposition, like the rigid canon of many religious systems, then it is not a step to freedom. A person's joy rests in the removal of layers of self-imprisonment and they become more joyous the more they are free. The majority of us are not free at the beginning and so there are many layers of self-imprisonment that need to be removed first as opposed to additional layers of virtue to be added, as suggested by other so-called religious systems. Buddha does not add to your imprisonment or teach you layers of virtue, he does not give you methods to numb down or narrow the mind, instead he helps you peel away that which imprisons you. So your freedom begins now, not after years of striving, not after years of prayer, not after years of mind meditation control, not after years of being dependent on a master; your freedom begins now in your intelligence, with that intelligence coming into operation.

---

[4] Yet to come to it there must be freedom from the known, freedom from all that drives individual human perception.

[5] This aspect of freedom is unchanging; funny that, to say that freedom can never not be free. To include the concept of *never* within *freedom* is one of the universe's little paradoxes.

Buddha's teachings are open to all. He invites all sceptics, all scientists, all non-believers, in fact anyone with an open, questioning mind. He wants your intelligence, he wants your enquiry, he wants your openness; he certainly does not want your obedience, not one bit. It is better to doubt than to believe and obey; only never doubt yourself. Who can you trust if you cannot trust yourself? You can begin with your own experience of joy and freedom and from this nurture a closer relationship with your inner being. And of course the more you go with Buddha, the more you realise that you cannot refute what Buddha is saying. This relationship that we are discussing is not really a relationship with Buddha or with other Eastern masters, it is a relationship with your inner Being; it therefore cannot be anything other than true. Buddha does not make philosophical assertions so that we can debate and argue, he is simply saying trust only your inner Being and your own experiencing and you will know what is right, what is real and what is not. You must find your own way, alone.

This is illustrated by Buddha's dying words to his disciples, concerned at the prospect of losing their teacher. He whispered to Ananda – his most loyal friend, disciple and aide – *'Ananda, Be a light unto yourself.'* Buddha was saying to Ananda, you don't need me, you are already that which you seek, you are your own light. The teacher you seek is already within you. Buddha was emphasising the importance of relying on one's own intelligence, he was advising not to be dependent on others, nor to rely on teachers. They can become a crutch and when this happens we stop listening to the wise teacher within. Truth is far too vast for any single human to have authority. Yes some knowledge can be handed down from one teacher to the next, but it is only wisdom when it is understood by you, for you. *Be a light unto yourself.* Jesus was not the first to say it; Buddha said it 500 years earlier, and Buddha was not the first to say it either.

It is hard to refute Buddha because Buddha refrains from making absolute statements. This is exactly the point. Truth cannot be stated, there is nothing to refute; Truth just IS. Please do try to understand this for yourself, it really helps: Existence IS, existence is 'what is'. Your mind may have been conditioned to respond to doctrines, but how can 'what is' be a doctrine? How can nature or the universe be a doctrine? A doctrine is manmade; Truth and nature are not. So first Buddha convinces your logical rational mind, he invites elements within you which respond to reason. You have to listen to Buddha because you cannot refute what he is saying without resorting to some kind of belief, judgement or fixed position, and as soon as such inflexibility enters the discussion Buddha has destroyed your argument. He holds up a mirror and with it you destroy yourself with your own rigidity. How can you be rigid when it comes to your own inner Being? Slowly you become more open, an inner feeling beyond reason begins to arise; you feel a deep realness brewing for you that is beyond your current comprehension. Only those with the sharpest of minds are attracted to Buddha's teachings; only minds willing to move against the grain of their conditioning begin to understand what Buddha is saying. The 'grain' is to obey and to believe as dictated in most religions; against the grain is to not obey, it is the state of 'non-belief'. So don't believe; instead enquire, investigate, show initiative and be open. Freedom has no dependency, only intelligence. His message to you is purely about your freedom. All wisdom is rooted in freedom.

Empty Space

BUDDHA ENCOURAGES INVESTIGATION INTO THAT which is false to uncover your inner Truth. What is your inner Truth is not the 'I', the 'I' is a false entity; your inner Truth is that which is your Being, your AMness, your awareness exploring existence. This feels intuitive, doesn't it? What we do not normally see is how this inner Truth is in fact all Truth. It is our inner consciousness expressing and exploring 'that which is' in an examination, exploration, embodiment and questioning process of all concepts known and yet to be; all in an attempt to gain greater understanding and so increase whatsoever is known.[6] We are discussing the Truth of all that is known – and this can only be all that is known so far, for it is forever growing and learning. That is what Truth does; it grows and learns. This growth is the growth of

---

[6] Please excuse this limited postulation of 'Truth', it is inserted purely to be helpful to this area of the discussion.

our inner essence forever expanding and our human life here today is part of this process.

'That Which Is' is the universe in process; it is Truth exploring itself into further Truth. It is the eternal growth of Truth into the infinite void of empty awareness; into what is the essence of the living universe – the infinite zero, the nothing, the black, the womb of all of existence from which only consciousness arose and which it now continues to expand into, exponentially. Every night in our deep, dreamless sleep we return to this womb of existence, this timeless void from which all energy arises. Buddha's teachings strip away all illusions and all dreams, including this dream we call life. No longer is our consciousness insulated by *ordinary appearances,* which is the product of intelligence or, more specifically, of computation or thought. The superstructure of the human brain has fallen and the shell between the old you and normal reality has dissolved. There is witness to the raw intelligence of reality in process and it is beyond description. There is the realisation that in this life we are enclosed inside a shell of perception that limits our understanding. With the Buddha and ultimately our inner Truth, that shell of limited perception is shattered. Only when there is existential experiencing of this can you experience true liberation, and the existential knowing that our inner Truth is 'that which is' exploring 'that which is'. Truth explores Truth; this is what Truth does.

Our awareness is pure, empty space. It is not conscious thought, it is just aware and nothing else. Awareness is the essence of life, it is the womb of existence, it is presence, it is pure empty AMness. In meditation you have transcended death, you have realised that which is going to die and that which will remain. What will die is the self and the body and what will remain is empty awareness and the ability of that awareness to see, and see everything. This pure awareness is the same awareness that pervades all life, for there is only one fundamental awareness which exists within Truth. Your awareness is deathless, it will always exist, it always has and it always will. You do not become deathless, you have always been deathless and in this realisation there is liberation. It is not just an intellectual, psychological or emotional liberation, such as the liberation of knowing that the self is false or liberation from your deepest fears. Realising deathlessness is the ultimate liberation; it is existential liberation. It is liberation to finally be your true expression – liberation that is beyond time, beyond physical form, beyond this life as we know it. It is the liberation of a complete communion with existence; liberation as an awareness that is free to explore the entire universe, all of its activities and its sensations. Freedom to explore, examine, feel, question and understand existence. The liberation of BEING with and of existence; feeling the freedom, joy, bliss and sensations of all existence. It is very difficult to understand and impossible to verbalise.

A master has realised the dream of reality. Much as relationships or possessions from a normal dream do not come with you when you wake up, your relationships and possessions from the dream that we call life do not come with you when you 'wake up' in death. All that you take is your awareness, your sentience and nothing else, nothing else at all. Understand the nature of this dream, make a home here but know it is not yours. Understand how life is a theatre created by a greater aspect of your own intelligence and all of this time you have been operating under the illusion of separation and isolation; an illusion that demands self-based perception. Don't be attached to the story of your life. Instead of being attached, laugh at the story of life. In your laughter, you have realised that it is all one big game and that the game is only real insofar as you think it is real. When you know that which is truly real, when you can see that what you thought was real is actually illusion, then you will laugh the belly laughter of immense freedom.

This is not to say that your life is meaningless and worthless; nihilism can be a most destructive force. Instead savour and enjoy this reality, it is real insofar as you can feel its realness, but know too that it is a dream and one day you will wake up. Perhaps you will now finally understand that there is nowhere to go, there is nothing to seek, there is nowhere but here. You are part of a vast interdependent system from which you cannot separate, there is nowhere other than here nor is there any moment other than now. There is no need for drastic action, there is no need to efface yourself or abandon everything. All that is needed is understanding; understanding of the essence of life and beauty. Know that all is momentary, and therein lies its greater 'suchness'. The essence, suchness and beauty of a thing lies within the moment; beauty IS when the moment IS and the moment IS when 'you' are not. Rewind if you please: beauty IS when the moment IS, for it is the nature of the mind to lose appreciation of beauty across time. It is because of the concept of beauty within Truth, in amongst many other concepts and reasons that are beyond our comprehension, that reality moves in cycles and is always in process. A rose bud is young, a rose flower is beautiful and then the flower withers away. It is beautiful because of this process, not in spite of it. Beauty is found in the essence of the moment; it is always found in the moment, and never in permanence.

The Message of Impermanence

BUDDHA'S MESSAGE OF IMPERMANENCE CAN be carried across into the way we lead our lives. Have relationship, have deep relationship with others, but know that it is unwise to be attached to another; attachment is the ego seeking permanence and where there is permanence there is no beauty, nor is there freedom. There is no beauty where there is no freedom. The very notion of a relationship forever bound is just that; it is bound in eternity and eternity is a mighty long time. Nor is it wise to try to possess another, for you are trying to possess that which is inherently free and possession of what is inherently free is simply not possible. Look inside yourself; see your desires, your attachments and your possessions, see how your whole sense of 'I' is made up of these things. Possession and attachment are foundations upon which you have built your sense of self. You can be attached to the body, you can be attached to an idea that you have formed about yourself in the mind, you can be attached to another person; these are three basic attachments that humans form, and which make up our first prison cell. Everything that you have ever done has been done with these in mind.

Realise that nothing is 'yours', not even your home, your family, your relationships: nothing! When you understand this deeply, only then do you realise the whole absurdity of attachment and possession;

you realise for the first time that the very idea of possession has been a mistake. How can you possess the contents of a dream? Possession is simply not possible. And then you realise that all idea of attachment is nothing but the response of your ego wishing to cling to aspects of this dream, and it is this clinging that will imprison you. In death, when your entire life flashes in front of you as it does in milliseconds, you are finally awake and aware of the extent to which you have enslaved yourself within nothing but a dream.

> "You are as the yellow leaf, the messengers of death are at hand. You are to travel far away, what are you to take with you?"
>
> *Buddha*

Sure, you can fill your life up with assets to make it more comfortable while you are here, but the idea that these are things which you possess in any real sense is nothing but illusion. Nothing is yours; you are on a trip, you are on a ride and one day that ride will end. To not have anything permanent seems frightening. What is the point of it all? Understand that you are on a journey and that one day you will have to say goodbye and travel on alone. Enjoy your assets, enjoy the people and places that are with you right now, imbibe the essence of all such moments, but understand that nothing is permanent and none of it is yours; you are merely witness to it all. Death is certain – more certain than taxes – and death will always separate you from whatsoever you cling to. Your possessions, like your relationships, are temporary at best; nothing on this side lasts forever.

> "He does not linger with those who have a home or those who stray. Wanting nothing he travels on alone."
>
> *Buddha*

I like to think of asset ownership as being analogous to the carrying of luggage on a long voyage of discovery which we call 'Life'. There may be some advantages to carrying a lot of luggage – you'll have more toys to play with and, yes, more outfits to change into – but ultimately excess luggage will only weigh you down. When it comes to what is important and what will essentially bring you joy, that being the exploration of the new and the freedom to roam (the whole point of the voyage!), your luggage will hamper your freedom. If you travel lightly, if you carry only a small bag, then you have greater freedom to explore and enjoy the voyage of life. If you carry a heavy load your movement is restricted. You want to climb a marvellous hill in the distance but you can't because you are weighed down by a heavy trunk and matching suitcases. You are stuck by the side of the road unable to deviate because your suitcases need their trolleys and trolleys only work on the road, never on the rocks or on the grass. You're stuck, truly stuck! There's a forest on the left with a beautiful stream running through it several hundred metres in. You cannot take your suitcases into the forest, they are far too heavy; you cannot take them with you for a swim, otherwise they will get wet. You could leave them by the side of the road, but if you leave them then they may get stolen and you cannot chance that. Always you must remain on guard, wary of others, stuck where you are because of your weighty possessions. Remember that whatsoever you try to cling to and possess – your partner, your home, your assets, your company, your reputation, your little diamond encrusted ring – all of that which you possess, possesses you.

Think of a small possession which you value very much and are attached to: a diamond encrusted ring. If one day you lose your diamond ring, the whole day is ruined. You have dropped it somewhere and you don't know where. It could be anywhere! You stress, you panic, you are tearing your hair out running this way and that. You are in dismay and you are devastated at this great loss. See how strange all of this is. You were perfectly happy before buying the ring, you lived quite happily without any knowledge of it, and so logic would dictate that you should be able to live quite happily without it again. But you can't live without it; now you feel terrible, now you feel a great sense of loss. See what possession has done to you; it is you that is now possessed, it is you who is running around like a loon after a tiny metal object.

Possession and attachment creep up on you. They creep up on you because all attachment goes unnoticed when you are not disturbed.

However when there is a disturbance, like when someone bashes into the side of your car or you lose something valuable, only then do you feel suffering. You only feel anger and frustration because you are attached; the car that was your possession now possesses you. Possession and attachment are fine so long as nothing goes wrong, but according to Buddha's teaching on impermanence, the very nature of attachment is that something is bound to go wrong. Everything that you possess will someday die, get damaged or fade away. It's a dream, an illusion to think otherwise. If you truly understand the dream, you come to see the problems which accompany attachment, like bumping your car or losing your ring, as a means of generating greater understanding. You realise that the accident occurred because more understanding about attachment was needed. There is no such thing as an accident without meaning. All events have meaning, in order to generate greater understanding.

Attachment is not only evident in our relationship to material things, but also in the possessive behaviour we demonstrate in interpersonal relationships. If you look around at the nature of the relationship between most couples, clearly many do not understand the truth that 'nothing is ours'. Jealousy in relationships is the obvious example, but possession can also be much more subtle and just as deadly. It seems that most of us, in our relationships, live by the concept of possession whilst calling it love. Do you think about your partner all of the time or do you only think about them when they are away? If you only think about them when they are absent, when your mind is disturbed, when you feel some form of suffering, then is your relationship love or attachment? This idea of missing someone only when they are away, do you call that love? Let's look into it more closely.

The very fact that you did not think about your partner when they were present, suggests what – possession or love? The nature of possession only reveals itself when you are disturbed. When you possess something – a ring, a watch, a car – rarely do you think about it. When you think of another person as your possession, either consciously or subconsciously, it is much the same and they go by unnoticed and unappreciated. Now when your possession is taken from you, missing or absent, it is only then that you notice; it is only then that you are disturbed. This noticing is a reaction of the mind is it not? It is a reaction and if you miss your partner only as a reaction, then you have reduced love to psychological reaction. Is love reaction? Is love the sensation of reaction? Reaction belongs to the mind. Is love the product of the mind or is love something that IS when the mind is not? A mind reacting can only be the product of ego resisting change; this is not love.

Reaction happens when the ego feels threatened, it is the result of the ego trying to establish some sort of communication in order to maintain its own security. The ego feels jealous and possessive of partners because it is trying to prevent any disturbance in relation to its possession. When its possession is safe, the ego does not need to think about it, so it can relax and feel at ease. This is why the ego invented marriage, a binding contract of possession, to keep itself in a state of ease. However when there is the potential danger of a disturbance, like a partner that could be leaving or straying, it is then that the ego reacts; it is then that the ego gets jealous. You are jealous and you call it love. You are jealous because you are caught up in the illusion of possession. Whatever love is, it is most certainly not possession.

There is no end to the things that the ego can get attached to – success, leisure, pleasure, addictive behaviour. If you have led a successful life, what you may find is that your success and your attachments bind you and entrap you, not in a dissimilar way to the suitcases mentioned earlier. You may become attached to the leisure that comes with success and because you like your pleasures, because they are gratifying, you want more. When your pleasures are denied you are upset, hurt and angry. You are used to a certain lifestyle. See how you have become attached to your pleasure. Your desires and your attachment are now two aspects of the same thing. Pleasure is wonderful but if you are entrapped and attached to that pleasure, then your pleasure is also your poison. The greatest joy is freedom and for that ultimately all you need is your head, your heart, your health and your humour. Know that with understanding you can be free of possession, free of attachment. If you need to give away all of your possessions, then have you understood? With proper understanding comes greater joy than you can ever know through attachment or possession. Ultimately, there is nothing to possess; possession is simply not possible. The only thing that is always ours is our consciousness. We had it when we arrived and it will be all we have when we leave. It is therefore the only investment worth undertaking. It is our only true possession; all other possession is illusion.

Breaking Chains

IF THERE IS TO BE wisdom, there must be the ending of even the possession of ideas. The mind must shut down completely, freeing itself of all philosophies, all methods, all preconceived ideas and all doctrines. A true master has to be against his own philosophy, his own teachings and his own methods. These methods are no more than props to help you along the way, like oars on a little boat to help you row to the other side of a river. If you keep on rowing and rowing and rowing, the other shore will only move further and further away, and you'll never reach it. The more you force it, the more it simply will not happen. The oars of method are only for use to give the boat starting momentum. Once you're moving, they must be dropped for this momentum to carry you to the other shore. You only arrive, of course, when you realise that there is no other shore. As with any form of attachment, if we become attached to the methods of masters and are unable to let them go, then they are no longer props for the mind, they are chains which fortify the sense of self. Any kind of dependency fortifies the self; dependency is the very opposite of being free from all influence, which is to be free from all identifications and thus the conditioning of the self. A master is only genuine if he is against his own methods; he does this to ensure that you do not become a slave to his words or his practices.

You must break all chains and all attachment to false idols so that you are not dependent upon others, systems or anything for that matter. This warning not to worship false idols has been misunderstood across history; it is a warning about the nature of dependency. But as history has demonstrated, the human mind is reluctant to let go. Despite the clear warning from our teachers, many Buddhists continue to worship Buddha, Christians continue to worship Jesus and

Muslims continue to worship Mohammed. Instead of listening and understanding, we follow teachers blindly and fail to realise how it is the 'following' that is the actual problem. We do not realise how such practices go on to fortify the ego and how anything that props up the ego can only take us away from our inner Being. All following props up the ego mind, but ego mind must collapse completely if reality is to come to you. It cannot happen if you are trying to force it, nor can you will it to happen. There must be a surrender to reality; allow it to enter you and in reply reality will allow you to enter it. It mirrors you; the more vulnerable, open and surrendering you are, the more existence will release itself to you. Let existence enter, intertwine and meet with you deeply and whatsoever you do will be matched. Merge with reality, become one with reality. It is more than a slow dance; it is more like a slow melt because it is a fusion – a deep existential fusion. If you are open to it, Truth will arise from within you; there is no need to search for that which you already are. It happens not through your action but in your inaction, in your surrender and your release. The superstructure of mind can finally collapse and the layers of falsehood that we know as the ego can dissolve. Underneath, lying in wait and always waiting, is Truth.

Growth & the New

IF FREEDOM IS WHAT YOU want, if freedom is the goal, understand first that entertaining any kind of goal is a form of attachment. You are attached to an outcome and so everything that you do moves you in that direction. Where there is a pre-determined direction, there is no freedom. Attachment is not freedom nor can it ever be freedom so don't make freedom your goal, otherwise you become attached to that goal. As long as this attachment remains, you will never be free; you are like a dog chasing its own tail. Attachment to a goal defines the future in your mind, rooting you in the past where the goal was formed. You are then past, dead to the now. If your future is defined from the past, how can you expect to embrace the new? Only the new can transform you, only the new can make you new; for what can transform you if not the new? You are old, all thought is old, so if transformation and thus growth are to be prominent in your life, then you must do more than make room for the new, you must embrace it, drink it, fall in love with it. Sometimes it will be hurt, sometimes it will delight; either way you are growing.

Understand this about the new: the only way to imbibe what is new is to be fresh and open to the new. You cannot seek what is new, you cannot prepare for what is new, you cannot define what is new; you have never come across the new before so how do you know what you are looking for, or what you are preparing for, or what you are defining? The new simply comes, and so you can either embrace it or resist it. If you resist you may as well be dead, if you embrace you allow the possibility for growth, art and transformation. Remember, the new can only ever be received; it comes to you, never you to it. You have to let it enter you, dance with you, commune with you, be one with you, merge with you and then one day in your life you will find that it *is* you. You are anew at each moment. Your life is a living, breathing moment of creation that is continuously re-creating itself; this has always been so, only now you can see it clearly.

You are fresh, vibrant and alive, you are luminous and radiant, you are joyful and most of all playful. You embrace life because in the potential for transformation there is freedom and energy. Life is filled with new openings, new challenges, new adventures, new freedoms at every turn and thus new wisdoms. You are like a child acting spontaneously and courageously; grabbing the immediateness of life, taking the proverbial bull by its horns. You are unshakeable now because whatsoever happens, happens; you recognise that life's pleasures, pains, successes and failures happen for your greater understanding and that all moments of life are an opportunity to learn and become wise. Soon you become more centred and more grounded, unshakeable like a mountain; you are a tower of strength. Embracing and being open to the new will transform you, lift you, enthuse you, mature you, become you, and then one day 'you' are not and only the new IS. Abandonment of the self each and every moment to what is new is true freedom and joy. This is what is truly sacred – not your cathedral, your Bible or your altar, but your freedom and your innocence to be open to that freedom.

Embracing the new in the name of growth and transformation takes courage. The ego is not, by nature, courageous. It fears the new because, as we have seen, it fears for itself; it fears its own death, and it contains this possibility by fragmenting itself into the thinker and its thought – its opinions, beliefs, biases, judgments and conclusions. If you find yourself rejecting what is new, rejecting change, then it is the ego at work. The ego does not like change; it never celebrates change because change threatens its very foundation. This is why the ego has a tendency to become stuck in its narrow ways of thinking; it is a form of protection undertaken to guard against the potential *continuity-ending* consequences of embracing the new. If you behave from the 'I', then when there is the potential for change, you choose to remain stubborn, fixed, unchanging, sterile and dead like a rock. This is true for most people; most people are stuck in their ways, not just the elderly. But if you understand that you are not your ego and that the past does not equal the present, then you can embrace change for the transformation that is possible.

Where there is the potential for transformation there is great energy. Now you are open, alive and vibrant; there is new adventure, there is possibility for change, there is the potential for growth and where there is growth there is freedom. Any understanding learnt from teachers should help recover your courage to embrace that which is new; to embrace freedom. Recover the courage to live and live fully, the courage to live and live dangerously – not recklessly (recklessness is for the foolish), but dangerously in the sense that you grab life fully and you take it, taste it, live it and live it intensely.

Courage is not something you need to go out and find, it is already within you – something that we *recover* rather than *find*. You have let your courage fall asleep under the dark shadow of the ego, a shadow that likes to stay fixed and certain. Your courage has been repressed and suffocated by your conditioned mind. It is the product of your blind acceptance of and your compliance to the rules of society, which by their very nature can only suppress. Courage is not to overcome fear, courage is to recognise fear and face it directly. When you face it, when you look into what fear is rather than looking into what it is that you fear, you understand that it is not separate from you. Fear rests in the ego's search for security; it is your craving for certainty. Courage is to no longer avoid this uncertainty. It is to break with habits that you have dared not challenge. It is to look into why there is panic when you break away from the hierarchical power structure that created you. It is to go against any system that promises certainty and therefore enslaves you, whether religious, political or social.

It takes courage to come face to face with that which is false within you and that which is true. Courage is to peel away the layers of the ego that cover your fundamental Being. You are not your ego, you are not the layers of the self, you are your Being and you have always and only ever been this Being. Only by surrendering and releasing the layers of what you *are not* do you come to that which you *are*. Only by understanding the false nature of the layers of the self do you come to that which is real, which is a non-self – what Buddha called *Anatta*. Only by negation do you come to that which is most positive.

When fresh, innocent and open to the new, you are always changing with the new. Resurrection is to transform yourself and be reborn to the new each second. Meditation is the awareness of the new each second. So a mind that is meditative resurrects itself again and again at every moment. Resurrection is to die to the past, transform and rise like a phoenix in each and every moment. Resurrection brings you to joy because resurrection is freedom. This is what intelligence is. This is what is truly implied by this word 'resurrection', which is so absurdly loaded by Christianity. There is nothing to learn, nothing to imitate; only see, only Be. Seeing is enough; Being is enough. Innocence implies no past, only now. No future, only now, because future is a product of the past. So we are discussing a mind that is vulnerable, gentle, innocent, open, chaste and receptive; only such a mind is capable of moving beyond itself, moving beyond the image of the self. Only such a mind is capable of seeing with absolute clarity. Truth is always in the new, not in the past, not in memory; it rests only in the new. Resurrection is the way of Truth. Resurrection has no dependency, no method, no system; only clarity, only freedom. What we call peace of mind is not a product of mind, peace of mind is no mind at all. Where there is no mind, then there is absolute clarity.

This clarity, this alertness is energy, pure energy; it is the energy of existence itself. It is the energy you plug into when you sleep, when you meditate, when there is that great contact with existence. It is the energy of the living, breathing, dynamic force of all existence; it is life, your life and the essence of all that you experience. Search within yourself, question, probe, investigate and you will find all of your answers. Think in terms of concepts and how Truth is the questioning of all concepts. What lies within your deepest realisations is something which is beyond mind, it is an existence where your ego mind has gone and all that is left is a fundamental ISness that IS, in this and every moment.

The only way to live is to live presently, and live every moment to its greatest intensity. To live in love, drop the ego. Egos fight each other, egos do not allow room for others to breathe, blossom and flourish. The ego does not like anything superior, it finds it difficult to adjust when it is not winning and so there is all the travail of comparison, measurement, conflict, jealousy: all of which can only imprison. Do you want to live consumed with winning or do you want to live free from that which imprisons? If you want to be free, be meek: be like a log floating in a stream. Ego momentum can drop and now there is nothing for tension to rub up against. Tension and conflict require abrasion, they require at least two sides, they require duality. All conflict or contradiction requires duality of mind. When you are soft, when the 'I' has gone, then there is the ending of duality. All conflicts and contradictions will drop of their own accord. Then your life is a life of harmony; a life of action not reaction. Then your life is free.

chapter five
Your True Nature

PONDERING OVER ONE'S INNER NATURE and the search for Truth are powerful drives; in fact, the search for Truth moves humans even more than the search for sex. If we are to be truly free, we must understand our inner nature and lay down fertile soil in our minds so that the flower of our individuality and personal expression can grow. This fertile soil is freedom from thought and it is the foundation of meditation; it is a mind in order, a mind not in conflict with itself in any way. If this groundwork is not put into place, then all that we do will amount to no more than a distraction or an escape from our sense of never feeling whole, never feeling complete. We tend to seek fulfilment through an idea that we have in our minds and it is this seeking, this struggle to achieve, this striving to be fulfilled, that is the very cause of our affliction. So the underlying question we must ask ourselves as we read on is: *Is there such a thing as fulfilment that is not an illusion of the mind?*

Let us first ask ourselves why we are constantly seeking fulfilment, and what do we mean by fulfilment anyway? If you feel the need for fulfilment, this suggests that you are not – or do not feel – fulfilled. This is the very human feeling of being incomplete and seeking completion. In those rare moments when you are fulfilled, or think that you are fulfilled, what is taking place and how long does it last until you are seeking fulfilment again, elsewhere? What is this consciousness that does not feel fulfilled? We must understand ourselves, our desires and our fears, most notably the feeling of incompleteness when we pander slavishly to the desires of the everyday. Ask yourself why you do the things that you do and why you are a slave to your thoughts. What drives you to rush around all day long? Is it simply because you, like those around you, cannot conceive of another way of feeling 'complete'?

It is this feeling of incompleteness that drives us to seek fulfilment through the pursuit of pleasure, and to seek peace of mind through the projections of our mind. These projections can take the form of politics, religion, economics and education – anything to distract us away from that inner discomfort. The command economies of socialism were designed to give people peace of mind at the cost of freedom; there is no peace of mind without freedom. Capitalism turns our search for fulfilment into a competitive economic drive to get ahead and meet with success. But this drive for success – a drive undertaken in the guise of finding fulfilment through the attaining and experiencing of further pleasures – is really a form of escape from that inner sense of incompleteness, from that fear deep within. We each hope to escape our sense of not being fulfilled. This is the great human escape. We focus our desires and act upon our thoughts; we distract ourselves and rush around in the search for fulfilment. Rarely do we question why we behave in this manner. You desire only when you are not fulfilled.

It is worth noting that in both the capitalist economic system (a system that thrives upon the activity of the ego) and in the Marxist system of the command economy, there is no fundamental freedom; no psychological freedom in the former and no physical freedom in the latter. If you are to survive, you are conditioned to conform to the system of economics in which you live (going to work, for example, and having the means to live) and if you are conforming then there is less room for individuality and expression. These systems thrive on our search for fulfilment, but both offer forms of distraction from our true fulfilment, from our freedom.

Our escape-orientated behaviour usually manifests as a craving for happiness through something external – a career, a reputation, an ideal, a contribution, a person, a family; it can be anything. We believe our fulfilment can be found through something like success because we think that success will provide greater freedom and adventure, or more power over others, or more security and peace of mind. Some of us seek fulfilment through family, trying to form a deeper connection in our relationships with others. Whatever the form it takes, our primary concern is finding what we believe will make us happy and that becomes the central focus of our life. We all suffer because our minds are contradicted; caught in the conflict between what we are and what we would like to be; we have become slaves to the relentless mental noise inside each of our heads. We are confused because we cannot see, feel, hear or touch a deep experience which every human, without exception, longs for in the depths of their being. It is our ignorance of our own inherent freedom and the elusive deep experience that lies within which is the main cause of our problems. We all long for this unknown something, and most of the time we do even not know what we are looking for. We run away from our sense of incompleteness and rush towards that which we think will make us happy and fulfilled. Our happiness and sense of fulfilment become dependent upon the object of our search. It does not matter what that object is, what matters is that we are craving and this craving never ceases. This craving is an expression of our sense of incompleteness, our dissatisfaction with our sense of self in the present moment; our sense that we misunderstand all that is implied by the self and the present moment, and that we are running away from the way in which we perceive the present moment.

We crave because we feel insufficient and unfulfilled and we feel unfulfilled because there is always a sense of emptiness inside that we do not understand. We have formed ideas about the self; for example, we see the self without activity to be a lonely condition. We think that success in or through something external will bring us completeness and take us away from this inner void. Because we do not know this inner void, we are trying to escape an inner fear of insufficiency and deep loneliness, and this is what motivates our ambition. As we shall see in this chapter, it is the activity of the self in its striving for fulfilment that both causes and expands this sense of inner void and with it our problems of insufficiency and loneliness. The movement of the self (its activities and its strivings) causes our sense of isolation in the world because it is always self-motivated, self-centred or self-indicative in nature. It is the activity of the self which makes us feel isolated and alone, and thus acutely aware of an inner emptiness inside, which we then try desperately to fill. And so we strive for success in numerous ways, we desperately seek fulfilment, but nothing that we do ever takes away this inner emptiness; it is always there, aching and pulling at us inside. We run away from our incompleteness, from our inner void of loneliness, by filling our lives with all kinds of activities and distractions. Our sense of self and ambition only make this worse. The harder we push the more isolated we feel, because the nature of the self is to always be self-centred and therefore cause further separation.

All ambition-orientated activity of the self compounds our sense of inner void and thus our loneliness and our feeling of inward insufficiency even further. The truth is that all activity by the self is self-enclosing and so we are caught in a cycle of our own making. We are seeking fulfilment because we do not know our inner nature and we cannot know our inner nature if we are caught up in the traps of the ego looking for fulfilment. The ego, engaged in activity to satisfy its lack of fulfilment, spins further traps of incompletion and loneliness for itself to fall into. The solution to the problem of fulfilment is to look inward; not to conform, not to imitate others or impose rules on oneself, but to watch the inner processes taking place and in this chapter this is what we will do, conscientiously and carefully.

Perennial Wisdom

THE NORTH AMERICAN INDIANS OBSERVED that the white man always looked tense. He is always frowning, always trying to do something; he never sits still and does nothing. Historically, the Europeans to whom the North Americans were referring have built their society upon fear. Notions of success and achievement are rooted in the fear of not becoming, of not achieving fulfilment. These fears manifest into a projection of 'what should be'. When the perceived pleasures of achievement and success are impeded there is frustration, tension, fear and aggression; and so continues the conflict. Deep inside, such people feel petty, small and limited. Thus the 'white man' is left feeling rather ordinary, vulnerable and insignificant, despite repeating the words of some poet to himself, or borrowing knowledge from a leading scientist. He seeks to become extraordinary, he struggles to achieve, he strives to become something grand, magnificent, noble and lasting; anything is better than revealing his inner vulnerability. This struggle to be extraordinary is the cause of human sorrow. Because we see only 'what should be' in this struggle, we cannot see and understand 'what is'; what we really are, what is our true nature. We cannot embrace our own vulnerabilities and see them for what they truly are. When your own vulnerability and littleness are embraced and seen for what they are with absolute clarity, an unfathomable strength arises. But man does not know himself, his inner workings and how they play out and so for him there is no completeness.

When we are still, when we relax, reflect and meditate, we can become calm, grounded and centred. But when we are rushing around trying to follow our passions, our drive for money or social status or this or that, we end up with the right leg running one way chasing after X and the left leg running the other way chasing after Y. It is no wonder the 'white man' (and this is now true of much of contemporary western society) is so divided. We are fragmented and torn; there is conflict, contradiction and disorder in the mind. We are what ancient Eastern traditions called 'dual'. We even deny aspects of opposing sexuality within ourselves. Let's spend a moment looking into this important point before moving on.

Yin Yang Wholeness

A GOOD STARTING POINT IS to learn to get in touch with our opposite gender energy; failure to do so is a part of this common feeling of being incomplete. If you are a man, it is most worthwhile to get in touch with female energy within you; if you are a woman, the male. It does not serve us to be only half of who we are, and this feeling of not being whole is the source of many of the world's problems. If you turn to others to complete your incompleteness, to a partner for example, you end up insecure and possessive. You are looking to another to provide you with the sense of feeling complete. This is evident in the modern language of love and romance – the search for a feeling of 'completeness'. Any such feeling can only be illusionary because your sense of completeness is dependent upon another and therefore unstable. All incompleteness gives rise to forms of behaviour to compensate and what results is not a mind in harmony with itself, but a mind in conflict; the need to compensate is a source of conflict.

In fact any 'need' is conflict. A mind in need is without freedom, it is imbalanced and irrational and this can only lead to further unease. A relationship where each partner feels incomplete very quickly turns towards co-dependency, which is the foundation of jealousy and insecurity. Needless to say, this is unhealthy for you, your partner and for the relationship.

We burden ourselves with a limiting concept of who we are, much of which has been drawn from the outside. Modern men are often caught up in the idea of being masculine, and they deny any femininity within. Women are often encouraged to be feminine, and reluctant to show any masculine traits or energies. This is not a natural state of affairs. We are all made up of both male and female energy. You will recognise the symbol overleaf; notice the seed of the opposite contained inside the yin and likewise with the yang; the whole symbol represents you. You are not one half with a partner making up the other half; you are both yin and yang energy. If you have a partner, it can be a great thing to help each other realise your respective opposite yin or yang energy in order to achieve greater balance both in yourselves and in the relationship. If you do not have a partner you can still achieve greater balance within yourself. The key is to get in touch with your opposite gender energy, then any potential union with another will be more healthy because you already feel whole.

The Taoist Way

THE MODERN MINDSET AND ITS obsession with success, achievement and ambition can never know completeness. It will never feel whole, it will never know peace of mind, no matter what it does – social reform, increased standard of living, 24 hour entertainment – unless there is love and understanding. Without love there is no virtue and without understanding there is no freedom; a world without virtue and freedom is a world in prison.

There is a law that exists within the universe and if we are in harmony with this law then we are happy. 'Law' may not be the best word to use as it suggests compliance and imposition, whereas 'way' infers greater freedom. The reality of what we are discussing is a combination of elements of the two. We use 'law' in order to emphasise the rightness of 'way'. For example to be healthy is the 'right way' to be, and to not be healthy is a mistake. So being healthy is 'right'. In this respect there is a law of health. Of course there are also many different ways of achieving healthiness – walking, yoga, sport, diet, a clean environment and so forth. Are you following this? Health is both a law and also a way. Bear this in mind as we discuss the way of joy and harmony.

There is a way which the Chinese call the Tao that gives rise to happiness. Buddhism calls it the 'The Shining Way' or 'The Dharma'. As soon as we step out of harmony with this law, this 'way', it is not that we are doing wrong, it is that we are making a mistake. That which makes you unhappy is a mistake. This is one of the laws of the universe. Becoming wise means understanding the nature of these laws. When in harmony with this law we sing, dance, play and are joyful at whatever life throws at us. Even the negatives that we all experience, such as the death of a friend or a relation, are understood in a more meaningful way and are easier to bear. If you are suffering and somewhere there is pain, then it is a sign that you have stepped out of harmony with the Tao. Balance has been lost somewhere and you are no longer happy.

There can be many out-of-tunes with the Tao but there is only one in-tune. *Samadhi* is to feel in tune with existence, or with the Tao, or the Shining Way, or whatever you wish to call it. The Tao is the river of life; to flow with that river is to float effortlessly downstream like a piece of timber. It is to be at home with the flow of existence, without tension; to be at ease, to be in the Middle, to feel no need to gain, to hold an unassuming nature, to be balanced with the movements of reality. When reality (like the current of a river) moves one way, there is no striving by the self to move against it and thus no source of friction, tension or extremity. It is to be beyond the striving activities of the self. You are like a drifting log floating with the current. Where life flows you follow, in harmony with that flow. No swimming against the current, no projection of 'what should be', instead simply yielding to 'what is', accepting the flow of existence.

The Self in Isolation

SELF-CONSCIOUSNESS IS THE WAY OF isolation. By self-consciousness here we do not mean being conscious of, and knowing, the self. We mean the type of thinking that particularly afflicts the younger generation: worrying about how you are perceived by your friends, polishing your persona and working on who you want to be. Let go of the trap of 'perception of self', the charade that is put up as your persona. Such self-consciousness is the way of isolation and the more self-conscious you are – concerned about what others think or what you may think of yourself – the more isolated and lonely you become. It doesn't matter how many names are listed on your SIM card or how many friends your Facebook page boasts; loneliness is an idea that rests in your mind and it is the result of the activities of the self, of thought.

For each and every one of us, loneliness is the consciousness of the self in isolation without activity of any kind, be that social, physical or psychological. All activity we undertake in life fills and expands the self in some way – your interests, your education, your pleasures – but when this activity is somehow thwarted and unable to continue, you notice the emptiness of the self and for some this can be so unpleasant that it leads to aggression. When you are conscious of yourself without activity, you feel something is missing; there is an emptiness inside that you are trying to fill, you feel unfulfilled and so there is the ache of not achieving fulfilment. This is all rooted in fear. You feel incomplete, you fidget and you feel discomfort. You yearn for an unknown something and so you do anything to fill the emptiness of the self, anything at all. We are not that fussy about how we cover up our inner void; we fill ourselves with all kinds of junk – TV, gossip magazines, computer games, a simple cigarette. The list is endless. Your whole life is spent seeking to fill this feeling of emptiness. Your whole life is dedicated to the search for fulfilment. Your whole life is spent distracted in the relentless craving to be fulfilled and no matter how the craving manifests – be that money, status, your entertainments, your God or the god of fashion – you are in a prison of craving and there is no freedom. All craving is the same and self-deception is inevitable when you crave.

Think of it a different way. If you feel that something is missing, what is it that is missing? If something is missing and you are trying to fill its place, and you have noticed that in life you are always seeking to fill this sense of incompleteness, then would it not be worthwhile to understand this sense of incompleteness properly rather than run away from it? To face it squarely, rather than try desperately to fill it up or ignore it? Any logical, sane, investigating mind can see the sense of trying to understand this inner feeling of incompleteness. Firstly it is important to understand that suppression, overcoming or conquering are all forms of running away. If you look a little deeper, what happens? None of these approaches really help to solve the problem. If there is something in your life which you always need to overcome, suppress or conquer, then do you not have to repeat these processes again and again for that something to stay down? Where's the freedom of this approach? Instead, there is conflict and disorder. But understand its nature and then there is understanding and, finally, freedom.

The Empty Inner State

YOU SEEK FULFILMENT BECAUSE THERE is a sense of incompleteness inside that never withers; it is an emptiness that you seek to fill. The ego mind thinks about this empty state and forms ideas about it, naming it as 'lonely' and then forming feelings around that such as fear. By naming this empty state and forming feelings around it, the mind is unable to see the truth of it with any clarity or understanding. However complex the names and feelings we associate with this empty state, this loneliness, we are still prone to misunderstanding. You may call loneliness 'consciousness of the self without activity', but what is consciousness and what is the self? These are terms that are often misunderstood. If you do not know what consciousness is or if you do not know the fictitious nature of the entity that we call the self, then it is futile to describe loneliness as we have above. Our description – the label we give to loneliness – and the feelings of fear that we have created around it have prevented us from seeing loneliness with absolute clarity. If we label it, and in this labelling we define it with terms that we clearly do not fully understand, then how can we see it clearly?

If we are afraid of something, if we are running away from that something, how then can we see and understand that something clearly? By running away from loneliness, we are preventing our understanding of it; inevitably therefore our fear of loneliness continues.

Loneliness has become a term, a description of something we think is actually real, but when we look beyond the description to see and understand that loneliness, we understand that it is not loneliness at all but something altogether different. We confuse loneliness with *being alone*, but actually being alone is not necessarily what we equate with loneliness and the feelings that surround that label. Loneliness is not the same as the actual state of *being alone*; it is an idea that we have formed around a word which we associate, in our minds, with being alone. Loneliness is the idea that we have formed in our minds because we have not understood the empty state, we do not know *being alone* the actual, the empty awareness which is the very essence of our Being. We don't see this, all we see is our fear of the unknown empty state; we are scared of it and so we call it loneliness and then we run away from it. The irony about this misunderstanding is that the more we run away from our fear of loneliness, the more isolated we become.

Our very efforts to find completion through our actions – our dependencies, our attachments, our ambitions and so forth – only increase our fear and thus our sense of isolation as the 'me' seeks to achieve and aches for its achievements. The 'me' strives to overcome loneliness by identifying with external things – our job, our country, our reputation, our possessions – or with internal psychological gratifications such as the wish to dominate or accumulate knowledge. However, all this activity only separates us from our true essence, from those around us and from nature. It fills the hollow emptiness of the self and compounds its driving momentum. Gratifications and attachments are not only self-absorbing, they also lead to self-deception. All attachment erodes the mind. It makes for prejudice, bias, bigotry and conclusion; the deathbed of sensitivity and discovery. Without sensitivity and discovery there is no intelligence, only illusion – the self-deception of freedom through accumulation, or even choice. We accumulate or choose because we ourselves are confused, we move in predisposed directions because we have not understood our inner emptiness. As we saw in earlier discussions of the ego, it is the process of the self – in whatever we do to run away from our deep fear of loneliness – that is both self-absorbing and isolating by nature. Your drive for success, your need to dominate, your dependency, your attachment, your possession, your reliance on systems and all that you do to free yourself from this deep fear of loneliness inside, are part of a process of isolation. As you seek to gain and find security what results is the increase in that which you are trying to overcome: your loneliness. You are in a vicious cycle of your own creation.

The self separates and although some of what it does can include others, it identifies with its motives and thus there is division. This division has an important function for the concept of selfhood within reality. Fundamentally within Truth, without these separating movements in reality there would be no time for consciousness. This is why technically there is no such thing as a purely selfless action in the realm of ordinary appearances, for what is a self is driven by the activity of the five primary senses, determined by your own DNA. That which separates creates time; that is why the process of the self belongs to time or space-time and only in the death experience is there the ending of time. This is a deeper philosophical point which we will investigate further in the book *Time is Thought*. For now, recognise that the process of the self is, by nature, divisive and isolating.

We rarely fully understand loneliness because this loneliness is not part of the fundamental essence of us, but rather part of the image that we have formed of ourselves. It has been defined by the 'I' as a feeling that belongs to the 'I'; but the 'I' can never fully understand aspects of its own nature without distortion. This is because, in the process of the self, the observer is the observed; the analyser is the analysed. The thing he is analysing – himself as the analysed – conditions the aspect of himself as the analyser. The analyser is part of the analysed. The 'I' is forming a judgement or view about something that it is fundamentally built upon and so it cannot see clearly without the distortion of this judgement. Because of this distortion, loneliness is misunderstood and because it is misunderstood, it is feared. The self is afraid of loneliness, this characteristic that seems intrinsic to the nature of selfhood, and it will do everything that it can to distract itself from the loneliness within, whether that takes the form of worshipping God or smoking a joint to get high. At the fundamental level there is no substantial difference; one may be socially acceptable and the other not, but the depth of the craving to fill our deep emptiness is no different at all. The self is running away from its emptiness, each time suppressing it through distraction, each time craving for something to fill this inner void; anything at all will do, even if it is an illusion. The more you run away from your deep fear of loneliness, the more you surround yourself in illusions seeking to overcome your sense of emptiness inside. Activity that is based in illusion breeds nothing but sorrow; although it may not be obvious at first this is the inevitable outcome. Despite its many forms, all craving is craving, and it is all rooted in a misunderstanding of the self.

Let us examine the nature of this craving to fulfil the emptiness of the self. The self sees that there is craving and separates itself from the craving. In viewing itself as a separate entity from the craving, the self fails to accept its fundamental limitation (*that it is craving*) and instead busies itself telling thought what to do or what not to do. This gives itself a task or a momentum which is its own form of security. This separate observing entity sets about trying to fulfil craving; it tries to fulfil the emptiness of the self through action – pleasures, activities and so forth. However it is this action that goes on to compound the emptiness of the self even further, for all action is self-centred and isolating in nature and this only expands the sense of a personal inner void. This is what most of us are busy doing. Our need to fulfil, our suppression, repression, sublimation, conquering and distraction, are all processes of conflict, fragmentation and contradiction that give momentum to the self. What we don't see is that by undertaking self-orientated activity, the self is actually reinforced because it feels increasingly isolated and in response it becomes even more determined to break that isolation, and whatsoever it does to break this action compounds its isolation even further.

This psychological conflict and disorder give momentum to the self; the self exists in this conflict. The self *is* this conflict and it seeks to continue this conflict because the continuation of conflict is its security. The self has become an observer thinking that it is different from the observed; it sees itself as an entity that is somehow separate from the craving that it is trying to fulfil. As long as the self holds the illusion that it is somehow different or separate from craving, then there is never the acceptance of its own limitations, there is always the struggle to overcome its limitations and then there can only ever be conflicting activities. This illusion is what leads to self-deception and the inevitable misery of the square box syndrome. What is happening is the self is forever chasing the mirage of fulfilment, but the mirage of fulfilment is part of the very process of the self. Such craving will never stop until the moment you die, unless of course you come to understand it.

Fulfilment is Not of the Mind

THE TRUTH IS THAT THE drive to fulfil or end craving is itself craving. The observer is no different from the observed; there is only craving. The self was previously trying to fill its inner emptiness because it felt separate from that emptiness, it felt that it was somehow able to overcome that limitation and correct it with activity. As long as thought separates itself like this, as long as thought does not realise that it itself is limited, then there's no escape from the fact that thought itself *is* that loneliness, that sense of emptiness within, simply defined by itself in thought. When thought realises that the self *is* that loneliness, that nothing that the self does will ever fulfil that loneliness and that its current activities only compound the loneliness even further, then there is the acceptance of the limitation of the self and its activity. In this acceptance we can face our fear of loneliness and see it with absolute clarity. When thought realises that it is through its own thought and striving activities that this sense of inner void and empty sense of fulfilment have been driven along, then it can see the nature of the whole process. It can see the limiting nature of the process of the self and simply cease cooperating with that process. This is done without an aspect of the 'I' trying to separate itself. When the 'I' stops trying to separate itself from the process and thought recognises that the self and the craving and the fear are not separate, then loneliness can be seen for what it is. There is clarity that loneliness is something that has been conceived only in thought and is not what actually is. There is clarity that the emptiness that has been so feared is something of an altogether different quality. Now there is no longer the distortion that existed around emptiness derived from our running away from it – like before in our suppression, conquering or overcoming. Now there is realisation that the observer is the observed, that the observer is that loneliness and that loneliness only exists as an idea in thought. Now there is understanding that what is real is the empty awareness of your essence; of 'what is' without thought. Now there is only pure emptiness, not a distorted view of what emptiness is (that we labelled 'loneliness', and feared) but open empty awareness that is experienced directly, understood and as a result no longer feared. There is the stepping beyond the old idea of loneliness that is the product of the limiting, isolating process of the self. The fear we ran away from for so long was a pre-existing notion that existed only within the observer / observed duality.

When we realise that loneliness is the result of an idea that we have formed around our empty state, we realise that we have created this fear ourselves. When our loneliness is faced directly and seen for what it is, we realise that we are our emptiness; we are that which is when the self is not because the self is the former loneliness and the former loneliness is the self. This loneliness was the fear that we, as the self, created for ourselves in thought and from which we were trying to escape through our various self-isolating activities. When we realise that this fear is our own creation, then the fear can cease. Our emptiness is our fundamental Being and now there is the experiencing of it directly. We see the beauty and freedom of it and thus no longer fear it. We are made up of empty awareness. This is our fundamental Being and as long as we are running away from it, suppressing it, trying to conquer it and so forth, we will never know it. If we do not know or embrace it, how can we understand our fear and ever know completeness? We will know only incompleteness and so our whole life is spent, until the day that we die, seeking to fill this sense of incompleteness. In embracing our fundamental Being, rather than running away from it, there is the realisation that loneliness is not a thing or an actuality but an idea. What is left is emptiness, aloneness and this is something altogether different that is beyond the self and any of its thoughts. It is absolute freedom, it is silence, it is peace beyond mind; it is freedom from all thought, the only true freedom there is. In this freedom there is completeness, there is fulfilment, there is love, and they are not the product of the mind. To come to love, there must be the facing of loneliness and the realisation and freedom of what truly IS, which is aloneness.

When you understand the falsity of loneliness, when you see it as a fear that exists only within thought, your understanding will bring you to aloneness. This 'aloneness' is to Be and be free from all conditioning and all thought. You see the falsity of escape into the illusion of fulfilment belonging to the mind, and you see that your running away from loneliness only reinforces your isolation and thus your feeling of incompletion and insufficiency. In aloneness, there is freedom from all outside influence; there is a life of autonomy, harmony and independent action instead of a life of constant reaction. There is no dependency and there is freedom from fear. You are finally free of the endless, deluded search for fulfilment.

There cannot be completeness or fulfilment until that which prompts us to seek fulfilment is understood, for fulfilment happens when we no longer seek it. That which prompts us to seek fulfilment is thought, and it is limited in that it can never know that which is not thought. Your denial of your fundamental Being, in your escape for the idea of fulfilment that you think the mind can bring, breeds nothing but illusion and its consequence, delusion. Let us return to our opening question regarding fulfilment that is not a product of the mind. The answer is that there is no such thing as fulfilment that *is* the product of the mind, fulfilment is what you already are; you have simply forgotten. Look around at the way our society is structured, all driven by the need to find completion through winning, conquering, distraction or suppression – all of which are activities of thought, processes of the self. Now you can begin to understand the mass delusion affecting all strata of society. Our entire morality is based on such delusion. Clearly we are making mistakes. There is no collective drifting with the Tao and we stand to learn our lesson harshly if we do not awaken, for the Tao will force us to change so that, as a species, we grow. 'The Tao' here is more than just nature; it is the intelligence of existence itself.

Calm Down

SO HOW DO WE GET to this level of understanding and freedom? The first and most important step is to calm down, sit still and do only that which needs to be done. Simply stop. Don't stress over that which is unnecessary. This might sound like laziness but it is not, it is simply the avoidance of the unnecessary. You can be active and remain calm; all the drama we create in our day to day lives is unnecessary. You can fill your day with activities, but how calmly do you perceive these activities? Ask yourself how important a task really is before engaging in it. Think of the story of Winnie the Pooh, the loveable if slightly slow-thinking bear who meanders through forest life with a calm, jolly temperament. Winnie the Pooh doesn't get stressed, he doesn't strive to achieve, he doesn't worry about being better and this is what makes him wise. If there is something that needs to be done he does it, but he does not stress over it. He lives in harmony with the forest, he does not try to conquer it or himself. He refrains from that which is unnecessary.

There is a series of TV adverts which I think summarise this more relaxed approach to life. Characters advertising a tropical rum are seen wandering along the beach in business attire pretending to get stressed on the phone. The tension of working life is ridiculed by the easy going island lifestyle. If you are tense and find it hard to relax then chill out, meditate. Become friends with the stillness of your mind wherever you may be – in the supermarket, in a traffic jam or on the train home. Meditating in the sanctuary of your living room at home with soft music, cushions and incense is one thing, but when you can find stillness in a traffic jam in the sweltering summer heat whilst needing the toilet, this is the beauty of being calm. Don't try to meditate – the effort will prevent you from relaxing. Simply relax; there is no need to control. Meditation is surrender and release. Let go of attachment to future scenarios that have not yet happened. Let go of past events so that they do not define you. See that your stresses and strains are largely of your own making, and allow the flow of life to take you. Happiness is in the 'here and now' – surrender to it, let go into it, and float gently downstream.

There has been a lifetime of programming placed upon you by society, by your peers and by your family, to 'be this' or 'be that'. Having internalised this programming, it brings you sorrow because you are caught up in processes that only compound your suffering rather than alleviate them. Your struggle to reach fulfilment so that you can escape your feeling of insufficiency and loneliness inside is a root problem. Allow expectations to drop so that these hopes to gain, achieve and become extraordinary can be abandoned. Only when you accept your ordinariness do you become extraordinary. If you are caught in desire, your mind is off elsewhere and you are missing the true treasures of life right now. The natural state of your Being is the state of ease, where within you do you not feel that ease? Look into yourself and your body. Where is there resistance to this ease? Understand the resistance within you. Where is it, and what is the cause of it? The greatest cause of disease is resistance to the state of ease; that is why it is called *dis*ease. Understand why you form attachment. You attach out of fear, so understand that fear. You fear because you fear loneliness and you are lonely because you do not understand that loneliness is thought exerting itself to a shape in response to a misunderstanding about your most basic truth: that you are empty. You are emptiness. Meditation will help you to understand and see this for yourself. Your investigation into attachment is not to detach, fight it or suppress it; it is an investigation into the nature of loneliness.

Do not try too hard to make things happen, if you do invariably they will not. Glide with it but do not push it too far; do not force it. If it is right, it will flow effortlessly. Let grace, let the strange attractor, let the current of the river Tao do its work. Understand the system of reality in which we live, look at nature and see how nature operates. What can we learn from how nature operates? Natural systems tend to operate in harmony, in their own simple rhythm. Is not harmony and simple rhythm the way of happiness? Relax and rest, but do not be lazy with your growth. Your inner voice is wise and immortal, it requires no further development. It is the 'self', the ego, that is the fictitious entity constructed out of your thought, so understand the nature of that thought; understand why you follow that thought like a slave. Instead, follow your intuition at every stage of life and watch how much easier life becomes. Understand how the pressures we place upon ourselves are self-imposed. Strip them away and what we have left is 'Being'; the love, order, compassion and bliss of genuine wisdom.

Peace of Mind

> "The way that can be spoken is not the real Way.
> The name that can be named is not the real Name."
> *Lao Tze, Tao Teh Ching*

IN THIS SIMPLE VERSE Lao Tze very powerfully and very appropriately recognises that the nature of wisdom is not found by following a system that can be spoken or defined; our categorising of a way of Being as the *'only way'* distorts the right way to Be. He is dismissing all system and all religion in one simple line. In the second line of the verse above, Lao Tze recognises the infinite complexity of the nature of the universe; our naming of it does nothing to add to our understanding of it. These lines are not intended to make us feel inadequate and unworthy, they are merely a recognition that the forces of the universe are much more complex than we appreciate and that our vocabulary does not include words to encapsulate that which we do not understand. Even now, 2500 years after the great Chinese sage lived, science is only just beginning to have an idea of the magnitude of the universe's complexity. In the great scheme of the universe we are tiny and insignificant but we are also rare and precious. There is nothing wrong with being tiny; in fact accepting oneself as tiny, small and limited, when we are no longer struggling to become something great, is a means of ending the struggle and sorrow of our daily lives. The struggle to achieve, to become great, to somehow distinguish ourselves, is the cause of much of our anguish. There is great power to be found in accepting this great truth; when we resist this teaching and continue to seek power and distinction, we only demonstrate to both ourselves and to others that we do not know who we are. We are not satisfied with what we perceive to be ourselves, we feel inwardly powerless and, because we do not understand our own absolute correctness, we cannot love ourselves.

What exactly does it mean to distinguish yourself, to be significant, to become a footnote in history? The children who are forced to study history do not care whether there were town squares named after you. It is all a product of the human ego; it is a mirage, an illusion of fulfilment created by thought. All idea of success, fame, achievement, attachment and possession are nothing more than illusions founded upon fear created by the human mind. They are a prison of our own making. True fulfilment does not come about because of the activities of the mind. Peace of mind is not a product of mind; peace of mind is to be free of mind. Peace and fulfilment come not from achieving a historic status or wielding great power over others; they are found in Being, in love, in the joy of here and now.

Individuals in Medieval Europe were so obsessed with their own significance that they even convinced themselves that the whole universe revolved around Earth and that they were made in the image of God[1]. Even today we are convinced that the human brain is the most complex organ in the universe. Out there in the great cosmos we are rare, nothing is like you or me. We are truly unique. As a consciousness within a system of consciousness, we are an aspect of this consciousness – a cell in its body, if you like. As part of existence, as a perceptual fragment of the whole, we are as precious as every other fragment. But this is not the importance sought by the ego, it is altogether different and more valuable.

The Challenge of Impermanence

LIFE PRESENTS US WITH CHALLENGES which are designed to bring forth greater understanding. They can be subtle in nature or they can be acute, and they can be presented to us in ways that we could not even

---

[1] A somewhat pathetic, insecure and shoddy god, it would seem!

have imagined; that is how life is. What is important to remember is that rather than force oneself, rather than strive and seek, your insight into daily challenges will lead you to life's own great lessons. In your greater understanding of these challenges which are embedded into life, such as those that bring forth leverage for transformative change, what you will find is that they become not less frequent or less necessary but rather more subtle in terms of how they disturb the mind once certain understandings have been reached. When we act against the grain of Dharma, when we swim against the current of the river Tao, we become exhausted and so life seems like an endless struggle. It is a struggle largely because you make it a struggle by remaining ignorant and closed to new understanding; by swimming upstream. The more blinkered you are, the more acute life's challenges tend to be in order to be thoroughly understood by you. For example, when one is free of one's attachments, one is already capable of living happily beyond certain difficulties. Economic struggles or disappointments are no longer an important consideration, when they occur. One is simply happy without the need of a financial cause. This is one of the teachings embedded in the Biblical quote below. In this and in other aspects of life, understanding overcomes the daily struggles of living in ignorance.

> "It is easier for a camel to go through the eye of a needle, than for a rich man to enter into the kingdom of God"
> *Matthew 19:24, Mark 10:25 and Luke 18:25*

Being happy in one's Being is the message deeply incorporated into the Tao. Harmonise with nature and its parent, Existence: it is a bigger force than you. Just as when you are swimming it is far easier to swim with rather than against the current. The current will always take you, the best thing to do is to let it carry you downstream. According to the Tao, the universe is and has always been an ocean of flowing energies in a constant state of flux[2]. Everything is related,

---

[2] A Mayan interpretation of these unique energies can be found in the Tzolkin.

interdependent, interactive and forever changing. As we have seen from the teachings of Buddha, reality is impermanent; so don't cling or crave for permanence otherwise suffering is inevitable.

> *Sutra 277:* "Everything arises and passes away. When you see this, you are above sorrow. This is the shining way."
>
> *Buddha*

Everything changes, it always has and it always will. Even though a situation is momentary, we often believe that the situation will become permanent. Through understanding we come to know that nothing is permanent; no moment in life, no asset in the safe, no relationship with another, not even your sense of self (and especially your sense of a 'higher' self), absolutely nothing is permanent. To accept this truth, that everything that arises will pass away, is a difficult pill to swallow. But it is the nature of reality, it is the nature of life and death, and the sooner you understand that this is the nature of existence, the sooner your suffering will end. Watch the Tao coming and going, see that existence is like a free flowing river. In this clarity one is above sorrow, as the sutra indicates. The understanding of impermanence, the understanding that the universe is a process, that its nature is always changing and only the law of change never changes – this understanding must be yours, deeply. All of the frustrations and suffering of clinging – to ideas, to possessions, to whatever – can be overcome through understanding. To cling is to want permanence but change is the universal constant, so to cling to what is always changing can only lead to frustration and misery. All things, without exception, arise and pass away.

When we flow with the Tao, we no longer project our fears into the future. If you try to excessively control the future, your mind becomes rigid and narrow. Only through insecurity and the relishing of the adventure and uncertainty of what the future brings will one become secure. If you obsess about security, your mind is filled with caution and fear. You fear the uncertainties of life, the 'what if's, and there are never-ending possibilities and 'what if's' to fear. Life is impermanent;

enjoy its fleeting moments. Each moment in time is brand new, never before has it existed, never again will it exist. Savour it, taste the 'suchness' of it but do not cling to it. Understand how the uniqueness and temporariness of everything gives it greater resonance. Reality is a process and its transient nature makes clinging impossible. If you try to cling to what is free flowing, you will only get frustrated and your frustrations will make you miserable.

The nature of ego is to possess, and our clinging nature is often an expression of our effort to feel fulfilled. We seek fulfilment in the things we desire and the things we possess. Virtually everything we do is geared towards acquisition and gain. Remember that we can only truly possess that which we can give away. If there is something that we cannot let go of or grant absolute freedom – whether a house, a consumable or a person – then we shift from being the possessor to becoming the possessed. The 'thing' we think we possess is now possessing us. Only that which you can give freely do you truly possess; no more so than love, which has no condition. Only in giving, only in showering others in compassion, are you love. There is only giving love in love. If you cannot give freely – your money, your time, your love – then what you cannot give possesses you. It is simple. How can you possess anything if you cannot give it away? Only by being able to give it away is it yours to give. The origin of your suffering is attachment and it is drawn from your ideas of gain and security, it is drawn from your non-acceptance of impermanence. To be beyond attachment is to be beyond sorrow and this includes attachment to your sense of self.

What could we possibly own that is going to give us a deep sense of inner peace? How many assets does one need before our internal fears cease, before fulfilment is ours? No amount of money or power is ever going to alleviate our deepest fears. No matter how far we run, these fears will always follow us. Like a rain cloud directly overhead following us wherever we go, living with this fear is your own personal hell. Every violent act, every selfish deed, every crime that has ever been committed can be traced back to the same root cause: a fear that exists because we feel separate from existence. Until we understand this, how can we hope to find fulfilment?

Impermanence is a truth of the universe. We are different from one moment from the next, nature grows, the planets move, everything is in process. We tend to think of the self as something static, but will you be exactly the same seven years from now? You will be quite literally a different person, as every cell within the entire body will have changed. Impermanence is the law; there is absolutely nothing we can say or do that will change this. The flow of change is like the current of a river. Accept it and let it take you effortlessly downstream, or fight it and expend energy trying to swim upstream. To cling and strive is to swim upstream, it is a futile waste of energy. It will only make you upset, frustrated, miserable and tired. Striving to distinguish the self and 'go down in history' is futile in the face of impermanence. If we can accept impermanence, in the self and in everything around us, then we are no longer frustrated by change, we are not upset because we have accepted this is the way it is. We can move beyond sorrow.

Ego identifies, ego becomes attached because the ego wants permanence; it wants everything to remain static. That is why we have a tendency to dislike change. Everything changes; not to see this fundamental law is to suffer. Understand that all is transitory and impermanent; your home, your family, even your sense of self. This may be difficult to accept because we feel lost without permanence. *"If all is transitory, if reality is an illusion and I am not what I think I am, then at least the illusion of permanence provides some satisfaction."* But illusion breeds untold misery if we are trying to cling to that which always changes. By clinging we are seeking fulfilment through a certain thing – an object, a person, a house. The more you cling, the more you become attached and increasingly dependent. Where you are dependent there is fear and where there is fear there is no freedom. We must learn the lessons of impermanence if we are to be free, free from clinging and dependence. The most obvious manifestation of impermanence is something that the Buddha talked about at length: the impermanence of the self, death. To be free of the fear of death is to have reached the ultimate freedom.

Death is a Transition

> *Sutra 287:* "Death overtakes the man who, giddy and distracted by the world, cares only for his flock and his children. Death fetches him away as a flood carries off a sleeping village."
>
> *Buddha*

BUDDHA KEEPS DEATH VERY MUCH at the forefront of his teachings. One of the problems of the western interpretation of Buddha is that we shy away from his teachings because death sounds morbid to the western mind; death fills us with fear. We are frightened because we do not understand that death is a transition, that it is a change in relation to the perception of what is, that it is the end of the self but not of existence. Death is not non-existence, but an existence that we cannot comprehend. Is death birth? Think of our only reference point. Birth to an unborn child would seem like death, the death of everything that child has ever known, the death of its life in the womb; without the perspective of what we know now, to the unborn child the birth experience could be perceived as a death experience. So without an understanding of death, some of the sutras can be interpreted as overly morbid in tone.

Just yesterday, as I write this, I went to the funeral of a dear friend who lived his life to the full. Rex most certainly pushed every button there is to push. It was a sad day and many wept for the loss. We weep because we do not understand. Are we feeling sorry for our friend or are we mourning our own loss of not being able to see him again? A few weeks ago, Rex and I had been discussing his adventures within his consciousness and they sounded incredible. Unfortunately we never got to finish the conversation. Rex was ready to go; his last adventure must have been so good that he didn't want to come back. The sly old dog went out the way he intended. We took comfort in the news that Rex died with a big grin on his face. At the funeral reception when another friend and I realised this, when we pieced together what had happened and the truth of it was revealed, tingles of primordial bliss rushed through the pair of us. My friend said to me, *"I feel a bit queer all of a sudden!"* which was a rather dainty comment from such a big man. We were touching universal Truth in that moment. Moving back into Truth brings one closer to the primordial state, to the very Being of Truth, the very life-force of all existence. This is the source from which all rushes and tingles of bliss arise; either in meditation, in the bedroom, on the dance floor or walking down the road. We both laughed, and raised our glasses.

The big misunderstanding around death arises because in reality very few people have experienced expansive inner consciousness. In western culture, continually harping on about death as something we should bear in mind so that we treasure moments in life with more resonance falls, to be frank, on deaf ears. In the presence of our perceived idea of death, we tend to clam up considering all such discussion depressing and morbid. Fear of the emptiness inside and a fear of failing to attain fulfilment in this lifetime, all driven by misunderstanding and ignorance, compound into our fear of death. Fear only exists in relation to an idea that we have about a certain thing, no more so than death. We fear death because we do not understand it. Try not to be put off exploring death because of preconceived notions about it that you have built up through your own conditioning. Unless you explore death and explore it without the distortion of what you think it is, to observe without view or judgement, you will never understand it. When you do understand it, you will no longer surround it with fear. Awareness of death as a potential around the next corner is important because it helps us truly savour the joys of the here and now as one-off moments in time that will never be repeated.

We need not take our awareness of death to the extreme. Like in everything, extremity only demonstrates tension, contradiction or conflict; that you are out of tune with the chords of reality. The more out of tune you are with the Tao, the unhappier you will be. Harmony in life is like tuning a stringed instrument – if you tighten a string on the instrument too tightly, the string breaks; if a string is too loose, it won't play at all. Your harmony, your happiness, your bliss lies in being correctly tuned; Buddha called this the Middle Path. Harmony is happiness and if there is misery, it is a sign that you are out of tune with existence; your strings need adjusting. If the conscious awareness of death is taken too lightly, many wonderful moments can be missed and pass you by without being savoured. If conscious awareness of death is taken to the extreme, this can be interpreted in such a way that the result is to never delay gratification anytime, anywhere. Such an extreme view can be very dangerous, an interpretation which can lead to the absolving of any responsibility for ourselves and others around us. Buddha is merely suggesting for us to be aware of life's harmony, to be finely tuned not highly strung, and to understand the transitory nature of all moments and all events. Awareness of this is enough.

The Purity & Clarity of Mind

IN THE BOOK *QUESTION MARK* you tried some basic meditation. When you found stillness from all of the noise within your mind, you accessed the holding area of your consciousness in that stillness. What can you say about that aspect of your inner nature? How did it feel? Getting in touch with this inner nature is the key to the consciousness totality experience. There is a fundamental purity and clarity of mind about this aspect of our consciousness; it is our true inner nature. If we take time to access it at regular intervals we immediately become more penetrating in our ability to see reality. There is an altogether different quality to our daily experience. You see art in every glance; you see the spectrum of colour inside every dewdrop glistening in the trees. You hear music, tones and rhythms inside ordinary sounds; in the pitter patter of the rain falling outside, in the songs of birds in the trees. There is a magical quality to your vision as you walk down the road. Thus there is a qualitative difference between what is seen by the enlightened mind, and what is seen by a mind that is caught up in the pursuit of fulfilment.

Your eyes are a little more psychedelic; you see art in every stone, in every flower, in every plant, on every blade of grass. Your vision of reality is different. You even see art on slabs of grey concrete on the side of unsightly city dwellings. Your vibration is different and more attuned. You are already here. Heaven is here but there must be attunement to see it. You must know perception and all that is involved in your perception. The greater your clarity, the greater your vision of the fundamental existence and the greater your kinaesthetic bliss. You walk in orgasm, you walk in art; there is nowhere to go, how can there be? The distortions of the ego mind are no longer clouding your perception of what IS, you are seeing Truth with less and less limited perceptions of the self. Clarity is the boundless blue sky free from the clouds of ego. This is why images of masters and deities in Tibetan art are presented in blue. The blue represents clear, non-dual wisdom, the wisdom that is beyond the duality and disorder of a mind in motion, a mind caught up in its idea of gain, a mind that is dual. Dual is discipline, sublimation, suppression, repression, contradiction, fragmentation, distortion, disorder. Non dual is clarity.

Love is Being

AS WE HAVE SEEN, LOVE – like anything – is only yours if you can give it away freely. Love that cannot be given freely is not love; if it is conditional then it is not love, it must be attachment or possession. Love can only be given, it cannot be taken; it is impossible to take that which grows out of you. Love is yours forever, even after your own death; the self will die but existence continues. Love knows no death, it is something which IS and will always Be. Fundamentally, Being and existence are the same. Existence IS. Existence exists. Existence is Being and this Being is Love. Your Being is Love. Existence is Love (this has been interpreted in a religious context as 'God is Love'; the sense is the same). Love is Existence. Love is what IS. Love IS. What is wonderful about these truths is that you already know them, you have merely forgotten them. The self can get caught up in permanence, clinging and searching, but your inner Being is Love, it is Existence. It transcends death, for it is eternal.

Your Being is a precious part of existence. It is like a drop of water within an ocean, yet the entire ocean already exists inside that drop that is your Being. This is difficult for us to understand because we usually think of existence in terms of mass and volume rather than as a vast consciousness with the natural characteristic of the 'whole of thought existing in every part of thought'. Jesus and Buddha employed the metaphors of a mustard seed and a holila fruit to describe this fundamental truth. They had an understanding of reality and its fundamental form, or rather lack of form, and they expressed this as metaphor. There is no absolute fixed physical weight or volume to existence; weight and volume only exist in our perception of weight and volume and this perception is intrinsic to selfhood. We will understand these concepts further with later discussions of holography and chaos mathematics in the book *Time is Thought*; what is important to understand now is the severe limitations of our misconceived sense of self. Until we can understand this, life will continue to be an uphill struggle.

To be conscious is to have remembered that you are love. We do not mean 'conscious' as in physically awake, but rather the consciousness of enhanced growth and understanding. Being awake in this way, one cannot hate another. When you are not conscious, when you are asleep to what is your fundamental nature, only then is it possible to not love. When you are your fundamental nature, you are love. Hatred – of the self or of others – is an expression of ignorance, of being asleep to your inner nature. You have to be full of hate if you are to pass it to another; like anything you have to have it first if you are to give it away. To hate you must first poison yourself and this is only possible if you are deeply asleep. To hate you must really be out of harmony with harmony, out of harmony with both your inner nature and nature itself. Remember, being out of harmony is a type of disease. If you are full of hate you are psychologically sick and this will arise in your body. Only when you are not conscious can you hate, but when you are conscious, you are like light shining into a dark room. Hate is the absence of light; hate is a consciousness that is asleep and your sleep begins when you are motivated only by your own gain. Your sleep begins when you are caught up in the activity of yourself. Your freedom begins in the release of the ego, when there is courage to move beyond the cravings and desires of the ego, when you are nothing, ordinary, empty; only then is there the showering of others with love.

The ego and the activities of the self are caught up in thought, whilst heart-led intuition is the route to love and your inner nature. Being one's heart is the key step to one's eternal Truth. Seeing the truth of reality and true intelligence in the heart go hand in hand; together this is the primordial state, the step beyond dualities, beyond all desire and all attachment. Just BE in the heart and the rest will follow. This is the first and only step. The first step is the last step and that step is freedom. Just BE your inner loving nature that you wish to express but hold back because you fear people will take advantage of you. It does not matter if they take advantage, let them; you can walk on unscathed and untouched because you are already complete. You are overflowing with passion for everyone, you are rich in this compassion, and they are poor. If they take advantage, it is clear that they are poor because they are confused and they are seeking fulfilment their own way; a way that conforms to the shadows of the ego. Their taking advantage of you only demonstrates that their understanding of fulfilment is incomplete; they are looking to complete their incompleteness through the idea of gain, but all such activity is illusion as we have demonstrated. It does not matter if others take advantage of your compassion, you can take the advice of Jesus and turn the other cheek. There is no need nor is there any wish to gain anything from others. There is no longer the fear of not achieving, your mind and your heart are mature; you are already here, life is enough. We seek fulfilment and get caught up in desire because we cannot see that existence is here, existence is enough. We do not know our true nature. In the understanding of this nature, there is gratitude and appreciation for the gift of life that we have given ourselves. Only when this point is fully penetrated is there freedom and is there bliss.

chapter six

Only Love Dispels Hate

> "In this world hate never yet dispelled hate. Only love dispels hate. This is the law, ancient and inexhaustible."
>
> *Buddha*

INSIDE ALL OF US LIES an inexhaustible source of love. When we love unconditionally, which is the only love there is, there are no boundaries as to how much love we are able to give. We are overflowing with love, it radiates from the essence of our Being; we are so tuned into existence that the source is endless. This, our basic quality, is the quality of sentience. It is the inherent nature of Being, of what is the essence of existence. It is the inherent nature of fundamental awareness; the non-ego state of life, Being, AMness.

Hate is only possible in thought and it is only thought, shaped as ego, which is capable of hate. The ego is made of thought and expressed in thought. It is only the ego which is able to feel fear because fear can only be sustained by thought. Fear exists only in relation to an idea about something. Fear exists when there is a thinker and his thought; but when the thinker is not, then there is no sustainable thought and thus no fear and no hate.

Who is the thinker that hates? The thinker is a centre of consciousness in movement, what we call the self. The self is a process of thought, a concept that exists in conflict and contradiction. On one side its thinking activities give importance, expansion and reinforcement to the 'self' – your career, your education, your beliefs, your religious ideals, your ambitions and so forth – and on the other side, you are seeking to abandon the self in moments of bliss, in moments of self-forgetfulness – in your cuddles, in your dance, perhaps during sex or when you are looking out over mountain tops or at glorious sunsets. The contradiction lies in this conflict – giving importance to the 'me' and emphasising the self on one hand, and striving to abandon the 'me', trying to lose the self in moments of bliss on the other. You are this contradiction and so long as this contradiction remains misunderstood and unresolved, there will always be fear within the foundations of your activity; there will always be a push to emphasise and reinforce the 'me' in some way. When left unresolved, this fear leads to hate. The contradiction and disorder in human society are clear to see; we certainly misunderstand. If we are not killing each other with our hands, we are killing each other with our thoughts – even in so-called 'civilised' society. The conflict of the 'me', the violence of 'me first', infects even the mind of a child when his toy is snatched away. So the nature of the ego and our emphasis on the ego must be understood if we are to live in a world of peace, not war; if we are to understand the inherent nature of existence, which is love.

Only an ego can fear, conquer, suppress, manipulate, dominate and hate. In the absence of ego, there can be no hate, only love. Fear and hate are thought; fear is thought that is preoccupied with the survival of the self and self-gain. Hate is the result of that preoccupation being exerted to the extreme. All exertion of thought is the ego in action, and the extreme result of such ego activity is, as we have seen, total isolation. Isn't this what happens when fear is indulged without end? Individuals acting in such a way become very isolated and lonely. When the ego exerts itself, in its measures to protect itself from its own fears, it is really working towards division and separation.

Because we have failed to address the problem of our inner loneliness, we each go through our lives looking for psychological security. We look to each other for pleasure or comfort or companionship and so in our relationships with each other we are seeking to gain in some way. We are seeking fulfilment through the other; we become dependent upon the other for our sense of completion. Without our problem of loneliness being resolved, without our inner fear of not being loved eased, we naturally seek and then demand to be loved, we seek and then demand comfort, we seek and then demand to be looked after. In these demands there is a power struggle to control and dominate so that we feel safe, so that all is well. The ego feels safe when the ego is in control, when it is not disturbed, but to demand love is to ask for love with authority, it is to claim love as a right, it is the ordering of love. Such demand, which is rooted in fear, must entail domination, manipulation and control; this is what is implied by the term 'demand'. This is not love, this is a mutual arrangement; you are using each other to alleviate your inner fears and find some sense of completeness through the other. This is co-dependency. We even create institutions like legally binding marriages to alleviate these fears. What business is it of government and law to be involved in a true relationship of love? Marriage can never be a contract. A celebration, a ceremony is one thing, a wonderful thing! But a contract is ugly because it is an expression of fear. This is the ego saying, '*You will love me, I must possess you, you are mine, you are my wife, you belong to me,*' which only serves to create misery and corruption, and which can only go on to breed further loneliness and isolation as the ego seeks its own security through domination or manipulation of the other.

Due to the limited nature of how we perceive ourselves, greed and aversion arise from the ego. Greed, for example, pulls objects and people towards us under the illusion that they will give us something. We may like to have friends who are popular, good looking, bright and smart; we may even think that by having such friends we will also earn such attributes. Such a desire is rooted in our feeling of insufficiency, a fear from which we wish to break free. Because we are looking to escape this fear, because our perception has been narrowed since the mind is looking for an objective, we are thus much more open to self-deception and so inevitably we form false perceptions of the friends and relationships that we desire. The relationship that ensues is bound to be one that is false. If this is the nature of your social network, as it will be for many of us, the illusionary nature of your relationships can go unnoticed for years. It is only when we are in need of a 'real friend' that the extent of our delusion becomes painfully clear. Conversely and in a similar context, once we push people or objects away from us our perception of them can become equally as distorted. It is our judgement, how we perceive and interpret whatsoever it is that we see, which lies at the root of all desire and aversion. It is our fear which prevents us from enjoying genuine relationships, both with ourselves and with others.

How can there be a healthy relationship between two people if they are using each other or dependent upon each other? Dependency can never be love; dependency can only ever be fear. Your relationship may last if there is common ground such as sharing a house, running a business or having children together, but if there is no communion and no relationship – which are not possible if you are still dependent upon one another – then there is no love, you are held together in fear. If you look at most relationships today, they are bound together out of fear. Rather than seek love as a solution to your inner loneliness, you must first understand and solve your loneliness and this will bring you to love. Relationship begins when you are not dependent upon each other and dependency ceases only when you have solved the problem of loneliness. You cannot escape loneliness, you can only understand it; only through understanding are you free of it. To solve the problem of loneliness is to feel complete; in this wholeness there is love.

Loneliness is awareness of the self in isolation; isolation from one's Being rather than geographical or social isolation. The expression of isolation can manifest as manipulation, sublimation, denial, domination, regression, repression, suppression, projection, rationalisation, psychological intellectualisation or displacement, and sometimes hate. It leads to avoidance and affiliating with others for support, or it can be expressed as compensatory behaviour like altruism. The defence mechanisms of the ego are numerous. Isolation is to be caught in the traps of the ego and this isolation is only possible when there is no relationship between you and your Being, between you and existence. What form does this 'relationship' take? You could live as a hermit in the remote mountains and still enjoy a communion with nature; this would be one possible form of relationship between you and existence. You are in harmony with existence; existence IS. 'Relationship' does not necessarily mean being in the company of other people; to be related means to be related to one's Being, able to stand alone, even in the company of others, and simply Be and be happy without the need for approval, change, improvement or the need to fulfil. In true relationship the self and all of its striving is no longer, and one is able to live a life beyond reaction to others, beyond reaction from your previous conditioning. It is to simply Be and be happy with what life brings; to recognise that life alone is enough. It is then possible for there to be an authentic relationship with all else that is – with animals, with plants and trees, and especially with other people. Authentic relationship is relationship with one's inner Being, it is the self-knowledge and self-empathy that must begin before true empathy can arise. In such relationship there is no isolation, even if you are 'alone'. When you can be alone and happy and not dependent upon anything, then authentic relationship becomes possible. Your relationship – both with yourself and with others – is a relationship of acceptance and love.

If relationship – whether with yourself or with others – derives from the self-serving ego, then that relationship can never fundamentally be *real*. It is a relationship based upon your idea of fulfilment, the ideal of 'what should be' or what you would *like* to be. This is not the real, the actual of 'what is' or who you are; it is a myth, an illusion, something that is self-projected. It is your escape into this conflict of opposites, between 'what is' (the real) and 'what should be' (the illusion), that breeds your confusion and resistance to what is real and what is true. To know oneself and be free one must know that which is true. To know what is true you must first identify the false. The ego and everything that it projects is false. You cannot know 'who you are' if you are seeking to escape and distracted by 'what should be'. This is part of the illusion of ego; it is a fiction, a form of self-absorption. Such an idea is self-constructed, not what actually *is*. Therefore this idea, this myth, is really quite unimportant. What is important is to understand why your vanity exists and why you are so mesmerized by the illusion of ego. Only then can you see 'what is', your essence, without distraction and without the resistance; without the judgements, condemnations and justifications that distort your capacity to see and discover Truth.

Remember that any idea of fulfilment can never *be* fulfilment, for fulfilment only comes about when your ideas of fulfilment cease. All ideas of fulfilment are forms of desire, and any relationship with what is perpetuated, propagated or maintained by the ego can only ever be false because the ego itself is false. Action based in ego – in desire or in ideas of fulfilment – is transparent and false. For example, if you have certain friends because of what they can give you, to climb the social ladder or to massage your ego in some way, then you are using them. This is not true relationship. Examine honestly the basis upon which someone is your friend, enemy or a stranger, and reveal how driven towards gain you have been. Is your relationship rooted in ego? Look into your life and you will find that this has been so, if not now then at least at some point in the past. To hate someone you once loved – and that hate can also be a form of satisfying the ego – is to never have loved them in the first place. Are they growing and are they happy no matter what they may have done to you? That is what matters. If we are love, if there is true relationship with our heart and with our Being, then when someone is unkind or unloving towards us we are able to understand and forgive them completely. There is no self-image that has been hurt, no offence that has been taken. There is no attempt at being fulfilled that has suddenly been denied. If you feel incomplete without the friendship or company of another then you were never truly complete in the first place. In authentic relationship we are already complete and thus incapable of being hurt. Innocence is to no longer hurt others, or be capable of being hurt. Where there is relationship with one's Being, there is innocence and there is love.

Isolation happens when there is relationship with your hurt ego instead of with your inner Being; it is the thought process that occurs when there is conscious awareness of your ego without activity. If you are feeling isolated then you have not embraced the freedom of simply Being, and without a relationship with your inner Being then of course there can be no relationship with existence, with nature, animals or people. There may appear to be relationship on the surface, but if you look closely none of this is truly authentic. In your relationship with your ego – when you are not in authentic relationship – things like popularity, the company of other people and the opinions of others really matter. However, no matter how popular you are or how many friends you think you have, your suffering is inevitable. There is fear when there is no relationship, but when there is relationship there cannot be fear. So relationship is very important, relationship is your joy. All happiness stems from relationship with your Being; this is the way of love.

Conforming to 'What Should Be'

THE ACTIVITY OF THE SELF at all levels leads to isolation. Ambition, power, dominance, suppression or the simple drive to change yourself and others in the name of self-security or self-gain; all such activities are isolating, always. Only when the self is not, when the 'me' is absent, when there is a relationship with your Being, can compassion, virtue and love flourish. The activity of the self is a movement of thought in relation to 'what should be'. Whatever your idea of 'what should be', there will be conflict between this idea and the truth of 'what is'. You live in accordance with your designs of 'what should be', conforming to this framework which contradicts 'what is' right now. 'What should be' is fundamentally disordered because in 'what should be' there is conformity and thus fear. There is contradiction between 'what is' right now and 'what should be'; that which you are striving to become in the future. You are striving towards some future ideal, caught up in psychological time, in complete contradiction to 'what is' in the present moment. This contradiction is conflict, this contradiction is rooted in fear; in wanting 'what should be' you seek to adjust from 'what is', you seek to escape. All escape is fear. You live this contradiction, and you become fear; it forms the very basis of your activity. The principal activity of the self is to run away from our fundamental Being, but we do all this because we fear not Being. Absurd, isn't it?

Conformity is to take action in accordance with the prevailing social norm or group standard; it is the process of transforming oneself in compliance with a blueprint design. Any effort of the self to conform is an expression of escape from one's fundamental Being. Transforming oneself to fit in with an externally (or even internally) imposed design is rooted in the non-acceptance of one's Being; you can neither love nor forgive yourself. Isn't this what most religious devotees are doing? Striving to be holy, to be godly rather than accepting themselves and simply Being? Such activity must end if we are to be free and if we are to love. Order, virtue and goodness exist in the moment of now, which is the moment of 'what is'; the moment of pure presence, the present moment. You cannot love if you belong to a sect, cult or a religion, because each of their activities implies imitation of others, living and thus conforming to a certain standard. In such activity there is naturally the contradiction between 'what is' and 'what should be', there is the conflict of being caught up in psychological time. Order, virtue, freedom and compassion are always *one* and *now*, 'what is' and not 'what should be'.

In this comparison with 'what should be' there is no acceptance of 'what is', there is no forgiveness. Instead there is measurement against others and the movement to go beyond others. There is competition between people which divides and separates one group from another, one sect from another religion. Such segmentation breeds intolerance, which cannot be love. Just yesterday as I write this, I saw on the BBC world news Armenian Orthodox Christian priests violently fighting Greek priests at the Church of the Holy Sepulchre in Jerusalem; the news scene revealed 'holy men' literally fist fighting over who has the rights to this sacred Christian church. All fragmentation is the result of the striving towards 'what should be'; it is the non-acceptance of one's Being, or the Being of another, in action. This fragmentation has been the cause of all the wars in history.

All comparison and measurement creates conflict and thus disorder. This conflict between 'what should be', 'what ought to be', 'what has been in the past' and 'what is' not only sustains but actually *is* the process of the self. The self is a process built upon this conflict. The 'I' thrives on the tension that it creates for itself; the 'I' will create new worries if it has to because without this tension – this contradiction, preoccupation or disorder – then the house of cards that we call the 'I' will come tumbling down. See that the 'I' is the conflict, it is the duality between 'what is' and 'what should be'. Without this conflict, the 'I' is not and so the 'I', being devious, will create conflict out of anything. Seeing and understanding the truth of this is of enormous value.

The 'I' is Conflict

WE ARE SAYING THAT THE duality of the preservation of the 'I' by the 'I', the preservation of its own process as conflict, will always continue because without this conflict the process of the 'I' will end. The 'I' is defending itself against its own ending, but the cost of this is a constant feeling of incompleteness. The 'I' is striving for fulfilment, not realising that fulfilment is the absence of the 'I'. It itself is the barrier to fulfilment, for fulfilment comes with the ending of striving and the 'I' is this striving. You are striving for happiness that will come to you when you no longer strive. That which you desire will be yours when you no longer desire. You are fighting a battle of your own making, and as soon as you stop fighting you win because you have already won. The absurdity is that you have been fighting a battle with yourself, where the battle *is* the self. The self feels empty, shoddy and limited and so it tries to do something about this; it tries to become something grand or achieve something that is noteworthy in history. See how it is your struggle to become, your struggle to achieve, that is the root of your sorrow. Let go of 'what should be' and embrace 'what is' and in this there is the ending of sorrow. If you allow existence to take you, if you float with 'what is' – what we have called the Tao – your completeness will be of its own accord. Buddha's First Noble Truth states that within the nature of selfhood your suffering is inevitable since the 'I' is its own contradiction, causing conflict and disorder. But you can still BE and not be your ego, you can BE because you already ARE. This is what it means to be related. When you are related you float with the Tao and what follows is harmony. Harmony is the ending of the 'I' and all its conflict; harmony is happiness.

The greater the sense of ego, the greater the conflict between 'what is' and 'what should be'. The greater the duality in this respect, the greater the sense of ego. It is a process which fuels itself. Modern history presents us with examples of the exaggerated expression of ego, demonstrating extreme inner conflicts, in characters such as Hitler, Mao and Stalin. A closer look into these characters' lives reveals isolation and loneliness, and the need to exert themselves according to misguided principles. Hitler insisted on sleeping alone; never did he allow Eva Braun to spend a whole night with him – his powerful loneliness needing to exert itself. Remember that all activities of the ego are self-isolating and self-enclosing. When the thinker exerts itself as a process of desire and fear, moving towards an ideal of 'what should be' that it has formed in its mind, this process is always self-isolating. The ego is driven, at all levels, by the wish to gain or self-preserve.[1]

---

[1] Even apparently 'good' or charitable activities can be driven by an ego wishing to gain satisfaction, in which case these activities will still, ultimately, be isolating. Only when there is no wish to gain and just pure compassion, no reason for you to help others but it is done anyway, is there humility and love.

We can see that the activities of the ego are isolating by observing ourselves and others, but why are they so isolating? The nature of 'me' holds certain characteristics that are common to each and every one of us, such as the fear of death and the fear of loneliness. In reaction, the ego is trying to escape the idea of death or loneliness that it has formed in its mind, and it tries to do this through action. As we saw in the previous chapter, our fears are based on our misunderstanding of what is empty awareness. This empty awareness is purely the absence of thought, but what the ego sees is something altogether different. All that the ego knows is the trepidation of loneliness that we have conceived in the mind, and by naming this trepidation as loneliness the ego confirms its apprehension. By naming and separating itself from loneliness, there is never a communion with loneliness. There is no realisation that loneliness is a state created, and sustained, by thought. As usual it is our distorting judgement that is the problem, and because of our view, opinion or judgement about loneliness we are always running away from loneliness, suppressing it or distracting ourselves. All our movements away from this conception of loneliness are self-isolating as processes. Our efforts aggravate the problem. We grasp, we attach, we compare, we are competitive, we become jealous, we strive to be better so that we are loved, we try to possess, we become anxious, we do so many things with this fear in mind. All are self-isolating processes founded upon the fear of isolation, but which in effect only compound our sense of isolation even further. We create only more misery, taking us away from the fulfilment that we seek. This fear, unchecked, provides the foundations for hate and evil; it is therefore worthwhile to understand the nature of these foundations if we are to save ourselves from unnecessary misery.

What is taking place in the deep levels of our consciousness? Thought is defending itself against its own annihilation because in pure, empty awareness there is no self and thus no thought. The self, the ego, is frightened of this emptiness and sees the moment of the self without activity as the ending of the self; as its own annihilation. Of course you cannot blame the ego for this; it is, after all, a process that is trying to prevent its own ending. And so the ego will always create activity in order to ensure its own continuance and permanence as a process. All of its activities are orientated with this sole and underlying objective in mind. So it operates purely for itself and the result can only be separating and divisive. Can you see this from your own experience?[2] Do you understand why the ego behaves in the way that it does? This is the nature of the ego. It is frightened of emptiness, frightened of its own destruction. What is the essential 'you', your Being, is frightened of nothing because this Being is invincible.

Our problems arise because thought identifies with itself, as the ego, and also with its fear of destruction. But our fundamental essence is not the ego; the ego is a fiction. The ego is a dictator hell-bent on its own preservation – even after death, in the form of either a soul, or a legacy, fame or a dynasty, as history has so clearly demonstrated. We are trapped in the limiting processes of thought, and unable to look objectively at these processes. Thought has failed to realise the limitations of its own thinking, and is trapped in its limitations by trying to solve the problems of thought with thought. Thought may separate itself as the ego and then tell itself that thought is limited and do something about it. This is different from recognition by thought that the ego and all thought is, without exception, limited. If the ego says that thought is limited, it will naturally try to overcome that limitation. It will separate itself and say '*I must understand*', but this itself is also a process. In this process of self-understanding, see how easily and quickly the process of the ego slips back into action. Whereas when thought realises that the ego is limited and that it can never break out of thought, then there is no movement away from this fact; thought recognises that even its current realisation is limited. Thought recognises that it is not possible for thought to ever completely separate itself from thought; how can it? Consciousness itself is thought in movement, it is its own content. How therefore can consciousness ever be truly objective? There will always be a slight distortion. Know simply that the ego is not you, it is not your essential Being, and that even self-understanding belongs within the realm of thought and cannot be separated from that thought. It is not an understanding that is

---

[2] Thus our use of the term 'selfish' – all such behaviour is rooted in the self and its drive to prevent its own annihilation.

known by some entity that is separate from you, like a higher self or an atman, it is an understanding that lies within the realm of thought and nothing more. True intelligence is being aware of this fact and understanding the limitations of that. It is recognition that the understanding of a process is itself also a process.

Observe the limitations of the actions of thought in relation to its fear. You are always operating in reaction, reacting to your deep fear. Understand that if you try to fight the fear of isolation through reaction, by striving for this or that or whatever you think will bring you freedom, what happens is that you only go on to reinforce the sense of isolation even further. Further to this, it becomes impossible for you to be free of reaction as you are always operating in reaction. This is not the way of freedom; free action over reaction. Rather than see the clarity of these facts and embrace them, the ego runs away from them pretending that knowledge and activity can bring forth freedom and fulfilment. We can all see this in our own life experience; the ego is always keeping itself occupied, always distracted and busy in the hope of finding fulfilment. How can we recover the state of love that is our inner nature? Until this problem of loneliness is truly resolved, there can be no love and there is only fear. For many of us, when there is a break in the busy activity of the ego, when there is an interval in its occupations, the mind feels incredibly lost and lonely. It is like the high flying businessman who takes a holiday and doesn't know what to do with himself. Without activity the ego feels lost because the ego is this activity; this is true for the majority of people in the world today. There is global fear, not love, and this is because the problem of loneliness has not been resolved.

Remember that loneliness is just a misguided idea about the fundamental empty state; it only has existence within thought. Far from being an actual thing, loneliness only exists as an idea in the mind. When loneliness has been understood, there is understanding that loneliness is a process of thought intertwined in the makeup of the self. In the cessation of the self, in true relationship with Being, there is the ending of loneliness. Now we are able to stand alone free, from our fear. Our aloneness is pure awareness that is free and unshakable from all influences, from the internal conditionings of the mind and conformity from the outside. It is the only true quality of freedom. We, as a society, don't know this quality; we know only the fear of what we think inner emptiness is. The consequence of this is that our entire society lives in fear and not love; virtually every action undertaken socially, economically, politically or otherwise is a reflection of this fear.

True aloneness is awareness that the self is activity and that this activity is binding and limited; this is a whole new dimension of understanding. Aloneness is the realisation that the nature of thought, the very make-up of thought, is narrow, mechanical and derived from the past. It understands that freedom does not exist within thought and, in this understanding, is subsequently free from all thought and therefore all conditioning, internal or external. This is the essence of freedom. Loneliness however is consciousness that observes the self without activity, where the observer has separated itself from the observed. Because of this separation it has not given complete attention to the essence of the thing that it has called 'loneliness' and it can never therefore truly understand it. When thought, or the thinker, tries to solve the problem of loneliness through action (in reaction), this shows that it has not understood. It has not realised that loneliness is a product of its own process. Loneliness only exists as a result of thinking, which is the result of memory and knowledge forming a view, opinion or judgement about loneliness. These views, judgements and opinions create beliefs and conclusions and any thought which operates within such fixed constraints is bound to be mechanical, isolating and enclosing. Even if thought penetrates further than this and sees that loneliness is the process of itself in perceived inactivity, this understanding can still bring about feelings of isolation and further loneliness, as it has failed to see that its very sensation of loneliness is part of the limiting process of the self. This sounds complex, but this is because we are caught up in traps of thought. There needs to be absolute clarity here. The moment there is complete attention to loneliness without attaching any views, labels, biases, judgements or opinions to it, there is the understanding of the essence and depth of what is the empty state and the beauty of this fundamental Truth.

Observe the world around you. People are not, on the whole, iconoclastic, on the contrary they like the mechanical prison of the mind; they are full of beliefs, opinions, conclusions and judgements which go on to form their habits. Any new ideas which challenge your system of thought – your religious beliefs, for example – are denied outright because they shake your foundations. This denial prevents you from seeing clearly, from looking objectively at 'what is'. There is disorder in your view of 'what is' through your own filter – you do not see 'what is' but what you *think* is. If thought is limited in this way, it cannot be free. Thought which operates inside a fixed space, such as limited view, creates all the disorder and conflict of the self, driven towards 'what should be' and 'what ought to be' – which are never free. Then there is comparison and measurement rather than love, there is more self-consciousness and fear, and thus increased isolation. Over time our sense of feeling completely and utterly isolated strengthens as we strive to find our own unique, misconceived idea of completeness – which becomes more unique and more specific the older we get. As we approach old age we become stuck in our ways, and this brings about unhappiness and loneliness.

A Loving Nature

IT IS ONLY THE EGO that is selfish. Look into the eyes of a baby; there is no ego and you can see his inherent, loving nature clearly. When we connect with people, when there is the absence of the 'me' with its ambitions and drives and motivation, we feel only goodness and love. It is the urge for power, a value deemed respectable and which has encouraged us to be selfish and competitive, that fosters fear and hate. What is it that seeks power? Hate is the totality of the 'me' while love is the absence of the 'me'. This ego conditioning is not the real 'you', your ego is the product of society but the essence of you is beyond anything to do with society. The real you is pure observation, the watcher whose nature is pure and clear, whose nature is pure love.

The objective of any spiritual investigation is to get in touch with this essential nature. In this nature there is the ending of all craving. There is absolute peace and where there is absolute peace we are no longer craving God, we are no longer craving for the highest or the greatest. We crave because we are suffering, that is why we strive for a goal. We desire to experience the infinite and we dress it up amongst lofty religious or philosophical ideals. See that our craving demonstrates that we live in fear and we want to escape from that fear. The objective of any spiritual investigation is not to experience the supreme, but to be of such absolute serenity, peace and inner harmony that the supreme is no longer relevant. Buddha has no craving for God because Buddha is already at one with his inner divinity. He is beyond fear, he is beyond sorrow, he is happy in his Being without being caught up in immature desires. There is no attachment, no craving, no aversion nor suffering; there is simply perfect order. When this order is complete, total and absolute, then you are home. There is nothing more. There is no further desire or fear, for the supreme, the utmost or for anything at all. Then you will know what it is to be free. You will know the beauty of that freedom, the beauty that is your very ISness. There is nowhere left to go. Such serenity, such calm, such wisdom! There is nothing to do but look into oneself, listen, attend, examine and be ruthlessly honest. Only in this way is there freedom, because Truth is Freedom. This is the message of Buddha. This is the practice of Vipassana: look, watch. That is all.

Cultivated Compassion

ONLY IN COMPASSION IS THERE enlightenment. Of course it is likely that others will react well to your kindness and open their hearts to you, but this is not why you undertook a selfless act; it is merely a consequence of that act. There is no motivation behind your goodness; you cannot help but do good since your goodness is already of itself. If there is a motivation, then you are looking to gain from your actions. If your compassion is authentic your goodness is shared because you are already overflowing with love; love is your inherent state of being, you and existence are in a state of fusion. How do we distinguish between the authentic compassion of inherent goodness, and the cultivated compassion which arises from selfish motivations?

Giving love to those who have not experienced it, helping those outside of our immediate friends and family, these are the contributions that bring us peace and joy. The very idea of cultivated compassion suggests that your happiness cannot coincide with the unhappiness of others, that it is impossible to be happy independently if others around you are suffering. Therefore when you act with compassion, you are indeed acting for yourself. For example, as you open your mind to the suffering of others, the magnitude of your own apparent problems is put into perspective. What in your life may previously have been unbearable is now much more palatable. What has happened is that you have become much more mindful of the problems of others and thus better able to put your own issues into perspective. By acting in response to the problems of others, you feel good inside and your own anxieties recalibrate into a more balanced and less egocentric point of view. Grateful, you are now more capable of being of service to others. Your happiness is a reaction to the recalibration that has occurred inside. Such happiness is still based on a reaction of some form; it is a happiness that is caused. Please note this.

Proponents of cultivated compassion always suggest that we should be mindful of our actions since it is unlikely that they can occur independently without there being an effect on others. Your happiness is linked to the happiness of others – your friends, your family or the strangers you may meet. Since we are all interdependent, it is impossible to separate our desire to be happy and the same desire in other people. There must, therefore, be consideration for others. This requires us to behave with ethics in mind; ethics enable us to distinguish the balance of our own desire to be happy with the equivalent desire in others. Ethical restraint is different from denial; it is an informed voluntary choice based on the understanding that all happiness is interdependent. This is the conventional view of ethics.

If you think that you must cultivate more collective happiness in order for our own happiness to increase, then this will be a projection of one of your ideals; it may be a noble, lofty ideal but remember it is still an ideal. Now let's examine this closer. Your happiness is dependent upon the happiness of others, it therefore has dependency, which means that it is a happiness that must have a cause. If you feel a genuine release from the disproportionate self-pity that you felt before, or if you are assisting others in order to create more harmony in your community so that you yourself will be happier, then fundamentally you are still operating for yourself. You cultivate more collective happiness for your own satisfaction. Your apparent selflessness is indeed selfish. Your selflessness is founded upon your desire for satisfaction through contribution. Your selflessness is pseudo. You are still operating from a mind that is wishing to gain, whether it is hoping to gain in the field of popularity or something 'nobler', like enlightenment. Understand that even here, even amongst the realms of lofty ideals, you are still operating within desire and the quest for satisfaction. You act because you want satisfaction and are therefore operating from the viewpoint of gain.

We are advised that in order to feel happiness within, we should cultivate an open heart so that we overflow with compassion and selflessness. By recognising our intentions and motivations to act, we can begin to see the benefits of selflessness, but in being selfless we are being selfish, we are acting out of the idea of a reward. By cultivating compassion and cultivating an open heart, the idea is that we overflow with love and compassion and it is this that makes us truly rich. Only by adopting such a worthy cause, by dedicating our lives to helping all those around us can we find real and lasting happiness. We are motivated to help others because we understand that our own happiness depends on their happiness. As we transform our spiritual qualities of compassion, tolerance and forgiveness, we position ourselves to better cope with the problems of life for both ourselves and others. Now is all that love? Is it really? Or is the self fundamentally still acting for the self?

This is not to discourage the practice of such noble actions, but to encourage understanding the nature of our 'good' actions. Know that you cannot practice an open heart, know that you cannot cultivate what already is; one can only uncover the selfish tendencies which block your inner nature, a nature which is inherently good. Once you understand your intentions and motivations, then you are closer to learning the true nature of the entity that wishes to be selfless. A self cannot wish to be selfless because the wish itself is a direction towards a gratification of some form. Selflessness is only possible when the self is not, when there is a complete absence of all motive, objective or direction. When there is clarity on this, so begins your authenticity and with it your uncaused joy – a joy that is free from all reaction. You are able to operate with authentic compassion, which is to operate with the complete absence of the 'me' – without a desire to gain, without any hidden motivations behind your action. Your action is thus truly authentic and your goodness is of itself. You are overflowing with passion for all and you are filled with the joy, love and goodness of existence itself as it flows into you, only to then dissipate outwards to others. This is an altogether different quality from cultivated compassion, a compassion which is at root false. Genuine compassion is not a product of the mind, it is already of itself. It is what is when 'you' are not. Something has changed kinaesthetically, now there is a different vibration; a vibration that celebrates the richness and perfume of life. All reality sits on a vibration and that is the vibration of bliss. Every cell inside zings with life. This is your potential and the potential of all those around you. Buddha called the relationship between enlightenment and compassion Bodhichitta. Happiness lies within the open heart, never within a heart that is closed, self-motivated or self-cherishing.

Only Light Dispels Darkness

THINK OF THE LOVE AND compassion that is your inner nature like the light of a flame within. It is like the light of an oil lamp surrounded by layers of thick black cloth, which represent the layers of your ego. Darkness cannot exist in the presence of light; if the lamp shines without being inhibited by the activities of the ego, then your light will fill the room; your love is free to Be. When this inner light shines freely, even if it is only a little flame, then you cannot hate another; it is simply not possible. You can only hate another if you are deeply unconscious, where there is no light at all, where the inner flame has been completely blocked by the dark layers of the ego. In the same way that darkness can only exist where there is the absence of light, hate can only exist when there is the absence of love, or more correctly when love has been blocked or inhibited by the dark shadow of the ego. Every time the ego exerts itself, it adds further layers that cover your inner flame, creating darkness in this absence of light.

This is the covering of love, compassion, virtue, joy and freedom: the presence of ego.

Your inner light can never go out because it is what you fundamentally are. Even those who commit heinous crimes retain this light within, however hidden in darkness. The light may have grown dim but it is still there, covered by the shadow of the ego; poisonous layers of self-interest and self-satisfaction. If the true nature of consciousness was hate, there would be no inner flame and this characteristic would remain unchanged, it would lock up every thought and emotion. It does not. Only thoughts governed by the ego block out your inner light and cause you to hate; it is a cage of darkness of our own creation. In this cage we generate a continuing cycle of unconsciousness, where violence breeds violence, war creates war, people hurt each other for gain or revenge; all acts of the inner ego dictator thriving on its own conflict. Evil only occurs when a mind misunderstands the nature of thought. This is why violence can never justify violence, and why the death penalty is the act of an unconsciousness collective mind. What does such a collective action say about society? Violence can never be justified, ever. NATO countries honour war like it is something glorious, noble, magnificent and even godly. You would never see a master with a machine gun in his hand, Buddha in a fist fight or Jesus throwing a hand grenade. Never!

Hate exists in thought and cannot be found in the present moment. In the present moment there is no thought, there is only presence; there is only awareness, only Being. Hate can only exist in the past or in the future, it cannot exist in the Now. We may hate someone when we think of what they have committed in the past, when we think of how they may have wronged us and now we want revenge. A thirst for revenge can only spring from thought; thought about past actions and future consequences. Fear is similarly based on our concerns for the future, or references from the past. Fear and hate can only draw from our interpretation and referencing of the past or future. When we look at someone in the present moment – where there is no referencing to past or future, no view or judgement – then they are simply over there and you are here. What they may have done in the past is no longer happening, nor is there the fear of what they may do in the future; hate is thus simply not possible. In the present moment, fear is not possible because fear cannot be sustained. This is the nature of the present moment. You can neither hate nor fear another without reference to past or future; it cannot be done. We are all caught up in psychological time, we live in thought about the past and the future, and that is why we fear. Fear breeds unconscious action, conflicts and contradictions in the form of aggression, tension, frustration and aggravation, all of which finally leads to hate, but when we remove time from the equation, hate has gone. Try it for yourself – hate and the present moment do not occupy the same space, hate is not present in a consciousness that is awake. When in the present moment, when the self is not, there is virtue, there is goodness and it is impossible to hate.

Insults & Anger

PERHAPS THE IDEA THAT OUR inner nature is love sounds alien to you. Perhaps anger and aggression have been a problem for you and you often find yourself reacting to insult. You are responding to memory, caught up in time. You are caught up in the past and the image that you have formed about yourself in that past. If there is authentic awareness of what is the shape of the self, if there is present moment awareness and thus freedom from psychological time, then whenever someone insults you, anger is simply not possible. Before you would have reacted angrily; maybe it might have taken 1 minute of anger before you woke up and realised what was happening. Maybe after some self-reflection that period of unconsciousness would be shortened to 30 seconds, or 10 seconds, 5 seconds, 1 second? Such reactions are only possible if you are deeply unconscious, if you are identified with the image that you have formed of yourself and are attached to your beliefs and values. You only react angrily when you are unconscious and unaware of what is your true nature; when you are asleep. When you are truly alert, when you understand the process of the self, then whenever an insult is thrown your way, you are untouched and unmoved. It doesn't take you a minute or even a few seconds to realise this; you are alert and unmoved in the instant of the insult. There is no anger that needs to dissolve because anger did not arise in the first place. Instead, you recognise the truth of the situation. Someone insults you: wait, watch and what happens is nothing but a further opportunity for you to see the situation with clarity.

If you respond to an insult, it is your choice to do so. The insult is only real if you allow it to be real. Now this choice to respond is not really a choice of freedom; it is rather a lack of choice because someone is pushing your button and, like a predictable robot, you are responding. Is that choice? If you are awake, if you are free, insulting words have no meaning; they are nothing to do with you. Insulting words are only meaningful when you are asleep, which means you have responded because you have identified with the image that you have formed about yourself, an image which feels insulted. Your response is rooted in ignorance and a lack of awareness. Somebody insults you, throws something unpleasant at you, why accept it? It has nothing to do with you. It is only meaningful if you accept it. Remember, you accept it because you are identified with the idea that you have formed about yourself across your life, which is with the image that you have of yourself. All of this is your ego in reaction.

When you are no longer identified with this image that you have of yourself, you are unmoved and unshaken and thus beyond sorrow. It even has the result of forcing the insulter to think again. Your inaction is a language that he doesn't understand and because it is so confusing for him, it will bring about greater self-reflection in his mind. This is your act of compassion, sprung not from the ego but from your true inner nature.

Not Opposite

LOVE AND HATE ARE NOT two opposing forces. There is only love, or love hidden behind the dark, distorting clouds of the ego (the layers of dark cloth in our earlier analogy). There is only light or a dimness of light. There is no true evil; only a lack of love. What we mistake for evil is love that has been hidden. The modern myth of Darth Vader in Star Wars expresses this very clearly. It does not matter how bitter, twisted or malevolent Vader becomes as he slips into the dark side of his ego, his son Luke Skywalker feels that there is still goodness in Vader despite the warnings of his Jedi tutors. In the end, Vader's compassion finally saves him from his nightmare of internal contradiction and disorder, where his quest for power had consumed him almost completely.

No matter how dim the flame of inner consciousness shines, or how many layers of cloth surround our inner light, it never goes out. So do not listen to teachers who tell you to fight hate, to fight darkness, to fight the work of the devil as if it is an actual force. It is like having a boxing match with the darkness, there is only a lack of light. You are bound to get tired and feel that the darkness is a superior force because you are fighting a vacuum. No one person is inherently evil, there can only be a lack of love stemming from the distortions of ego which are covering your inner flame. These distortions are the twisted thought patterns of the ego which are forever seeking self-gratification. If there are enough of them then they can shroud your inner light, casting everything into shadow. This is the darkness of unconsciousness. To feel hate you must be caught up in the ego, completely consumed by your own self-isolating, fear orientated thought patterns. If you hate another, know that you have become that hate; you have identified with that which shrouds your inner light. You have identified with thought, thinking that this thought is somehow separate from you when it is not; they have become you. All hate begins in the mind and, to hate another, hateful thoughts must first arise within and fill you with poison. These toxic thoughts can appear to take over, they can consume the self, but they are not (nor can they ever be) the essence of you. The greatest freedom is our inner freedom; freedom away from the desires, fears and isolating activities of the ego. When we look inwards at our inner Being, we feel lighter and more in touch with our fundamental nature. Love is the flame of consciousness that rests within each of us. The more we explore, the more conscious of this we become. We uncover our fundamental nature. You are love; it is your competitive ego which hides this from view.

All of the unease evident in our society has an antidote in love. This antidote has been there since the beginning of time but many have not noticed because they have been asleep, dreaming of ambition and self-gain. Love is most powerful, existence is most powerful. It is a wonderful ecstasy; a way of being that is healthy, cleansing and effortless. There is ease, rather than the state of unease which is characterised by 21st century stress and tension and which manifests in the body as disease. To hate requires energy; it consumes us, exhausts us and depletes us of vital chi energy. Love is the vibration of effortlessly flowing chi. Notice how those who are happy, who are in love, radiate well being and good health. Such people glow; this luminosity can be traced to DNA emitting light with greater strength. When we are joyful, we shower our compassion onto others. It is effortless and unbounded for love has a beginning and no end. It is universal, never selective. We no longer feel isolated from one another, we no longer compete for each other's energy, instead we are filling our energy from existence and it is a supply that is inexhaustible. The more you share, the more you receive and the greater is your outpouring of bliss onto others. You are in the bliss of the present moment, where hate is not possible. You are in relationship with existence; you are in love.

chapter 7

Good & Evil

Are good and evil at opposite ends of the same spectrum, with goodness at one polarity and evil at the other?

For centuries we have imported our idea of right and wrong from our religious texts, we have imported our sense of goodness from the words of key figures in history and transferred these into law and convention. For centuries we have cultivated goodness from the outside. The question for humanity is where has this led? Freudian psychologists would argue that civilisation prevents humans from descending into savagery, and that humans need a strong ego in order to uphold a sense of right and wrong. But if individuals' perception of goodness is a product of conditioning, then surely it is therefore a product of evolution and time, what we can call cultivation. Can we say that goodness flourishes from cultivation, in an evolved and 'civilised' society?

Freud may have seen us as essentially 'savage'; with society a 'civilising' influence as it strengthens the ego, but isn't civilisation itself also savage? The starvation, poverty, misery, war, destruction, pollution and financial imprisonment of entire countries through debt; is this not aggressive, acquisitive, competitive, violent, brutal, cold and callous in nature? Though we may be less physically violent than we were before the 18th century Age of Enlightenment, violence is still pervasive in the world today. The more 'civilised' humans become, the more we create our own psychological disorder as we strive towards various ideals. Our ideals, whether political, religious or otherwise, create fragmentation and where there is fragmentation there is conflict; not only internal conflict but outward conflict between one group and another. Though we may consider our society to be civilised on the whole, to have stepped beyond savagery (and remember that 'savage' and 'civilised' are also subjective terms) the conflicts of the human mind still continue. Contradictions are still present in the civilised mind, and occasionally they manifest externally in the form of violence and war. Even within Europe, that supposed bastion of civilisation, we have seen recent atrocities in the Balkans and violent crime rates in cities in the UK. There are still wars all over the modern world, with violence between conflicting groups of 'civilised' humans. Though we may feel more comfort, safety and luxury in our homes, very little has fundamentally changed. The developed world sells guns and arms to the developing world and then speaks of *'Peace and goodwill to all men.'* The United States, Britain, France, Russia and China are the largest exporters of arms around the world; many of the same nations who participate in peace talks at the United Nations. Despite rhetoric about human rights and universal harmony, global arms trading continues apace and an inherent sickness lives on in modern culture, amongst groups of people and between human societies and the natural world.

If our morality is derived solely from the process of socialisation, then goodness and evil are purely subjective. In one country a soldier is a protector of civilisation, someone noble, lofty and brave; in another country that same soldier is a pawn of military occupation, an invading barbarian who will murder in the name of his mission. In this respect goodness and evil exist only within conditioned viewpoints.

Look inside and observe your feelings about war. Maybe you support war; maybe you think that war is sometimes necessary. Look inside and watch. Check the conclusion which you come to, and you will find it conforms to a past prejudice; perhaps it brings you comfort to see someone else's son sent into battle (just as long as it is not your son) so that you can continue your life of patriotism and luxury. If your view is free from any distorting prejudice, you will see the truth that you have been happy to live a life of luxury at the cost of someone else's blood. You will find that you are more interested in your own moral judgements and conclusions, and how they make you feel, than in the truth of any given situation, such as war. Your conditioning enables you to quickly reach conclusions, while a master is not quick to judge because a master lives beyond such conditioning. So if you have rushed to a conclusion then you are no longer living freely; you are living according to a conditioned pattern. Your conformity can only lead to disorder as you deny 'what is' and replace it with 'what should be' (that being your conclusion), thus stepping into illusion. In this illusion all that is really happening is that you are adding more layers to your ignorance. Your conclusion masks your ignorance. In the light of this, reconsider your perception of right and wrong; it is a shocking insight when you realise just how much of your morality is pre-conditioned.

What is interesting to observe is that in most cases, evil is not evil in the mind of the individual committing the 'evil' act. An American soldier in Iraq may consider himself the protector of global democracy, while an Iraqi insurgent thinks of himself as the defender of his homeland. Subjectively each party feels that he represents goodness and it is the other party, the enemy, who is evil. This subjective justification extends into most case studies of alleged wrong doing. Whilst humanity is largely united in its view that the actions of Hitler, Stalin and Mao were amongst the worst atrocities our species has ever seen, in the eyes of those three individual dictators their actions were justified in the name of a professed 'perfect ideal'. The 'end' in their respective minds justified the 'means' and they did not consider themselves evil – in other words, their egos had decided on a 'what should be'. Most people do not commit 'evil', according to their own model of the world, it is simply that their model differs from those of others, and in the grossest cases may be warped relative to the social norm.

> "The nature of the universe is such that ends can never justify the means. On the contrary, the means always determine the end."
>
> *Aldous Huxley*

The behaviour of psychopaths is an extreme example. Their callous behaviour is characterised by the manipulative drive for self gain, satisfaction and the exertion of power and influence. They do not care for their victims, they do not feel empathy and there is little comprehension of the consequences of their actions in terms of the suffering imposed on another. Many do not comprehend love or hate because, more often than not, these are states or emotions that they have never experienced. Their victims are no more than a means to an end which is fully justified in their mind. Unlike the sociopath, the psychopath very carefully plans and organises his action. And for both their principle concern is *'will I get away with it?'* and *'is the subjugation of another satisfying?'* The means to an end is always pre-meditated and the difference between the two definitions is in the degree planning, and also in the capacity to execute such a plan without detection. Once again we are discussing some form of ideal, some form of 'what should be' that they are striving towards. That end may not be justifiable in your eyes or in those of wider society, but the individual has justified it to him or herself. This is the key point. The actions of psychopaths are beyond our comprehension, the stuff of movies, and easy to dismiss as 'evil', but from the perspective of the evil-doer it is action taken in response to his or her beliefs, ideals and perceptions. These actions are justifiable according to the psychology of these psychopaths, according to the information that they have constructed and the choices they think they have available. The point to consider is that most psychologists think good and evil function perceptually within the frame of cultural and psychological conditioning.

Civilisation is the destroyer of nature: fact. The world is still a world of conflict and war[1]: fact. Efforts to solve the problem of goodness at the level of society – through rule, through law, through force and through convention – have failed to put an end to corruption in human society. We should not overestimate the capacity for civilisation to bring forth goodness. Surely goodness begins at the level of the individual; if each individual within a society is corrupt, that society will also be corrupt. When you understand yourself and in this understanding come to genuine goodness, when everything that you do is good, then society will be good.

What it is to Love

THE HUMAN CAPACITY FOR EMPATHY is closely related to our notions of 'goodness'. Can we dismiss the idea of empathy and compassion as natural human qualities? Does empathy have religious, philosophical or ideological roots? If this were true, compassion and empathy would be a matter of opinion; to make love a matter of opinion is to turn it into a means of gratification.

Compassion is understanding, a matter of comprehension and the direct perception of another. It is acquired, or more correctly

---

[1] The USA has bombed over 50 countries since WW2, many secretly.

uncovered, through self-understanding; then one is able to understand the pain of another freely and effortlessly. One can feel the pain of the world and not be diminished by it. If diminished then we are still at odds with unresolved issues, still reactive to the disturbances of the ego. This is signalled by our search for security and our aversion to any kind of disturbance. It is the desire not to be disturbed that causes us to avoid 'what is', to run away from it. The avoiding of 'what is' is fear. The ignoring of 'what is' is ignorance. Disturbance and pain are symptoms of that ignorance. Disturbance is a matter of misunderstanding and it always coalesces inside the image that we have formed of ourselves. It is this self-image that must be understood.

Our desire not to feel the pain of another, to walk on by, is a reflection of our desire not to be disturbed. But once understanding is clear, once the ego is recognised as the false entity that it is, it need not be self-affirmed or protected from disturbance since there is nothing to protect. To negate compassion on the basis that you are depriving others of their own experience or understanding is no more than a justification of the ego. It is the ego saying *'do not deplete me, I have limited energy, I need to be preserved'* or perhaps, *'another's pain is necessary to learn the avoidance of pain'*. Such conditioned thought forms are rooted in self-justification. To practice antipathy in order to know empathy is sheer nonsense. Empathy comes into being when antipathy is understood. Antipathy is not the opposite of empathy, just like hate is not the opposite of love. There is only love and what is not love. To sense, nurture, listen and help others, understand why they are disturbed or why they feel pain. This is empathy; what it is to love. Everyone comes to understanding in their own time. The intelligence of empathy recognises this and listens without dispensing advice, or will only offer advice when asked. Such support, care and affection are all given freely without motive. Empathy and compassion are only authentic if there is relationship, a heart-felt and sincere communion with another. Then there is connection with reality, with existence and nature. When this connection is real, then there is no sense of depletion. Compassion is then unlimited. Existence replenishes because existence is compassion. There is no isolation in such relationship. It is then difficult not to act rightly, to act without integrity, because there is a kinaesthetic dissonance from reality, a separation felt in the mind-body. Such empathy runs far deeper than the cultivated empathy of rules, regulations and social convention to moderate behaviour. This is the empathy of the heart, not the mind.

Remember that it is the ego that is attached and thus fears; it is the ego that is identified, prone to labelling and thus attacks one border or defends another. What is it that we need to change? Is it more weapons or is it a change of consciousness? More war, more organised massed murder or more celebration of Being? War or music? War or dance? War or art? War or freedom of expression? Music, dance, art, freedom and love or victory, glory, violence, suppression and conquering? One is freedom, the other imprisonment, which do we want? Guns generate more fear and more violence, how can that be the solution? For the insanity to stop, we must realise that *'society is me and I am society'*. If society is to change then I must be that growth. Perhaps one day we will grow up and teach our children how to celebrate their Being, rather than celebrate their patriotism, competitiveness or victory over others.

> "Quietly consider what is right and wrong. Receiving all opinions equally, without haste, wisely, observing the law."
> *Buddha*

All prejudice is rooted in social conditioning; values taught in schools, by our parents, by the laws of our courts. (Cast your mind back to the chapter in the book *Question Mark* titled, *A Mind Beyond Judgement*.) This is evidenced in the fact that different societies around the world have different moral values; we all have different views, opinions and prejudices. What makes one society right and the other wrong? Western social values preach competition and ambition, yet to some this is what makes it socially immoral. When faced with an ethical consideration or a moral dilemma don't decide, don't rush to a conclusion, and in your stillness the inner eye will see. The inner eye can see as it receives all opinions equally. It is not quick to judge, nor swayed by popular values. Devote as much time as is necessary to the search for Truth and Rightness; you will be surprised at how often the answer is immediate and instinctive. If it takes a little longer, it is important that you are not impatient for a conclusion that makes you feel better. Observe how your conclusion regarding an ethical dilemma makes you feel. Does it make you feel more secure, does it make the problem disappear? You may form a false perception of knowing what is right and what is not and in this perception suppress the truth of 'what is' in order to feel the satisfaction of knowing you are right. Your conclusion may suit you, but is it rooted in Truth?

When you operate from pre-conditioned judgement, goodness and evil will appear to exist as relative points along the same spectrum. But when there is no judgement, you will see that goodness and evil are not together on the same spectrum at all. This is because within love there can be no judgement, nor can there be hate. If love has hate within it, anywhere at all, then it cannot be love. If goodness has evil within it, relatively or perceptually, then it cannot be good. Goodness is indivisible, goodness cannot be fragmented; there is no evil within goodness for goodness is of itself. It is whole and complete; never incomplete or fractured.

In order to see this for yourself you must be quiet and silent within. Then there are no old prejudices, views, thoughts or beliefs interfering; now you can see clearly, without reference to the past. All thought is old, all thought is past and the past prevents you from seeing the present. But when in the present moment, when there is no thought, there is no distortion between you and 'what is'; there is simply the clarity of 'what is' without any filters. In this clarity you automatically know what is good and what is not; it is no longer an intellectual evaluation, it is a knowing. The inner eye knows because the inner eye is already wise. Love or fear. 'I' or the absence of 'I'. Humility, or the search for something. The inner eye will see and the inner eye will know, but for the inner eye to see there must be order, there must be no contradiction within your mind. Goodness and virtue can only arise out of order. Order is virtue and virtue is goodness.

Absolute Good, Not Absolute Evil

WHEN ASKING THE QUESTION, *'Is there absolute good and absolute evil?'* we are often still thinking in terms of a spectrum of relative good and relative evil with the absolute of each at either end; a question of gradation, if you like. Traditional Christian terminology would define absolute goodness as God and absolute evil as the devil, but do these reference points have any functional meaning or value? Let us consider these points. Firstly, many do not believe in God or the devil so for these individuals such references can only be treated as metaphorical. For those who do believe in the devil as a separate and equal force to God, this belief acts as a distortion to the clarity with which you can consider questions of evil and goodness. Please consider the following so that we can demonstrate this simple distortion.

To continue in terms of God and the devil, if God is everything and everywhere, how is it that hell is not a subset of God? Is hell a place or is it a concept? Can hell possibly exist outside of the body or thought of God? It cannot hold for God to be everything, with hell somehow outside of everything. Nothing can exist outside of the whole, otherwise the whole is not whole. How then can the devil exist outside of God? The devil (Satan, Saturn, Lucifer, Bael or Jahbulon) along with the other 71 demons named in Aleister Crowley's (1904) book *The Goetia*, are considered to be independent entities in Christian thought. In Eastern thought evil is also commonly perceived as a separate yet equal force to goodness; a famous ancient sculpture at the Cambodian temple at Angkor portrays Hindu demons in a tug of war with the gods. Christian texts depict the Satanic fallen angel that fell out of favour with God and is now active as an opposing and equal force. The fallen angel represents pure evil and is a worthy adversary to God as they continually battle for our souls. How can there be a separate entity – the devil – existing outside of universal wholeness? If we assume that God is everything then the idea of evil existing outside of God, as some kind of separate entity, is not supportable. We can dismiss the idea of evil existing as a separate entity or concept outside of universal wholeness; we can question the idea of evil and goodness as two equal and opposing forces.

This universal wholeness is all Truth. Evil exists within Truth since Truth demands that evil, like any concept, must be explored. The essence of evil must be explored if Truth is to be maintained. Evil therefore must exist as a subset concept *within* Truth, since nothing can exist outside of Truth. If you wish to call Truth 'God' or 'Allah', by all means do, but what you need to understand is that since the universe has provided for evil, then if you use the devil as your reference point for evil (even if just metaphorically), then such a reference must co-exist within Truth. To revert to traditional Christian terminology therefore, the devil must be a subset of God. Evil, or the devil, may represent a perceived opposing force in relation to our human experience, but it is still a subset concept that coexists within Truth. Now if hate can only exist in the totality of the 'me', then hate – and its archetypal representation in the form of the devil – must be related to the feeling of separation and isolation of the 'me' that we have discussed so far. In the extreme of isolation and fear, in the extreme of our ego-based activity, we find and become our demons.

The Devil in You

SO THE CONVENTIONAL IDEA OF the separation of God and the devil, of good and evil at opposite ends of the spectrum, can be reconsidered more maturely if we think of this separation in terms of the isolated self within the whole, that being the ego, isolated from existence, which knows no relationship with Being. This is what we have been discussing as the great trap of the ego, a trap that knows no completeness and leads so very easily to isolation and hate. The 'devil', then, is a subset aspect of you; it is your ego in extreme fear and isolation. It is still meaningless, however, to talk in terms of absolute evil; the devil within of fear and isolation is never absolute because the ego is a fictitious entity of thought and is not what is fundamentally real. Only your AMness, your Awareness, your Being – that which exists within Existence and which is, in essence, one and the same with Existence – only this is what is fundamentally real and therefore absolute.

So the Lucifer of religious myth is an aspect of fear and isolation within ourselves that we have projected onto an outside other. In this context, 'Lucifer', the 'light bringer' or the 'sun', is really another name for the ego. Lucifer lives within each and every one of us as the ego, and the extremity of ego we call Satan (or again Lucifer), which we know already to be fear and hate. It is the archetype of Lucifer as the ego coupled with the Sun (or the various solar deities) as the differentiated self, operating in a similar manner to the astrological archetypes, which (in our solar system) enabled the fragmentation of subsets of consciousness from the whole and allowed the possibility of perceived independent existence. The Biblical references and prophecies relating to the rising of the Anti-Christ in the Book of Revelations could be simple representations (in the form of an analogy) to describe the twentieth, and now twenty-first, century of the self; centuries where the ego is king.[2]

With this new perspective let us now return to our question: *'Is there absolute good and absolute evil?'* Evil cannot be absolute because it can only exist as thought or concepts of thought and, as we have established, all thought can cease. (In practical reality, apparently evil actions may not actually cease nor are they likely to cease, but in relation to our question, the fact that they *can* cease is the fundamental point.) Because evil can cease, because it exists only as thought and thought can cease, evil cannot be absolute. For it to be absolute it must always *be*. There is no such thing as permanent thought. Only the void of empty awareness always is; the awareness from which all thought arises and falls. This emptiness, this empty awareness, is what you fundamentally are; it is the order that lies underneath all of your disorder. This order is eternal and absolute, but to come to it all disorder must be negated. To return to an analogy, it is the clear sky of order that lies eternally behind the dark clouds of disorder. It is the blue sky of empty awareness that is permanent, absolute and eternal; not the dark clouds of ego-based thought which pass across and block out that sky. Some individuals may live out their lives under a dark grey

---

[2] The era black magician Aleister Crowley called *Thelema*. Crowley espoused a form of libertinism based upon the rule of Do *What Thou Wilt*, which is the essence of Satanism or the doctrine of Lucifer. Also espoused by Albert Pike (1809–1891), US Grandmaster Freemason.

sky of continual ego-based thought, and after a while they may conclude that the sky never changes and is therefore absolute. This is a misconception based on limited understanding.

Absolute Order is Absolute Goodness

IF THERE CAN BE A mind in perfect harmony, then it is possible for there to be absolute order. To return to the question as to whether this order – this goodness – can be cultivated, the question translates as to whether harmony can exist in a map, in a plan, in accordance to a blueprint or design. Can it be cultivated through time? The evidence from world history, that being century upon century of imported goodness from religious law or political view, suggests not. Yet if you look into yourself with clarity, do you not feel an inherent goodness within? Do you feel that this goodness is something that you can learn and import or do you feel that it is part of you? If it is inherent, then it is part of your fundamental nature and need not exist according to a design laid down by the human mind or by society. So look inward and find out; is that flame of goodness alive? If it is (and the author, like many before him, has found that it is), then realise therefore that it will be the same for others. And if you realise, as an individual component part in a society of many, that '*I am society and society is me*', that '*You are society and society is you*', then these realisations will also be universal. We can all share this realisation. Then what is fundamental to me – this goodness – and what is fundamental to you – also goodness – can translate together into a society of goodness.

If goodness is something to be imported – an ideal or blueprint of 'correctness' – then in order for goodness to be expressed in our outward behaviour and relationships, we have to spend our lives striving towards these ideals. We are aiming to live and to behave in accordance to a pre-designed pattern. If goodness stems from design, from externally imposed ideals, then it must be the product of thought, possible to be cultivated by thought. As we have seen, anything that exists in thought cannot be absolute. If we seek order – in our quest for goodness – through planning and movements of thought towards an ideal, that order must exist as a pre-designed pattern that we have created. We end up living – or trying to live – in accordance to that pattern, just as most religions have dictated throughout history. As we have seen, this kind of conformity – in living according to a pattern, design or any form of blueprint – is rooted in fear; the fear of not achieving our desired goal and the avoidance of what we are, as we are. Goodness is not something to be imported. It arises from a mind in order, a mind of freedom. It can be reached through perfect order within one's own mind, not through a process which is based in fear.

Goodness is love, which is to accept, honour and celebrate one's Being and the Being of others. Remember that freedom, virtue, order, love and goodness all exist together; we have established that there cannot be one without the other. There cannot be goodness without virtue, there cannot be virtue without order and there cannot be order without freedom. There cannot be freedom when there is conflict and conflict exists when there is fear. All fear derives from the contradiction between 'what is' and 'what should be' and this contradiction is the foundation that lies within all forms of conformity. Freedom, virtue, order, love, harmony and goodness are facets of the same absolute Truth; conformity, contradiction, fear and disorder take us away from this absolute Truth, leading to all kinds of misery and suffering.

Finding this perfect order within the mind happens in the moment of Now. Freedom exists in the first step, not the last step. If your first step takes you towards a pre-designed pattern it will entail conformity and imitation in order to reach your goal, and where there is conformity there are all kinds of tensions and contradictions. Fear, hate and conformity belong to the language of time, whereas goodness, freedom, order and virtue belong to the language of Now. If your first step entails conformity, you no longer imbibe your own Being, right now at this very moment, because you are distracted towards behaving a certain way (a different way) in the future. This is not the acceptance of one's Being; this is not love. In this language of time there is conflict, tension, fear and, potentially, hate; thoughts that are carried into the past or the future and which overshadow the perfect order of the mind. Someone offends you and you want revenge, this thought is nourished within your mind; your offence exists because you are looking into the past and identified with your self-image and your revenge is held in your thoughts of the future. All is sustained by thought. Where there is no thought, there is no revenge and thus no hate. When there is awareness of the nature of thought and how thought is the holding mechanism of all fear and all hate, when that thought is negated by understanding its true nature, then that thought can be let go. Then there is present moment awareness (the only true absolute), there is the total relinquishment of the self and the essence of compassion and goodness.

Goodness is the order of the intellect and the heart speaking as one, it is what arises when heart-felt intelligence can see the disorder within itself. Goodness arises from a mind that is no longer in contradiction with itself, from a mind of stillness where there is no conflict between one side of the mind and the other; free of the idea of becoming. It is a mind of innocence, of presence, of serenity and silence, a mind without conflict, just pure clarity. A clear mind sees how thought takes shape and then craves for security and permanence, it sees the disorder within and in this observation the disorder ceases of its own accord. Once you have seen the true nature of disorder then you cannot go back to it, it is not possible. When you have properly understood an inner conflict then it is no longer a conflict. Just as when you understand a mistake, you naturally do not repeat it. You do not need to take a vow not to make that same mistake again. What is the point of taking a vow? If you need rules and promises, clearly you have not understood sufficiently that the mistake was a mistake. If you tease a cheetah in the wilds of Africa and it attacks you but you survive, you know not to tease another one in the future. Vowing never to do so would be pointless; if you have understood that such an action would be dangerous, then it is natural that you do not do it again. It is effortless. It is the same with disorder and conflict in the mind; once you have seen them for what they are, through understanding, order arises naturally and effortlessly.

Intelligence is the ability to see and move away from danger, physical danger obviously but also psychological danger. Now can we be free of psychological danger if we are forever running away from it, or avoiding it, or trying to control it? If we are running away from danger, we are not able to understand it. Also we are creating this illusion that we are somehow separate from our psychological disturbance and therefore able to overcome it or defeat it. The truth is, there is no separation. We are the jealousy, anger or hurt; we are the disturbance. So it is the disturbance that must to be understood; why it arises in the first place. Now if you overcome psychological pain, sublimate it, suppress it and so forth, according to the various blueprints laid down by society or by a system, this needs to be repeated again and again for the pain to stay away. You are therefore caught in the trap of reaction. You have not understood the nature of the disturbance which is you. When these understandings are clear, empathy is a natural action; right action, never a reaction, never an effort.

This order, and the goodness which accompanies it, is not a blueprint that can be imposed. It is 'what is' when the conflict of the mind – the movement of thought one way, and then another way – ceases through understanding. As we have seen, it is our psychological contradictions and conflicts that cause tension and thus disorder. This disorder is the process of the ego, it is the conflict of a mind in motion focused on self-preservation and self-gain[3]; focused on its search for 'what should be'. Evil is the extreme of this focus on self-preservation and self-gain, evident in notorious human examples. Unlike the perfect order of what IS, this evil cannot be absolute. Evil is an aspect of thought, an aspect of ego. To say that it is absolute is to deny the fictitious nature of the entity called the ego, to assert that thought is permanent and that the inner flame of love and Being can somehow blow out. This is simply not correct. The falseness of the ego can be demonstrated, thought will always arise and fall away, and your awareness will always be aware. The inner flame of love and Being will shine, always: Truth dictates it.

With the careful observation of fear and hate, there is observation that the 'I' is our behaviour; that the behaviour is no different from 'me'. This very observation is enough to see and understand why we act the way that we do; the very act of observation is present moment awareness. All behaviour is wiped away and what is left is freedom, virtue, order, love and goodness. They are not connected to

---

[3] Like the craving for security.

the movements of thought in any way, they ARE when thought is not. They ARE because they always ARE; they are truths that are eternal. The emptying, the negation of thought reveals what is good and what is good always IS. It never ceases nor can it ever cease. It is our non-dual nature that IS when thought, when the self, is not.

The non-dual nature of our inner consciousness will always remain clear and pure. Dualistic concepts such as the individualistic demands of the ego are like clouds in the sky, they are cumulative and they can build and build but they can never be absolute. They may temporarily cloud over the eternal, clear blue sky of our non-dual consciousness but they can never occupy that non-dual consciousness. Purity is the fundamental nature of all consciousness. It does not matter how many issues we build up in our lives, how cruel or self obsessed we become, how many layers of 'me first' selfish thoughts arise, our inner nature is like this clear blue sky – it can never become irreversibly polluted. In whatever manner fear and ego may cloud our sky, they will never be the sky.

> "Evil and good are not equal, even though the abundance of evil may amaze you."
>
> *Qur'an 5.100*

It is this fundamental purity of our awareness that allows for absolute goodness. It is what IS when all thought ceases. Evil may be cumulative but it is never absolute. Goodness is absolute. Goodness only IS in wholeness, it is never fragmented; there is no such thing as partial goodness. You cannot cultivate goodness through your will since goodness is what already is. You get to goodness by negating what is not good. This is not done by conquering, overcoming or suppression; it IS only when there is understanding of what is not good. Sometimes we have to go into the depths of darkness within our minds to emerge with new strength; to capture inner treasures we never knew we had. Growth follows the confrontation of our deepest fears, so our darkness can represent times of growth and transformation, ego death, healing and new inner power. Moments when we face our fears are our defining moments, but too often we do our best to avoid fear, following religions that are designed to comfort us and alleviate our fears. This only postpones our growth and keeps us immature.

You have to face what within you is tense and in contradiction. What you will find is the activity of the 'me first' self with its closed-hearted nature. But this is not your inherent nature; your inherent nature is what already is non-dual, what is not in contradiction. You cannot cultivate goodness, goodness is not something that fits a certain design. Goodness is what you already are. When you look within and understand your fears and contradictions, in present moment awareness, you will see the truth of this. What you fundamentally are is not the self – the self is thought which divides and separates, striving for this ideal or that goal. All of this conflict is the very source and foundation of the disorder within, and this disorder is the movement of your mind making up what you see and do daily as the ego self. This disorder is what clouds your non-dual nature; it is not permanent.

Please take a break from reading and make a cup of tea. Before you do, please open the kettle lid and take a look at the water inside; it is both clear and pure. Now flick the kettle switch on and watch the water bubble up (obviously be careful!). When the water is boiling it is no longer clear; we cannot see through it. This water is representative of our consciousness. When the disorder of boiling and bubbling ceases, the water returns to its clear natural state. If we were to take out and examine a single droplet, we can see this nature with clarity. Until we stop and become still, the bubbling thoughts of our mind will obscure our clear essential nature. It is in the disorder of these bubbling thoughts that fear and hate can develop and thrive. Let the water calm down into stillness, be calm and still and see what happens. Hate disappears. There is no absolute evil, but there is absolute goodness. This absolute goodness – this order and love – is the fundamental Truth.

Principles of Separation

INTERESTINGLY THE PRINCIPLES OF SELF-PRESERVATION and self-gain, as expressed in the survival of the fittest principle (attributed to Darwin and not Howard Spencer), exist in nature. If evil resides in these drives towards self-preservation and self-gain, does this imply that nature itself is evil? To say that nature is cruel, indifferent and unforgiving is one thing – an accurate thing – but to say that nature is evil seems absurd. Yet when we look at principles evident within natural systems, they seem similar to what we have been discussing. We must not rush to a conclusion without knowledge of how nature itself is constructed or at least understand some of its empathic and co-operative principles – something which we will cover in the book *Time Is Thought*. For the moment however, let us consider the purpose these principles could serve in nature. It seems that nature requires principles of separation within itself in order to exist.

What we must recognise is that without these principles of self-orientated action existing in life, we ourselves would not exist. This is not just from the perspective of the evolution of our species through natural selection, but also from the perspective of a conceptual necessity for selfhood within Truth. Your very self-existence is based upon the principle of perceived separation from wholeness, which itself derives from movements of self-preservation and self-gain operating within the differentiated activity of the self. All of this activity must co-exist within Truth, at least partially, if you are to exist as a self. Your self-existence is founded, at least in part, upon principles that we have identified as being within the concept of evil; the isolation of the self from existence. These concepts are part of reality's mechanism to understand itself, part of the movement of time itself. To deny the understanding of those aspects within you because they may seem evil is to deny the very foundation upon which you – as an individual 'self' – exist. This is why it is futile to deny the presence of what we conceive to be darker, separating aspects within us. For without them, without going into our own underworld, we will never have an understanding of Truth and we will never realise that even the physical universe itself would not exist had these principles not been introduced within

Truth. You as a self and the universe as a theatre cannot exist without the causes of separation existing within Truth.

One last thing (and it is a slight tangent): darkness is not necessarily evil. Although darkness is often associated with evil in metaphor – and this can help to explain certain points – the two concepts can also be completely different. For example, there is no freedom without communion with the womb of all existence, which is the dark void of empty awareness. This absolute darkness is the true nature of existence – of God, of Allah, of the Source, or whatever name you wish to call Truth. It is not light, God is not light; this is a projection of the human mind and its inner fears. For millennia we have been traumatised by darkness, feeling unsafe and undefined in its black formlessness, and this fear has been carried deep into our collective consciousness. This is why we associate our deities with light. All Truth arises from the void of nothingness; the infinite black void of emptiness. This absolute darkness is fundamental to life. When we meditate on this, we know the beauty, freedom, love and immensity of the inner void, of what is the dark void of awareness from which all things arise.

chapter 8
Fundamental AMness

FREEDOM IS NOT REACHED THROUGH activity, but everything in this world is geared towards activity. Our way of life is shaped by the wish to succeed; in this current 'century of the self' where the ego is king everything we do is to gain, even (and especially) in the spiritual search. Immature minds are only interested in what is good for 'me', and this interest is carried into their choices about spiritual systems. We follow systems in order to break away from the ego (which we know to be activity), not realising that the following or chasing of any objective, no matter what that is, is actually just another form of activity. We may try to abandon the ego through action, but all action is activity. Effacing is activity; it indicates an objective for the 'I' to cease. Who is the entity holding this objective? The objective can only exist in the movement of thought towards 'what should be'; this psychological conflict which we know to be the foundation of the self. Self-healing and reinforcement (the essence of New Ageism) strengthen and expand the ego by creating yet more activity. Why act to strengthen that which you know to be false? All that needs to be done is to live an authentic life, true to your Being rather than the inauthentic desires, fears and subconscious guilt complexes of the ego, and then all will happen of its own accord. The ego is clever and narcissistic, and it will reinforce itself whenever and wherever there is an objective, motive or direction; wherever there is activity. If there is an objective, then you have not understood that the goal is to live without a goal.

If there is a goal, you already know what you are looking for. Your search is already conditioned to be a means of achieving what you desire. Your search is no longer a search, open to real discovery, but just a means of gratification. Your occupation to find Truth is just another source of satisfaction. Can the known – you as knowledge, memory, experience and conclusion – know or have any understanding of the unknown? Won't what you understand simply be another modification of you, the known? Surely for the unknown to be, the known must cease otherwise what you find is just another, modified aspect of yourself? Therefore all pre-determined objectives must cease. There must be no motive in your search, just curiosity. There is no point tethering the investigation before it has even begun. A mind of purpose can meditate and meditate, waiting for something to happen.

There is no end. Are you enjoying Now? If so, enjoy it some more. The objective is to have no objective – just enjoy your own Being-ness. The end is not the end, it is Now. There is no end nor is there a goal, there is only 'the Way' and the way is Now – the enjoyment of your Being right here, right now. The individual with the 'me first' mindset asks, *'What happens in the end?'* only because he wants a goal; he is striving towards a 'what should be', an ideal that his mind has created. He has not realised that striving creates continuity, which prevents discovery. The new only comes into being when that which exists within the field of time – 'me' as thought – ceases. All that continuity must cease otherwise Truth is not Truth, it is modified past – which is desired, pre-conditioned, self-projected.

If you are such a person and you recognise that, accept it and go to the end of it in order to understand it. Understand that continuity does not liberate. Continuity – the word, the idea (of oneself and of 'what is') – operates within the field of time. This prevents one dying to the past (or future) and resurrecting in the Now, into what is new. For the unknown to Be there must be constant renewal, which means operating beyond the limiting parameters of psychological time, beyond the 'me'. When this is understood, one realises where the path of self-gain and self-interest ultimately leads, and comes to understand the isolation and loneliness as discussed in recent chapters. In understanding the process of the 'me', one has already moved beyond it, reaching this conclusion by oneself rather than learning it from another. If you try to move away from the 'me' with effort, like the devotees of various systems and gurus, you reinforce the 'me' in a different way and so you end up chasing a mirage. Only in the moment of Now is there no 'me' and is there freedom. If we strive to become egoless through specific practices, this confuses because the word 'practice' suggests the idea of something 'to do'. There is nothing to do; it is a practice of non-doing, as Buddha refers to it. We are discussing not only the ending of the ego but the death of everything about the self – every action, every thought, every subconscious thought, everything – without actually dying; shutting down the superstructure of the mind and the brain's filtering mechanisms. Then you will experience that which you truly are. You will taste death, you will know what happens at death, you will know exactly what is going to die when death comes knocking at your door and you will know exactly what will remain. The first time you go beyond death, you will know what part of your mind is mortal and you will realise that awareness, AMness, the essence of Being, is not mortal. Love knows no death. It is the greatest realisation.

Pure Vision

GOING BEYOND DEATH, ONE IS able to see 'pure vision' – the wiring under the board of reality – and experience the great void of emptiness. It works this way because reality is not what you conceive it to be. Think of this: when you have a dream and you play a character in that dream, everything around you exists outside of 'you the character that you are playing'. Your mind has created the tables, the chairs, the room you are standing in and you are there as a character standing in that dream, in that room which is all taking place within your dreaming mind. The laws of physics in your dream may appear perverse (dreams can be like that), but you can still feel, touch, hear and watch; you interact in response to your sensations and you can experience locations you have never before conceived. Sometimes it can feel nearly as real as waking reality. All of this was created by your consciousness. Now take this a step further. Could not a consciousness have created a dream within which there are billions of characters, billions of perspectives (of which you are one) and each of these characters calls that dream 'reality'? As a character, as one of billions of single perspectives of AMness, your reality and the reality of others is only separated by perception. This is the central principle of selfhood.

We should be cautious not to be too literal; the following is inserted for your consideration only:

> What distinguishes is 'I'; what is the same is 'AM'.
>
> 'I AM'. Let's break this up:
> 'I' = my perception of being individual. 'AM / AMness' = that which IS (in the first person).
> 'That which IS' = that which IS.

> Conceptually, 'I am' equates to 'I' + 'that which is.'
> I (individual) AMness (that which is); the first person perception of 'that which is'.

The only thing that distinguishes me from you, you from your best friend and you from your partner, your child and every stranger that you do not know, is the perception generated by selfhood, the foundation of the concept of 'I'. Is this the clever use of words, the clever use of concepts or does Truth work in terms of concepts and how they bind together? Let us consider the following sutra; it is something that you can test from the certainty of your own existence.

> "In seeing, there is just seeing; no seer and nothing seen. In hearing, there is just hearing; no hearer and nothing heard."
> *Buddha*

What Buddha is saying is that the only thing that is truly real is your AMness, your awareness, the observing aspect of your consciousness, the centre of no centre, the holding capacity for communication exchange of all sensation and awareness of that sensation. We are individual because AMness is split up into individual perceptions which go on to form the 'I'. Fundamentally, there is no 'I AM', there is only 'AM'. Just observation, no observer and nothing observed. The 'I' is what makes you separate and individual. It is the self; that which you think you are but you are not really. The content of consciousness may be our memory and our knowledge, but consciousness itself also includes our awareness. You still are when you look within yourself to recall a memory. You still are when your mind is searching through its own databanks to bring up some lost knowledge from somewhere. When you peel away every aspect of the 'I', like layers of an onion; when you take away everything that has ever been said about you and everything that you have thought about yourself or anything else for that matter; when every last layer has been peeled, all that is left is pure, empty space. This pure, empty awareness is the fundamental truth of Being. It is what you are: emptiness, empty presence. You are fundamentally empty of all these layers, there is nothing left of anything that you conceive. Yet in this emptiness there is a door to a different dimension; suddenly you are more, not less. You are what you cannot even conceive, but it is so alien that nothing recognisable from this life remains. Yet curiously it feels like home, like it has always been home. The 'I' is part of the dream we call reality. When the dream is taken away (like at the moment of death), everything you thought about yourself no longer holds. All your relationships, passions, hopes, desires, attachments and business affairs are all part of the process of that dream. Take away the dream and they are suddenly meaningless. So everything that you think you are, you are not. Your idea of 'self' is part of this dream, the accumulation of a personal story that is running in this dream. Take away the dream from your perception (as happens in the moment of your death) and the substory of your life as you knew it stops running.

You realise that what you see is not real and your body is not real. We can all appreciate that the image we hold of ourselves is not real, but can you also appreciate that the self, with all of its perceptions, might not be real either? Of course your perceptual awareness is real right now, but can you accept that one day this too will end? Your craving for a soul demonstrates non-acceptance of this. As physics has discovered, everything you see is not actually real; it is only perceived to be real. Time itself only exists in the presence of our perception of it; time is thought. In sleep we create our own dreams and this principle extends into our waking reality. Reality can be the product of our own affirmations. We perceive reality to be real, which is why we call it reality; it is the most real reality that our consciousness has ever experienced. Although it is the hardest hitting reality that we can conceive – it certainly hurts when you break a bone! – it is not the hardest hitting reality of all. Only once this other, more primary reality is experienced can we see that conventional reality is really no more than a shared dream. Given that most of us cannot conceive beyond the level of ordinary appearances, of conventional reality, we perceive it to be real and it is real. It is all that we know and perceive, and it is only perception that matters. This is very important to remember:

your perception determines your reality. This is why, in these pages, we have repeatedly sought to change your perception. What you perceive to be real will be real to you, until you alter your perception. Reality is real because we perceive it to be; it is not as real if we alter our perception. This is what a Buddha does.

Buddha says reality is the ultimate illusion. This concept, known as 'Maya', can be very difficult to understand. What is real? The tree may be real or it may be an illusion, it may simply be a construct of mathematics formulated in the brain. Most people believe that this Eastern doctrine asserts the outside world to be illusory. The true meaning of the term Maya refers to the illusory way we think about the outside world. The difference between these two definitions could not be more significant. When you look in the mirror and see yourself, the image that you see is a reflection. That reflection is also an imprint created by your mind, your sensory processes. Are you that imprint? Are you sure? The imprint is only a reflection in the mirror – it is not actually real. If the reflection is not the real or actual, how then can you be real? But if I am real, then the appearance that is my reflection must also be real. Which one is the reflection and which one is real? Are they both real, one real and the other not, or is neither real? What we know of consciousness is only what consciousness decides about or discovers of consciousness. Consciousness has this unusual monopoly over itself. Consciousness is its content.

When in a dream (unless you are lucid dreaming) you perceive that dream to be real. When you wake up from the dream, only when you realise that you are in your bed looking around your bedroom and you conclude that *'Yep, this is reality,'* do you realise that your previous dream reality was, in fact, a dream. Extend this principle further to the entering of Consciousness Totality and the witnessing of the primary reality; it is so intense and hard-hitting that you suddenly realise that your entire life as you knew it has been a dream. It is the ultimate wake-up call from reality. This is why Buddha refers to those who are 'asleep' and those who are 'awake'. Normally we cannot conceive outside the parameters of our character in this reality, we fall foul of mathematical incompleteness theorems. Reality seems to go on forever out there into space but according to Buddha this is only in your perception. Since our perception is what matters, our reality is real and valid and it extends out there into space. This, though, is not the final truth. Buddha demonstrates a way of seeing the essence of who you are such that there is no seer and nothing seen, but only seeing; where there is no subject / object, no demarcation between observer and observed; where they are together, not separate. He shows us how to step outside the system of physical reality. Buddha shows us an experiential way to the ultimate reality, to the ultimate truth. Do you believe it? It does not matter. If Truth is Truth it does not need defending. Such experiencing requires no belief; the truth of it is invincible when you know it to be real.

> "Believe nothing, no matter where you read it, or who said it, no matter if I have said it, unless it agrees with your own reason and your own common sense."
>
> *Buddha*

If you understand yourself, there is no need to believe in anything. When you can drop everything that you have ever known, when you can wipe the slate of your mind clean, you become alive for the first time in a way you could never have conceived. Stay within the confines of your mind, within memory and knowledge, and you will suffer because there is no freedom in thought. It is the nature of thought and the nature of the self to entail suffering because there is no freedom[1]; this is Buddha's First Noble Truth. In the absence of the 'me', when the self is not, there is freedom from thought; there is Being, love, the essence of beauty and what Buddha called 'Nirvana' – the state of bliss. The cessation of suffering is attainable; masters have reached this in the past and others will come to it in the future. This is the Third Noble Truth.[2] You become alive in a way beyond your comprehension. You wake up from the dream! In a dream, when you play

---

[1] Also, because the nature of reality is impermanent.
[2] In case you were wondering what the Second Noble Truth is, it is something we have discussed before: 'The origin of suffering is attachment.'

a character in that dream you are still in an environment created by your mind. You created it all. Reality is not so dissimilar. Know that it is a dream, know how the system of consciousness works, become a master of that system and then you are free. Old concepts of religion, worship, prayer and approval, not to mention newer concepts of consumerism and brand identification, are no longer relevant as factors that drive your mind.

> "And wisdom is sweet, and freedom."
>
> *Buddha*

In this and previous chapters, we have insisted upon the importance of understanding the self because of the freedom to be attained in such wisdom, such genuine understanding. Meditation furthers our understanding of the process of selfhood and this gives rise to wisdom and freedom. We become wise because we are aware of that which is false. When that which is false is negated, we are our own truth. Only when we are true can we be free – free not only from our subconscious guilt complexes, condemnations and justifications which arise from leading an inauthentic life, but also existentially free. Wisdom is to be free from continuity, away from our various projections, which only create self-modification and thus ignorance and illusion. To see there must be renewal, the ending of the word, the idea, the continuation of the 'me' with its activity. When there is no longer a 'me' as centre, no longer a distorted or modified 'me', then that which is beyond the 'me' can come into being. As we understand ourselves, so too do we understand reality; the investigations into self and reality are the same investigation. In death there is life, the ultimate form of life. Life is death; the death of the 'me'. The 'me' can die, but love has no death. To live fully, you must die; either now in the present moment or at the end of your conventional life. Reality is but an extension of you. All you have to do is look deeply enough within and you will see what Buddha and other great masters have been speaking of. Jesus was not the son of God, he was an aspect of Truth, of the WHOLE, and so too are you. You cannot exist outside the whole. The whole is in every part. The mustard seed of the Kingdom of Heaven is already within you; you only need to strip away your layers of falsehood as Buddha suggests and Truth will find you because all Truth is already within you. Only by removing that which is false do you come to 'that which IS'. Then you know what is real and what is not. Then, in pure vision, you see the wiring under the floorboards of reality and the intelligence behind all motion. In attaining this insight we become free, we understand our inner nature. If you want to call it 'divine' call it divine, it does not matter. These are only labels.

Remember that 'divinity' is more like a system, it is indifferent to our various beliefs. It does not care how it is conceived and it does not judge, it only IS. When you know the system is not a personality, that God as you perceive him will not save you, that the universe is not selective (love is not love if it is selective, it is only love if it is universal), then suddenly it dawns on you that you are on your own. In this realisation you take responsibility for your own growth; you can no longer rely on this father figure called God to look after you. If you are to be free, you can no longer be lazy when it comes to self-knowledge. It is down to you to understand the ways of the self and your inner nature; a nature which is not confined to the parameters of mind-body or space-time. Look inward and see what happens. If 'divinity' is real, it will become apparent and there is no need to search for it. In genuine understanding of reality, in the insights of pure vision, the unnecessary strivings of life no longer have consequence for you. You will no longer worry or be driven by the need to gain and your suffering will come to an end. Previous hopes and desires no longer matter because you are already in bliss. What place is there for desire when one's essence is already bliss?

It is a transformation beyond your wildest dreams. It is the alleviation of your three greatest fears: the fear of not feeling love, of not being enough and the fear of death. These fears of loneliness, insufficiency and death are ideas that exist in thought, and they prevent our communion with 'what IS'. They give rise to continuity, which always fragments, disintegrates and decays. 'What IS' is our aloneness and freedom, our absolute correctness, pure life and love itself – what greater returning transformation could there be? Physical life may not be eternal, but your awareness and love are eternal. It is beautiful when we have the insight to see it. God is dead, God belongs to an age of worship, fear and approval; Consciousness Totality is liberation across all time and all fear. What better news could we ever ask for? There is a primordial condition within us, an essence which is pure and uncontaminated by the activity of the mind. If this essence is allowed to surface in a state of pure presence, in total awareness of the moment of NOW without modification by the ego mind, then Consciousness Totality, the capability of seeing all Truth, will come to you in its rawest and most beautiful nature.

Overcoming the Perception of the Ordinary

YOU ARE A DIVINE BEING, you are part of this world and yet you are also more than this world. You observe this world but you are not of this world, you are a single perception whilst more perceptions are possible. To find the divine within, one must be aware of that which is false so that one can be true to oneself and therefore free. You cannot destroy this inner truth, it can only be hidden and it is hidden behind the layers of the ego. Your consciousness operates, fundamentally, on the principle of freedom. To see, feel, hear, touch and Be Truth, freedom is essential. Can intellectual analysis penetrate this Truth? Analysis belongs to the field of the known and what is known by a human mind cannot encompass all Truth. Can it be an existential experiencing of something beyond our comprehension? This is the moment we call Consciousness Totality.

What we are discussing is not knowing Truth or intellectualising Truth or even understanding Truth, what we are discussing is Being Truth. It is something that is very difficult to understand because we usually conceive of Truth as a set of ideals, formulas and concepts, and whilst these elements exist within the thought structure of intelligence, such truth is just an abstract idea, and not the actual. Truth is existence itself and all elements therein. Truth is all Being; it is not comprehensible intellectually. So the notion of Being Truth is not as absurd as one might think. Buddha says to know existence we must Be existence. To know existence is not a movement of mind, it is the non-movement of Being; free of motive and direction. It has a different dimension to a purely intellectual approach. Whilst you may argue that we need to understand something intellectually before we can know it, this is not the case. Intellectualising about what love is does not make the experiencing of it, the knowing of it, any more authentic.

Think again of Winnie the Pooh, *'happy as a little bear can be'*, spending time with his friends whenever he can. Compare him to his friend Owl, intellectual Owl, who spends his time pouring through books and learning as much as he can. If Winnie the Pooh was to fall in love, he would be overjoyed, bouncing around full of joy, hugging and kissing his new partner. He would share his joy with his friends. Owl on the other hand would look up 'Love' in the dictionary, search for its definition and try to understand it before really experiencing it. Would such intellectual understanding make Owl's experience of love any better, any truer? Of course not. In fact, his intellectual understanding would likely detract from the authentic experience. It is the same with Truth.

The point is worth emphasising: if you can experience, in the essence of your Being, that you have an immortal awareness with the ability to access all areas inside the vast consciousness of raw existence inside your mind; if you can truly go to this then what difference does it make to intellectually understand it? Intellectual understanding adds little if anything at all to your experience of *being* your inner divinity.

Limitations of Ego

THE ACTUAL EXPERIENCING OF TRUTH arises in meditation. The non-existence of self is the experience of what happens at death; it is the end of limited perception and the seeing of all Truth. In meditation we can truly experience something to be beyond the physical human form, we can have a mock death experience in which all is revealed. We will understand how the awareness inside us is the interface of life with all moving intelligence – what we call existence – in process. Existence is a non-ego state and it is the movement of all intelligence. To merge with existence is to witness and comprehend the deeper workings of existence. When there is a union of awareness without the limited perception of selfhood, when there is awareness without the ego state, then there is a deep connection with existence. This connection is so complete that the word itself is misleading; it is more like a fusion.

To understand beyond the self, there must be observation beyond this image that we form of ourselves and the ending of all movements of thought, both conscious and subconscious. Only by understanding the nature of ego and the entire composition of consciousness will the self drop of its own accord. We must learn about all aspects of the entity that we perceive to be the 'I'; our *individual* sense of self. We are not individual despite being conditioned to think that we are; principally our desires and fears are identical. Each of us is the entire book of humanity and this book can be read in a single glance, without missing a word or ever skipping a page. What is the 'self' and what are the layers of our self-perception? You are not your name, title, property or accumulations. You are not even your memory, knowledge, desires or fears. You are as nothing; neither the various escapes from that nothingness nor the observer of that nothingness. You and nothingness are together, as one. This nothingness is emptiness, pure AMness. We must explore deep within until we know, with every essence of our Being, the ultimate truth of the non-existence of the 'I' and the absolute existence of 'AM'. The shift from 'I Am' to 'AM' is monumental to a pure view of reality and it can be experienced prior to one's death.

> "I have been reading your Descartes. Very interesting. 'I think, therefore I am.'
> He forgot to mention the other part. I'm sure he knew, he just forgot: I think, therefore I'm not."
>
> *Katagiri Roshi*

But who or what is the entity that understands? It is very important that we are clear about this. If the 'I' understands that its consciousness is its content – its memory, knowledge, etc. – and that the nature of thought is limited, fragmentary and enclosing, then the 'I' has separated itself from the limitations that it perceives about thought. The 'I' is imposing itself upon thought, declaring that thought is limited but that the 'I' shall not be. This is what most spiritual seekers are doing, caught in the relationship between the thinker and his thought and therefore tethered by the net of thought. They understand that thought is limited, yet they are seeking not to be limited, and this is a form of fear. Their seeking not to be limited only limits them further; this problem is particularly acute in those whose self-effacing activities are carried out in the name of freedom, such as the famous Indian ascetics. Whereas when thought or consciousness realises that it has created the 'I' and acknowledges the tendency of the 'I' to separate itself from limited thought; when it understands that its content is all of its consciousness and that this content – including the 'I' – has limitations, then there is no pretending that the 'I' can be anything more than limited, narrow and small. This is recognition that all methods towards freedom are nothing more than narrowing processes. Quite a different understanding is taking place.

Let's explain this again. When the 'I' sees that thought is limited, it tries to overcome those limitations and of course it feels validated because thought is limited. There is thus the effort to overcome that limitation, there is method and system, there is conflict and an imposition towards a 'what should be' or 'what ought to be'. There is disorder. However, when thought realises that the 'I', and all thought, is limited, it does not try to overcome those limitations. It realises that it can't do anything about it; it cannot change this fact. It is not trying to impose this conclusion or that pattern and then separate itself from the limitation, it is merely seeing very clearly the limitations of all the constituent parts of the 'I' and all of the limiting aspects of what make up the content of any consciousness. In this recognition there is simply understanding; there is no conflict to change 'what is' into 'what should be' and without the conflict to change, the 'I' is not. Then the foundation for meditation has been laid. Consciousness has realised that the ego exists in the conflict to change 'what is' into 'what should be'. Where there is no conflict, the 'I' is not; it drops of its own accord.

There is the embracing of and surrendering into 'what is', that being inaction rather than action. Thus begins authentic meditation.

There is no path to Truth. For Truth to Be you must cease and when you cease there is contact, a sublime connection with existence. Adopting a fixed path injects the fear of adjustment into the minds of seekers, aggravating the very problem of seeking itself, which is the antithesis of love. If you adopt a new pattern (following a certain ascension plan, for example) to break out of your existing pattern, you are still operating within a pattern. You are still conforming and so of course there will be fear. Action in accordance to any pattern is based on certain evaluations. Right action can only be action that is free from pattern or evaluation, like this whole idea of 'becoming' or the need to ascend. Freedom is found in *being,* not becoming. Ideals, values, beliefs (*'I must do this'* or *'I must do that'*) are all forms of becoming, all rooted in fear, and therefore self-perpetuating in nature. They reinforce the very structure of the ego. Any purported system is a clear example of the ego seeking continuity and permanence.

It is a conceptual requirement that ego must drop of its own accord for there to be non-ego state awareness. Behind the scenes there is the harmonisation of concepts within Truth; the experiencing of the non-ego state of existence cannot be experienced by the entity we call the ego. The two cannot sit together. This is logical and scientific. Look again at the problem of ego: how can you be beyond ego? You cannot do anything! It cannot be done through action, only in inaction does ego drop of its own accord, because action (the conflict to change) is ego.

The effacing and denial of all that we perceive to be the 'I' only leads to misery and distortion. If you force the ego to drop, rather than allowing it to do so of its own accord, this is activity by the ego, a self-effacing process which only goes on to reinforce the ego. As an activity, effacing indicates an objective by the ego for the ego not to exist. But this objective is itself activity and we are trying to abandon the ego (which is activity) with yet more activity; clearly this is not logical at all. There should be no activity, no process at all; no imposition of any form. Even to say 'should be' in the sentence above is misleading; 'should be' entails a process, a conflict, a non-acceptance of 'what is'. 'Should be' is an objective; in that case the ego continues to exist in order to set the objective; who or what else is the entity with the objective? An objective for the ego not to exist can only be held by the ego, for where else can an objective reside if not within dualistic thought? The moment there is effort to abandon activity, there is conflict and where there is conflict the ego returns. See what cunning tricks the mind is playing? Setting an objective for the ego not to exist is absurd; you have not understood that there is no goal. Where there are goals, objectives and conflicts there is no embracing of 'what is', and thus no love. Instead, allowing ego to drop of its own accord is to surrender into and the embrace 'what is' – which is love.

The Ghost in the Machine

FOR MANY OF US, THE belief that we are no more than intelligent, self-aware lumps of flesh, skin and bone prevents us from exploring the possibility that we may be much more than the physical body. Our beliefs have determined our internal maps of reality and as such limit our investigation. We cannot accept that thought is limited, and this leads humanity to revere thought and overestimate its possibilities. We do not find evidence to suggest that we are divine beings, and we perceive this to be our limitation. If we cannot at least momentarily entertain the possibility that we may be more than flesh and bone, then we do not move beyond our perceived beliefs and there is not the energy for growth. In being open to this possibility we find the patience to understand our true nature and gather potential for a communion with our fundamental essence. If we are convinced that we are entirely mortal and unremarkable, we stay locked up in this perception and so we do not even bother to start investigating. Rather than simply believe, we can use our awareness and power of observation to experientially explore our inner potential, and later apply the logical reasoning of concepts and how they are framed together within Truth. (This is what the New Approach entails, as detailed in the book *Question Mark*.)

There is much about consciousness that we do not understand. If we think of the 'ghost in the human machine' and where the control centre is inside this machine that is our living bodies, what can we say of the whereabouts of our fundamental essence? Where is our control centre? Where is our essence, our spark of consciousness, that which gives life to our body and which seems to be absent at the death of the physical body? This life force is in every cell of our body, but also sits in other dimensions of reality that we do not see. We have a more subtle, energetic and conscious body that is visible to masters in Pure Vision.

Within the body are channels of energy flows that do not correspond directly to physical veins or the nervous system. Still disputed by many Western surgeons, this energy life force is variously known throughout the world as ch'i (China), prana (India), ki (Japan), waken (North America) or kurnba (Australia). It is no coincidence that these are all locations noted for a dense concentration of meditation masters and shaman. These are the same energy flows manipulated by acupuncturists to improve health. Acupuncture works by inserting extremely fine needles into the body at designated meridian points (as laid out in the 24 volume *Nei Ching* Chinese medical text) to influence the flow of chi throughout the body to assist healing. If we were to inject harmless radioactive tracers into these acupuncture points we would find that the tracers follow the traditional Chinese meridian paths inside the human body (this was carried out by Doctors Darras and Vernejoul in 1992).

There is an intertwining life force matrix that extends throughout the whole body. It is a life force which interacts with every cell of the human body, where the cells themselves also have a consciousness. A heart transplant patient who is lucky enough to get the donated heart of an ex-marathon runner will very likely take up jogging after the operation. There is encoded memory and consciousness in the DNA and cells of the donated heart. Science is now suggesting that even electrons have some kind of consciousness. According to cell biologist Bruce Lipton, much of the genetic material of a cell is contained in its nucleus. It has been asserted that the nucleus is effectively the 'brain' of a cell. Yet if we remove the nucleus, it is possible for the cell to survive several months without its genes and it is in fact fully capable of complex responses from both outside and inside the cell. This led

Lipton to contend that the cell's membrane – its outer boundary, the only organelle common to all life – is actually the cell's brain. Think of it like a bubble with things inside being controlled by the outer bubble – this brain boundary gets to interact with the outside world and control what is going on inside. The peptide receptors and the effector proteins all reside on the cell membrane. Such cells have been found to possess consciousness. If the control centre of even a cell is unclear, what therefore can we say about a person? Consciousness seems to exist without a centre or location.

Food For Thought: Powers Within

DO YOU SENSE THAT YOU have within you powers you are not even aware of? Telepathy may be real, precognition may be real, mediumship may be real; just pop into your nearest spiritualist church and take a look. Remote viewing activity seems real; governments have been running programs since the 1970s although much of this activity is denied today. All these phenomena have been recorded and although such recordings are hotly contested, they are all explicable according to the logic of consciousness. It is the perceived limitations which we impose upon ourselves that prevent us from exploring our potential. There are many stories of people being able to move items with their own thought; Qui'gon masters can move objects without touching them. The power of penetrative insight should not be underestimated. People have cured themselves from sickness, disease and, in rare cases, even cancer with their own thought[3] or, more specifically, their understanding of the nature of thought. Try to avoid being cynical about the power of the mind. Equally though, be mindful of the application of thought to attain freedom. Thought is corruptive, often dishonest; thought is a product of time. Thought is limited and what is limited will always be restricted. It is meditation, and genuine understanding – not the activity of the ego, not thought – that will lead to liberation.

---

[3] We know Placebo effects work; just think about why this may be.

chapter 9
Sensation

OUR SENSES CRAVE HEIGHTENED AND more intense experiences; our eyes desire interesting and beautiful sights, our ears want to hear pleasing sounds, we want to smell wonderful aromas, feel the sensation of touch, taste the finest and most exquisite foods and of course avoid as much unpleasantness as possible. We are all driven by sensation and there are many kinds of sensory attractions and aversions available to us as potential experience. Sensation is the activity of the senses and how this activity is translated by the mind. Sensory perception cannot exist without some form of interpretation and the mind is the instrument for this process; the mind is thus the mechanism for sensation. Without a brain interpreting the sense of touch, for example, it is not touch. The experiencing of sensation is the reaction of the mind to the activity of the senses. This reaction is continually changing in response both to new information that is being received through various sensory inputs and to how this information is being interpreted. How the mind perceives, receives, interprets, translates and thus processes information determines our reaction. Our experience is made up of all reaction to sensation.

We have physical or biological sensation through the five primary senses: touch, smell, sound, sight and taste. We also have other sensations in the form of psychological abstractions such as status, security, satisfaction, power, prestige, submission, fear, domination – even, perhaps, contribution. Whatever these abstractions may be, the mind-body feels stimulated in response. Say for example that the mind-body wants the feeling of satisfaction and it is looking for it through sex, the mind-body feels something during this process and so we are still operating within the realm of sensation. Sensation can also take the form of emotion. When you feel humour, happiness, heartache, fear, anger, offence or jealousy you are moved; you are subjectively experiencing and subjectively feeling sensation. There are also intellectual or philosophical stimulations such as the appreciation of elegance or style or perhaps the solving of a riddle. All of this is sensation. Sentience is the capacity to feel sensation. Your sentience is your awareness of feeling, hearing, seeing, tasting and smelling; when coupled with thought it is your capacity for conscious experience. It is clear then that there cannot be life without sensation, for there cannot be life without the capacity for perception. This capacity for perception is sentience and it is fundamental to all life.

Without the perception and contact of the senses to generate the experiencing of sensation, you would not be alive. It is the experiencing of sensation – of the physical, the emotional and the psychological – that is life, and makes up your existence. Sensation is what is real to each and every one of us. Some sensations can be shared, either directly – like the more psychological sensations – or indirectly, like those emotions we share in empathy. Other sensations are unique to us. A raindrop lands on the back of your hand: you feel a cool, wet sensation on your skin. To you, this sensation is very real; it is real because you *perceive* it to be real. When a raindrop lands on the hand of another, it is real to them but not to you. We are not negating its reality in terms of their perception but, in relation to our distinct and unique perception – that is, in terms of our own subjectivism – it is not real. What is real to you lies only within your perception of the real, only within your mind's reaction to sensory input; without perception and contact then there is no reaction, there is no experience and thus no sensation. There must be perception and contact with a flower for you to experience that flower, to know *experiencing* of it. The mind needs the perception and contact of its sensory inputs to recognise and generate reaction to sensation. Sensation cannot be separated from the process of experiencing, because experience is the recognition of and reaction to sensation. Experience can also be felt in reaction, such as the experience of a flower from the memory of a flower. Here there is reaction to a previous sensation without current contact, so memories too stimulate sensation.

What is also true of sensation is that, in keeping with the law of impermanence, all sensation arises and falls. Sensations may naturally come to an end, freeing your awareness to move on to the next sensation, or conscious awareness finds a sensation unsatisfying and so it goes in search of a better, more gratifying sensation. For example when you become bored of a previous sensation, like the sensation of sitting still in the same the position for too long, you go in search of novelty within a new sensation – you feel like stretching your legs. Conscious awareness is constantly moving between sensations, usually in the direction of what is more comfortable, gratifying or exciting. If you look into yourself, you will find that this process never ceases, nor are you ever truly gratified.

The mind perceives something new, engages with it through the senses, reacts to it and either likes it or dislikes it and so thought as memory is created. When we like a sensation and want more of it, we call it pleasure, and when we don't like a sensation and try to resist it, we call it pain. These pleasure and pain sensations move into memory and become our remembrances of pleasure and pain. These remembrances naturally help shape our ideas of what is pleasure and what is pain, both now and in the future. So our ideas of pleasure or pain actually draw from the past. Is that right? What about pleasure that is happening right now? This happening right now appears to be immediate but it is not; your idea of 'right now' is rarely truly right now, unless of course we are dealing with basic survival sensations that are not often open to interpretation, such as rudimentary pain.

Let us look to everyday living and examine the apparent immediateness of sensation. Consider the sensation of touch, which we feel automatically. There are nanoseconds between touch and our registration of that sense of touch, and we all feel that this touch is immediate or close to immediate.[1] Then of course there is your psychological reaction to this touch based upon your interpretation; there are a few milliseconds of time in between the feeling of touch and your mind's interpretation of that touch. Someone slaps you on the back, is it friendly or is it aggressive? Your interpretation determines the experience. These milliseconds determine your experience and it is this interval of time between perception and experience that we are interested in. It makes sense that we cannot know whether a sensation is pleasurable or painful until our mind has reacted to the information that it perceives. Thus your reaction, although it appears to be immediate, is not actually happening in the moment of Right Now. It is based in the past, albeit only a few milliseconds in the past. You only know sensation as pleasure once you have decided that you like

---

[1] It is interesting to note that some scientists have documented recognition of touch prior to actual touch.

that sensation; your decision is drawn from the past – no matter how close to the present moment this past actually is. This is vitally important to realise. It is also important to recognise that, underneath all of our apparently advanced consciousness as sentient beings, we are also still animals and we each still possess basic instincts. Many of our interpretations to sensation are automatic, and there is little we can do or say about it. Rudimentary pain can come under this instinctive category.

Think of moments when you are having foreplay sex with your partner; your partner is touching you in a most sensuous way. Pleasure comes when your mind has interpreted the sensation of that touch and decided that it likes it. There is an interval of time between the sensation that is happening and your reaction to that sensation. This interval may be a fraction of a second but a fraction of a second is still an interval, and it is the knowing of this interval that is key if we are to understand desire. You will have also noticed that there have been other times when that same person has touched you in a similar way and your reaction to that touch has been totally different; you were not 'into' the sex at all and the chemistry was just not there. Our notion of pleasure or pain lie in our reaction to sensation and this reaction has many roots. This is why some people adore certain things and why other people do not. You may be a sexual person or maybe you are not much into sex at all. Maybe you love Marmite (the British sandwich spread) or maybe you are one of those people who cannot stand it. Or perhaps you love both sex and Marmite, at the same time. (What a ghastly thought!) Pleasure is sensation that thought has reacted to and turned into pleasure. Pleasure is thus a verbalised label which we use to describe sensations that we, as sentient beings, like and want more of. Sensations that we don't like and want to resist, like the prick of a needle for example, we call discomfort or pain.

On the subject of needles, notice how some people can insert a needle into themselves without any pain at all, they are completely disassociated. This is an interesting phenomenon. Understanding pleasure is not dissimilar in its shape to the understanding of pain and when there is understanding of both then there is headway in the understanding of desire. Have you ever noticed how there can sometimes be a significant interval of time between damage to the body and your feeling of physical pain from that damage? I can think of many examples from my own life when I have been cut deeply and have not noticed the pain of that cut until actually seeing the wound, or the resulting blood. Please hold onto this notion of intervals of time between awareness and interpretation.

Desire Definitions

WHEN THOUGHT GETS INVOLVED WITH sensation, everything changes. As soon as thought gets involved in the process of what it is to move towards, feel and experience as sensation – what it reacts to as pleasure or pain – it has projected itself in the form of desire. Desire is thus projected thought, it is the output of a mind projecting itself onto sensations that it likes or dislikes. The nature of desire rests within our reaction to sensations and the directions of these reactions. These reactions have shaped the very nature of the ego because the ego is the accumulation of all such reactions. The knowing of desire is thus found in the knowing of your mind's reactions and these reactions are themselves drawn from the past because they are your mind's response to sensation; they are responses that operate from the past. Desire can be thought of as the directed movement of thought within your mind for you to have conscious awareness of further pleasure sensation (or less pain sensation). Or, more specifically, desire is the movement towards perception, contact, relationship, recognition, interpretation, reaction and thus experiencing of pleasure sensation. It is the process of thought that has given shape to the pursuit of pleasure sensation or the avoidance of pain sensation.

Over time the constant movement between one preferred sensation and the next, or away from an undesirable sensation towards the next, creates the habit of moving between sensations. Thus begins the thought process of desire, which in effect simply describes our will to move in these directions. We naturally like some sensations more than others, and it is how we value each of these in our recorded memory that determines our tastes and preferences and, therefore, our current or future desires. So in relation to will, desire exists as a form of thought that has taken shape to describe the movement of our will to pursue pleasure and avoid pain. Fundamentally, this is the movement towards fulfilment or denial. These definitions are important if we are to understand desire fully, thus freeing ourselves from the trappings of desire.

Fulfilment

AS WE SAW EARLIER, THE search for fulfilment is a strong drive in human nature (Chapter 5, *Your True Nature*). Each of us hopes to find fulfilment in experiencing life's pleasures (which include the avoidance of pain). Look closer at what is happening. The experience of pleasure or pain itself can be broken down into the drive towards various sensations that we like or do not like. This is determined as much by the interpretation of our mind as it is by the sensory input information coming into that mind. Your interpretation is as valid a factor in your reaction as the sensory input itself; reaction is not only dependent upon sensory input but also dependent upon interpretation. Too often, the mind has a tendency to concentrate its efforts only on improving or altering sensory input, with less attention on the interpretation of that input. This is important to note.

Our daily experience is a method to soak up, test and explore our relationship with sensation. This is what we are all doing; this is what it is to experience. It is the movement towards certain sensations and away from others that drives all of our activity. When we like something, it is important to realise that it is the sensation that we really want (or wish to avert) as opposed to the external factor that is the current cause of sensory information coming into the brain. So if the sensation can be reproduced without the need for certain external stimuli, can we agree that this would be a useful tool? Please think about this for a moment before you agree or disagree. We are saying that desire rests inside the movement of thought, expressed as will, to reach towards or avert certain sensations. Desire is the movement of thought that is focused solely on the gratification of or aversion to sensation; it is a process of fulfilment or denial. So if we are to understand desire, we must know the nature of the relationship between our conscious awareness and sensation, that being our perception, contact, recognition, interpretation and reaction to sensation. A good starting point from which to understand this is the identification process.

Identification

WHEN I EQUATE MYSELF TO a sensation, I am identified with that sensation. When we say or think, '*I am jealous*' or '*I am hungry*', the 'I' is equated to jealousy or hunger in the present tense. The equating of the 'I' by thought to sensations such as jealousy, hunger, anger, laughter or despair is the identification process. What is happening is that thought has created this entity called the 'I' and identified it with a sensation; this entity that we call the 'I' is considered in thought to be jealous or hungry in the present tense, yet at the same time also considered to be a separate entity from the jealousy or the hunger. There is a contradiction.

Thought likes to create a sense of permanence with its identifications; it stores up identifications within its memory and from this collection of memory, built up across a lifetime, it forms an image in its mind that it knows as the self. The mind, or more correctly thought, constructs an identity of its own thoughts and identifications and calls this thinker 'I'. Now it does this in order to create for itself the notion of permanence because all sensations and reactions to sensations are impermanent. It likes to store up memories because the factors that create memories are always coming and going and, if it did not store up such memories, there would be no continuity. Understand that without any permanence in time brought about from the collection of memory, the 'I' – the observer, the experiencer – is lost. And so the thinker, the experiencer, is created, enforced and strengthened to create a sense of permanence within a world of impermanent arising and falling sensations and reactions. If you think about your life experience, every element other than 'you' comes and goes; it always has and it always will. There is a contradiction between the idea of permanence and the reality of impermanence and it is this contradiction, this conflict in time existing within thought, that is the very process of the self. Please take a moment to mull this over.

When we identify with a preference for Sensation A or Sensation B and when this identification has continuance in thought, which is the same as saying a continuance in time, then there are a series of remembrances building up within memory. These remembrances naturally help shape our ideas of what we like and don't like, and what we think. What is happening is the building blocks of our personality are taking shape. Through the identification process – through the experiencing of various sensations and our thoughts in reaction to these sensations, both live and in memory – we form our tastes and preferences, which are key elements in the construction of the self. Each identification forms a new layer of ego, and the more layers you add, like the layers of an onion or the outer shells of a Babushka doll, the more they coalesce over time to form personality. The ego is not a tangible thing, but is constructed out of layers of thought in the form of identifications.

So our identifications determine our identity. They thus determine our drives, our desires, our frustrations, our fears and so forth; in short they coalesce to form our whole sense of self. For example, if you like the feeling of power that comes with bossing people around, then clearly you have identified with the psychological sensation that power brings and so it is likely that you will desire positions of power. You may not even be consciously aware of this, for the mind can be very subtle and very clever at creating scripts that you are unaware of. Transactional analysis, for example, is a good therapy to uncover such scripts. The more one identifies with movements towards certain sensations, the more one is driven by the desire for that sensation. Our desire is the process of fulfilling our attractions and denying our aversions. One's personality is formulated out of one's attractions and aversions and from these identifications our desires are formed. The whole movement in the process of fulfilment (and of denial) is desire. The self is a process, a construction of action, reaction, initiation and response – a momentum based upon its desires.

The Shaping of the Self

WE ARE FUNDAMENTALLY SHAPED BY the cravings that we hope to satisfy in our search for fulfilment. Underneath are the root sensations that we like and want to experience more and, of course, the sensations that we dislike and want to experience less. It is this process which drives our actions. Naturally we each wish to follow our own preferred patterns of sensation as much as we can, but what we often forget is that many of our allegedly freely determined, preferred patterns of sensation are actually the result of previous conditioning. They are thus less freely determined than we might think. Such patterns are embedded deep within our psyche and are formed from a lifetime of reaction to sensation, reactions that have given us our life experiences to date and thus our subsequent memories. From these memories – and their relationship with various sensations – associations are built up and it is these associations that form the conditioning process.

Memory is the result of reaction to sensation, but it also determines our current reaction to sensation; there is an interdependent cause and effect cycle in operation. Memory is the accumulation of experience and yet at the same time memory also determines the way we interpret and perceive new experience; it influences all reaction to sensations. In simple terms, what is old is influencing how we perceive and interpret what is new. Obviously our associations can re-construct themselves in our daily activity, but it is not often that we see this happening. Humans are creatures of habit, on the whole rather dull and often closed to what is new in terms of sensation and new experience. Most of the time, we follow repeated patterns of behaviour. These patterns form our psychological maps and scripts. When we look at our habits and our addictive behaviours for example, which themselves constitute a large proportion of our daily activity, we are most certainly drawing our current experience of sensation from reaction to sensation that is past, drawn from our associative memory.

Let us look at this cycle of cause and effect using different terminology. In the conditioning process of the past, the mind records our reaction to various sensations and then forms memories about them, labelling them as either pleasant or unpleasant. The mind has formed ideas about them in a summary relating to the experience. This summary is forever changing, adapting and being modified in accordance to the reactions of similar experiences in daily life, but its core usually remains fixed in the mind. A reaction can be anchored and associated with a certain sensory experience and then stored as memory; if we would like that sensation again we simply repeat our behaviour to repeat the reaction, and this is how our habits form. The ideas that the mind has created around certain experiences are the images that exist in memory. For example, if the mind likes the sensation of distraction from boredom whilst smoking a cigarette, as soon as a situation of boredom presents itself, immediately you reach for a cigarette. The image that the mind has formed and identified with is one of *'cigarettes relieve boredom'*. This is a script and if you relate to that script, then you are identified with a psychological sensation. This tiny little identification is but one of many identifications made by someone who considers themselves to be a smoker. *'I am a smoker'* is a form of identification. *'I smoke, I drink, I am a yogi, I am funny, I am .... anything'* is identification.

Any identification process – such as relating cigarettes to the relief of boredom – adds another onion layer onto the self. Our preferred sensations and our associations of those sensations with certain experiences formulate the identification processes which construct the self. Desire is formulated from sensation – either the mind trying to re-create past sensations or its periodic quest for new sensation. Much of the time we like to stick with what we know, but not always. There are times when we seek new sensation to break away from our indifference to old sensation, or maybe we feel a lack of sensitivity to current sensation and we want greater intensity. Perhaps we perceive that our current behaviour is limited and we would like to escape our general feeling of dullness. We want to live, we want to experience, we want to break away from the old, from the norm, from the treadmill. We want the new, and so we desire the new.

Karma

HOWEVER, WE DO NOT KNOW what the new is; we have never seen it before so how can we know what we are looking for? Instead, our future imaginations drive what we do today, but these imaginations have been formulated from the past. These imaginations are formulated from the image that the mind has created around both our sense of self (our identifications from past experiences) and what we think certain future experiences will bring us. This happens by default of the nature of the sensations recognised within an experience (or what we think that experience may be in the future) and what has accordingly been translated into memory. So our past memory determines what we become identified with and this shapes what we desire today. As one sensation reinforces the desire to seek out the next sensation, so begins the process of cause and effect. If this process continues without an awareness of what is happening, how it is happening and why it is happening, then our perception of what fulfilment is narrows, and subsequently we become shackled to this narrowed perception. Until we wake up, for a very long time we will continue to seek fulfilment only according to this narrow perception. This cause and effect process and our self-imprisonment within it is our karma, and it is a self-binding process of our own making. All karma can cease if there is awareness of what is the process of karma. In this process the future is being determined by the past, and when we place our identifications on top of one another, thereby adding more layers onto the ego, the ego gets constructed out of the desires from a mind that is past. Our sense of self is the product of our own karma, of the past; even our hopes of the future are formulated from what is past.

The 'I' is introverted desire. We know that the ego is also built up of memories (of compliments, flattery, insults and achievements) and our knowledge, beliefs, values and attachments that we have accumulated in our life to date. Remember that the ego is not a tangible thing, but is a process of these memories, expectations, beliefs, hopes and all the rest of it; driven forward primarily by desire. Think about it. How much of what you do is determined by the people or places that you want to see, activities that you want to do or items that you want to own? All of it. We are constantly changing this or that, improving our surroundings or our appearance, thirsting for gratification in any way possible. Gratification of your desires is what drives you, it is a fundamental part of you and there is no point denying this truth. All desire is projection of the ego and it is the desires of the ego that largely construct the ego. The ego is a process not a thing; it is the momentum that is being carried forward based upon what it is that you desire; where your desires are based on your projections of fulfilment or denial. Ego and desire are two parts of the same process; a process directly linked with that of karma.

Seeking Permanence

WE KNOW THAT THE EGO strives to create the idea of permanence, the question is why? Let us consider what would happen if the ego did not form identifications. There is, as we have seen, an interval of time that exists between sensation and thought; a moment of awareness of sensation without thought behind that sensation which we can call pre-intellectual awareness. For most of us this interval is a millisecond and so to us it seems that pre-intellectual awareness is merely an idea. Yet you have numerous examples of pre-intellectual awareness from your own life – those moments on a mountain top or looking out at a sunset. Here there is a sense of bliss and this can continue for a considerable interval of time, but as soon as thought enters and says, *'Yes this is fantastic. How beautiful!'* the ego has identified with this moment and thought as pleasure has been created. We then form memories of these moments, and seek to repeat them, adding to the layers of the ego. Without identification, your awareness exists only within the perpetual moment of now. Despite what many masters say about the freedom of this moment, it is important to remember that without thought wishing to hold onto memories of experiences, these experiences of perpetual moments of now would be enjoyed and then forever lost, since without some form of identification, without thought identifying with certain sensations to create an image of some sort of permanence, then the self is not. If this was your only state of being from which you could never escape, you would have no personality at all. So it is clear that for the self to function, some form of basic identification is needed.

Ego is momentum. The mind likes to keep busy striving for things, achieving this and that – a new house, a new car, a new job, a new wife, a new husband. It is this process of striving for new objectives that drives the ego. When there is nothing to do, the ego feels lost. In order for the ego to gather a sense of permanence, it must keep moving; it must keep driving forwards because it *is* that momentum. Can you see this? Look into your own life. When you are waiting for a train or a bus or maybe you have finally finished decorating your house, what do you do? You don't know what to do with yourself; you feel lost, twiddling your thumbs and feeling uncomfortable and unsettled. Maybe you pass the time by smoking a cigarette – at least this feels like you are doing *something* – but underneath you smoke only in order to keep yourself occupied. You only think that cigarettes relieve boredom because you are identified with this belief.

The ego sees that the nature of all sensation and all thought is transitory and so it tries to create a sense of permanence within a world that is impermanent. The ego – the process of thought – is forever seeking its own security, for it realises that without any sense of permanence, without memory of the image that you have of yourself through identifications with your job, your status, your home or your family, then you are nothing but emptiness; you are nothing but empty awareness. You – your sense of self – are the image that you have created about yourself; this we have called the ego. This image is the entity that most of us call the 'I' and it is seeking a permanent state. But the nature of ego is impermanent and so it will try tooth and nail to create a sense of self – even the idea of a higher self or soul – that is permanent. It does this because without permanence this 'I', the ego, faces its own annihilation. It fears the emptiness within, where there is no sense of self. It seeks permanent thought as something separate from the moving thought from which it is constructed; it creates the observer as separate from the observed, the 'I' that is separate from the anger or jealousy, the illusion of something fixed, unchanging and permanent. The illusion of permanence stems from this perceived separation. Even though the anger and jealousy are transitory, by creating the 'I' as a separate, distinct and permanent entity that is separate from the jealousy and anger, so begins the illusion of permanence. The result is the creation of psychological time in the conflict between permanent thought and impermanent thought, between the illusion of the 'I' and our reaction to sensation. The ego (and ultimately the 'actual' of physical selfhood) is, after all, a process and if the momentum of that process ceases, then the self ceases and with it ends our own, unique relative time. This is what Buddha is trying to help you understand. Understand that the self identifies, desires, attaches and even fears in order to ensure its own continuation.

Continuity: A Summary

REALITY – BOTH EXTERNAL REALITY and our internal reality – is in a constant state of movement; it is an impermanent process that is forever changing. Our thoughts, our feelings and our sensations are forever and continuously in a state of changeability. So as one sensation comes to an end – when it withers away, becomes dull or we simply become insensitive to it – the mind seeks out the next sensation and so the habit of moving between sensations is embedded into our basic activity. The ego is looking for the continuous experiencing of sensation, it is wishing to make sensation permanent because it itself is not permanent. By making its identifications with sensation into something permanent, the ego seeks to make itself permanent[2]. We desire because the ego is trying to create permanence through continuous sensation. Desire is the process for the continuation of sensation, and thus our sense of selfhood; without desire, there is the discontinuation of activity and the ego loses momentum and ceases to exist.

Let's summarise this chapter. We attach thought and labels to the processes of sensations, leading to identification and adding layers to the self. Our will moves constantly towards the pursuit of pleasure and the avoidance of pain, that being the process of the gratification or aversion of sensation that gives continuity to desire. Desire is the

---

[2] The ego desires in order to prevent its own ending. Desire and fear are interrelated.

projected ego and the ego is the incorporation of desire. The momentum of selfhood is the continuous movement of will, as desire, between one sensation and the next. Without a basic version of this we simply could not function as individuals. Desire is a product of conscious and subconscious thinking and what thinks is the self; so thinking gives continuity to desire. If we can understand that desire is a process that we each peddle along with thought, then we can gain both understanding of it and freedom from the psychological mechanisms that drive it. If this mechanical process of desire cannot be understood, then your life is bound to be forever imprisoned by it, forever enslaved by a process that is of your own making, that is your own karma; the rest of your life will be utterly sorrowful, stuck inside a prison of chasing one desire and then the next desire and then the next desire, until the day that you die. Freedom from this process is joy. When we look into our own lives, it feels like a constant struggle to find continuous and satisfactory sensation, always we are engaged in a repetitive rat race where our desires are never fully satisfied for long; we are in a perpetual state of dissatisfaction. Any satisfaction is at best temporary and old desires for sensation are soon replaced by a new set of desires for sensation that may again be fulfilled briefly, but never for long. They will always be replaced by a further set of desires, and the same problem repeats itself. The nature of desire is that it will never be fulfilled.

Thought sustains and nourishes desire. Thought determines 'like' or 'dislike' based upon ideas formed within the mind. These ideas, or preferences, are a reflection of what thought considers pleasure or pain. Pleasure is nothing more than memory; an idea of gratification that the mind has determined. It is a system of preference, a means for the mind to find stillness and bliss, to lose itself or get lost in union with another. The seeking of pleasure is an escape from our daily routine, where there is indifference to 'what is'. All indifference arises because there is a lack of sensitivity. We are not aware of the true nature of sensation – which is impermanent – and, by seeking to make sensation permanent, we lose sensitivity. There is little sensitivity if we are constantly seeking stimulation, as most of us are in the modern world. The search for stimulation is no more than a psychological escape from what we *are*, from 'what is'.

We seek to escape because we are reacting to an idea of fulfilment; the idea has become all-important and so the idea comes before action. Only action that is free from idea is true action. Action based on bias, preference or prejudice, in response to our thoughts about fulfilment is no action at all, only reaction. All reaction entails conflict between 'what is' and 'what should be'. The process of becoming between 'what is' and the state that I seek is simply a projection of my mind. It is our struggling towards an ideal that makes for conflict; it is the disintegrating factor that is the product of our conditioning. We are *this* and we want *that*. This is our daily activity; a self-projection, a modified version of 'what is' – we as ourselves somewhat modified. It is the mind fooling itself with ideas of fulfilment, the idea of a lasting higher state. The struggle towards any ideal never brings freedom – which is the integrated state, or state of completeness – it leads only to disintegration and fragmentation. The idea of permanent pleasure and our struggle towards it breeds only illusion, and of course freedom can never be found in illusion. For this illusion to cease, it must be seen for what it is. The seeing itself is the integrating factor, not the effort to become what you are not, or the struggle, striving, achievement or maintenance of that which the mind has nourished and sustained as desire.

Because of the transitory nature of all sensation, the more we try to seek happiness through our identifications with sensation, the narrower our perception of fulfilment becomes. What follows can only be perpetual dissatisfaction. Because of the transitory nature of reality, because of the impermanent nature of the universe, if we cling to sensation then it is bound to change, and if we are attached to that sensation we are bound to be upset. What is happening is we are clinging in the face of inevitable change; it is like trying to grab hold of something liquid; it will always run through your fingers. We seek happiness and fulfilment through sensations and gratification. We are always seeking happiness through something; our possessions, the acquisition of money, getting our face on TV, aspiring to be like the models on the pages of fashion magazines, or through adhering to certain religious beliefs in order to reach God. Whatever it is, the seeking of fulfilment through something – it could be anything at all – results only in sorrow. This is because you are distracted from knowing your inner nature, which is not identification with sensation, it is only sensation. When there is only sensation, meaning complete and total sensation of all senses, then there is extraordinary bliss; there is inner completion. Wisdom is completion, a unified wholeness. Wisdom is to know one's inner nature, a nature that is without a centre. There is no wisdom without ending the search for fulfilment.

chapter 10
Desire

BEFORE WE BEGIN OUR ANALYSIS of desire, it is important that we clarify certain fallacies existing within conditioned viewpoints in relation to desire. Our desire represents our search for satisfaction. Everything that we do, we do for satisfaction; even what we do for others we do ultimately for our own satisfaction, and this is without exception. The fact is that there is no such thing as *non-interest in oneself*. Recognising this fact, and recognising the fallacies of denial which exist within certain segments of society in relation to this, is vital if we are to tackle desire – a concept which has dominated human life since the dawn of history.

We hear about enlightenment, we want fulfilment and we seek these outcomes. We hold a perception as to what fulfilment is, or what enlightenment is, and by holding onto these perceptions our awareness is automatically narrowed down into a more limited field of view. We form beliefs about enlightenment or fulfilment and then stick to these beliefs in the hope of achieving our goal. Over time our views generally become increasingly fixed, rendering our activity towards these pre-determined ideals completely self-defeating. The nature of anything pre-determined is that it takes on a direction. Moving in a direction is a movement of thought and so immediately you are caught up in psychological time. The corruption begins because we are moving in a direction. Instead of understanding the value of Right View and Right Intention, which is to have no view and no intention, we are occupied in seeking our perceived goal.

As we have seen in earlier chapters, humans give themselves goals which define directions of movement in the name of fulfilment. It is desire which fuels the process of finding fulfilment as an action or a movement. As we now know, the question of why we desire is a question of understanding the nature of why we seek continuous sensation and the relation of thought to sensation. If our freedom is to be authentic, we must understand the nature of this process completely without the distortions produced by the mind; without the limited views or beliefs that, as humans, we generally hold. We must be free to observe the nature of desire without any judgement, justification, condemnation or fixed perception so that it can be observed with clarity, free from the usual conflicts, projections, tensions and contradictions.

You only have to look at the way some of our belief systems deny and suppress desire to glimpse the depth of misunderstanding about this most important concept.

So how do these belief systems distort our ideas about desire? Religious traditions instil the idea that desire is bad or sinful, but this only creates further misunderstanding around the primary activity of the individual – the search for satisfaction. All desire, regardless of its shape, is the search for satisfaction. Maybe you want physical satisfaction – food, sex or sleep – or perhaps you want psychological satisfaction such as sitting next to God, contribution to others or power and authority; whatever the form it takes, the underlying thread is that you are looking for satisfaction. We are not saying that desire is good, but to say that desire, the search for satisfaction, is 'bad' is utterly nonsensical because anyone who thinks this way clearly finds their beliefs or morals satisfying. You may be happy to deny yourself the physical sensation of sex because of your religious beliefs, but you are only doing so because the psychological satisfaction is greater for you. All psychological satisfaction is sensation, is it not? So the religious devotee is actually advocating movement towards satisfactory sensation, this time psychological as opposed to physical. It is still desire, albeit in a different form. Understand that if you wish to free yourself from a certain form of satisfaction, you do so because you seek an even greater form of satisfaction. You have exchanged one satisfaction with another, greater satisfaction. You are still operating within sensation and fundamentally you are still operating from self interest.

Understand that everything that you do, you do for your satisfaction; even a saint is satisfying his own saintliness. This is not to be cynical, but rather to practice the kind of complete and utter honesty which brings one to freedom, especially when it is turned upon the self. Everything that we do is geared towards finding satisfaction in some way and so our primary interest in life is ultimately in ourselves. Don't say that this is not true, don't say that others come first and you second because this is simply not the case; not ultimately. Whilst you may place others in front of yourself, satisfaction is the primary concern of your life, no matter what you say. It gives you satisfaction to place someone ahead of you – even mothers place their children ahead of themselves because it gives them satisfaction to do so. If you give up your life for someone, or you accept torture on behalf of your army, you do so because it gives you some kind of satisfaction – however obscure. By not doing so, you will be unsatisfied; perhaps you will not be able to live with yourself. Your movement away from dissatisfaction is itself a movement towards satisfaction, so there is no such thing as *non-interest in oneself*. You may claim not to be interested in yourself, or driven by satisfaction, but you will always wish to move away from dissatisfaction, even if that means sacrificing your own life.

You are motivated by your desire for freedom and happiness, or because you want to contribute to others. You are doing this because of the satisfaction that this will bring you. This is what motivates you, you want satisfaction. You may disagree with this on moral grounds but what you think does not change the truth of the matter – even holding onto the moral high ground gives you satisfaction! You are still acting within sensation, a sensation that is more gratifying. You act selflessly because to do so makes you feel satisfied. Don't deny what is the main objective of your life – which is to find some satisfactory sensation – by negating it with one of your projected ideals. Understand that you only hold moral ideals because to do so gives you satisfaction. Satisfaction is the primary concern of your life; even the movement away from dissatisfaction is a movement towards satisfaction.

You seek satisfaction because you desire change. Something is missing; you feel incomplete and you hope to find completion. We seek completion through another person, through reaching an ideal, through various actions that we have decided must be so. We are always seeking fulfilment through something and, so long as this search continues, we will always attach great importance to the object of our attention. We become dependent upon and attached to the object, thus beginning our self-imprisonment.

Religious objectives are a clear example of this form of self-imprisonment, and one which we have dealt with in earlier chapters. The religious ascetic denies physical pleasure in his or her pursuit of the greater pleasure of an afterlife in heaven or the psychological satisfaction of religious achievement. Even in its milder forms, this type of religious bargaining is highly hypocritical. Making sacrifices in this life in the hope of pleasing 'the boss' and entering heaven is driven by desire for a better future, a future in a different life. Notions of heaven and the bliss of the afterlife are a form of projected desire. On one hand religions teach that desire is bad, whilst on the other hand bribing their followers with promises of paradise. Such teachings are pure hypocrisy; desire is still desire.

In fact, religious forms of desire are often rooted in a deeper greed, because worldly desire is transitory whilst religious desire is for an eternity of bliss which death cannot take away. Within this concept of heaven, there exists the notion of an eternity of gratification, one where every wish is granted. Heavenly satisfaction is not transitory like it is on Earth, now every wish is granted immediately. No matter how quickly our wishes are granted, desire still exists. It is materialism with a different and greedier name, and as such it keeps you locked out of the present moment, out of contact with existence. Rather than understand your desire, you are encouraged to desire a heaven where desire is ceaselessly satisfied; it is the most monstrous invention ever conceived.

Riding a Bike

EGO IS THE INCORPORATION OF desire. Ego is made up of all of the identification processes that run hand in hand with various sensations. Desire is the movement of thought that describes our will to find and maintain gratifying sensation; the process of thought that has given shape to the pursuit of pleasurable sensations or the avoidance of painful sensations. Desire is, in effect, the process of gratification; the movement of ego seeking satisfaction. By 'gratification' what is meant here is *preferred* sensations; the demonstration of preference in relation to sensation. This is the way in which we identify with sensation. Desire is therefore a process of finding and maintaining identifications that we like or averting identifications that we don't like. It is the central process upon which the ego is built, since the ego is made up of all of our identifications with various sensations. Desire, then, is essentially a process of fulfilment; even what we deny we deny because we seek fulfilment. The ego, having formed ideas as to what fulfilment is, seeks sensation that it thinks will give it gratification. The ego tries to make this gratification permanent by seeking one sensation after another in an attempt to continue gratification. It is this search for (or avoidance of) sensations which we identify as pleasure (or pain) that is the movement of thought as desire. The ego is a momentum that is pedalled along by desire. Let us investigate this process further using the analogy of riding a bicycle.

I like to think of an old British Penny Farthing with its huge wheel at the front and tiny wheel on the back. Each turn of your foot on the pedal represents a movement towards a sensation that you have identified as something pleasurable, or a movement away from a sensation that you have identified as pain. Each turn represents a desire or an aversion (note that an aversion is simply a desire turned upside down). As you pedal the bike along with your desires and your aversions, the bike moves and this momentum is the process of the ego in action and reaction. The ego is built upon the momentum of desire – a process, not a thing – and without that momentum the ego begins to wobble. (Likewise it is easy to wobble on a Penny Farthing, for it is a most poorly and absurdly designed bicycle!)

Take away our identifications – such as our beliefs, values, desires and aversions – and most of us would barely know who we are. The foundation upon which we, as humans, are built is made up of these identifications. Everything that you think you are has come from the outside and it is based upon the image that you have formed of yourself in response; a response that has been based upon whatsoever you have become identified with. So if we stop pedalling the bike, if the identification process with our beliefs, our values or our desired sensations comes to an end, then of course our sense of self will slow down and eventually cease. It will continue for a short while, in the same way as a bicycle will carry on rolling down the road after you stop pedalling, however eventually its momentum will cease. Just as the Penny Farthing starts to wobble and then grinds to a halt, so the process of the ego grinds to a halt.

It is important to remember the risks of self effacement. If in the 'letting go' of your identifications you become a shadow of your former self, if you have effaced yourself such that little or no spark of vitality and enthusiasm remains, then you will remain unbalanced, sluggish and wobbly like a slow moving Penny Farthing. This slow wobble will continue until you have fully understood the whole process of the ego. Your misunderstanding is sufficient to keep the bike pedalling along, but at such a wobbly pace that the ego will never drop of its own accord. Effacing the self can actually strengthen the momentum of the ego, pedalling you along for years as a ghost of your former self. If instead you clearly understand the pseudo nature of ego personality, then you can say goodbye to identifications freely and without effort. The desire process will then grind to a halt of its own accord, and your true individuality will shine as you feel free and alive for the very first time.

Ending the process of the ego is not something that you do through action: this cannot be emphasised enough. Actions such as following a religious system or effacing yourself in some absurd ascetic practice only add to your ego's momentum. Ending the process of the ego is something that happens only in the inaction of letting go. If you try to do this through action, then you are still caught in the desire for an outcome, for satisfaction. Understand that it is the movement and the momentum of your pedalling desires – your desire to drop the ego or your desire to be humble or your desire for Versace or whatever it is that drives your bicycle – that distracts you from the present moment. Anything that distracts you from the present moment prevents you from knowing fulfilment. So in your everyday drive to make pleasurable sensation continuous, in whatever way gives you satisfaction, you are pedalling along the very momentum of the ego. You are denying yourself the lasting bliss that will be yours automatically and effortlessly if you stop pedalling the bike along. Your struggle to achieve your desires is the actual cause of your sorrow. The fulfilment that you desire comes into play when you no longer desire; it never comes into play if you seek it through desire. All desire must cease, but only of its own accord through awareness and understanding, never through enforcement or action. Desire is nothing more than propelled ego. Understand what propels the ego and then you will understand desire.

How can desire cease without us making it cease? This may seem contradictory until you can understand desire's inherent nature. Through genuine understanding, all that needs to happen will happen without you needing to do anything about it. You cannot satisfy desire because desire is, by definition, the movement of thought that exists when you are not satisfied with the present moment. How can you satisfy that which is, by definition, perpetually never satisfied? Desire is a state of dissatisfaction with the present moment, which means that your awareness is not here and now. Dissatisfaction, and therefore desire, is only possible when you are looking to the future or the past for fulfilment, rather than observing and understanding the present moment of Now. As we discussed in the book *Question Mark*, all problems rest in the past or the future, never in the present moment; this includes the problem of desire.

Desire is always one step ahead of you. You will never catch up with it nor satisfy it, yet some hope for change always remains. This hope for fulfilment is what fuels your desire in the first place. Conceptually, desire means that something is missing, something is wanting; it signals that you want change. If you seek happiness you must be unhappy right now, the very fact that you want happiness shows that you are unhappy or dissatisfied with the present moment. Now is not enough, you are unhappy today and so you desire to be happy tomorrow. You are making a projection out of a state of unhappiness. Tomorrow is a projection of what you think tomorrow will be, but always that projection is based upon ideas that are drawn from the past, because they come from memory and memory is past. All projections that you form are formed from thought, and so all projections are formed from the past. Understand that your idea of the future, which is drawn from the past, is merely a projection of desire. Otherwise the future does not, psychologically, exist.

If you are unhappy right now it is because you are not here right now; your mind is focused on tomorrow or troubled by what is past, which means that you are caught up in desire and psychological time. Your unhappiness will not be solved by tomorrow's achievements, but by understanding the present moment and the processes which colour it. Unless your understanding changes, then you will be unhappy tomorrow as you stay contained inside this projection of your desires. The nature of your thinking, desiring mind – seeking change and believing that tomorrow will somehow be better – is to continue this cycle forever as you are fooled by this dreadful concept of hope. Only an immature religion makes hope a virtue, distracting its followers from living in and understanding the present moment of Now. Christianity makes hope a virtue and, in the largest Christian country in the world, hope is the foundation upon which presidents are elected.

The Magician

THE TRICK OF THE EGO is to distort our perception of almost everything, especially objects of desire. To illustrate this, imagine a magician like David Copperfield in front of an audience with his box of tricks. The audience is in awe of his illusions and is thus inclined to believe that they are real. When the magician creates the illusion of a delicious cake, members of the audience rush over to take a slice. As soon as they reach out, the magician turns the cake into spiders and immediately the audience runs away in fear. We are just like this deluded audience. We believe in the appearances of the dualistic mind, chasing after cakes (or rather the gratifications that we have decided are pleasant, according to our own identifications) and then we run away from these cakes as soon as they turn into spiders. The one who is awake is like the magician; able to enjoy the scene, but because he knows it is an illusion he is not caught up in its illusionary drama and so he remains unmoved.

He is unmoved because, just like the magician, he has clarity; he is not stuck inside a narrow perception like the audience. As we come to understand the nature of our identifications, the way in which we perceive objects of desire changes. We are able to understand their true nature with greater clarity rather than simply be their slave; a process which itself determines much of our identity. Just as what we strive for and achieve (or fail to achieve) shapes our sense of self worth, our tastes and preferences equally determine who we are. What we desire and what we identify with moulds our personality. If you are unaware of the extent of this process, as you strive towards certain goals that your mind has decided must be achieved, then you can create an entire life drama for yourself that is both inhibiting and exhausting. You are bound to feel that life is a struggle and whenever your life is a passage to reach certain goals, then love will always be an elusive state of Being. The very nature of struggling and striving blocks you from reaching fulfilment.

Think of objects of desire as you would a rainbow. We all know the rainbow exists, yet no matter how fast we run towards it, it will always elude us. Knowing this, we are prepared to stand still and appreciate the rainbow for what it is. It is better to appreciate its stunning beauty, enjoy its suchness, enjoy its quiddity and accept that it is impermanent and it will never be ours. Understanding that it is transitory does not mean we need enjoy it any less. An understanding such as this can save us from much suffering and its principle can apply to all objects of desire, including our interpersonal relationships.

The ego tricks you into believing that you are no more than your thoughts, and you can easily spend your entire life dictated by these thoughts. If you examine them, if you look closely, they are full of contradiction and conflict and they can be very erratic. If you were to write down every thought that comes in and out of your mind within a 30 minute period, you would be in for quite a shock. Your thoughts in this period, or any reasonable period for that matter, will be chaotic, random, inconsistent and most certainly contradictory. When you read out your list, you find that you are like a discombobulated madman inside; your mind is dual. One thought is going left, the next thought is going right; there is conflict and disorder all the time inside your mind. These are the thoughts that are driving you every minute of every day. Realise that you are primarily driven by what is fundamentally a consistent state of contradiction.[1] It is no wonder that you feel exhausted and tired. Think of how peaceful it would be if these thoughts could be attuned with one another, if they could rest in harmony with one another, so that there is order, so that you have a mind in accord with itself. Would that not be a calm, tranquil, peaceful

---

[1] In the inconsistent, dualistic mind, it is only contradiction which remains consistent.

way of being? To bring about this order, you have to be aware of the conflict in your mind, aware of the illusions and distorted perceptions which bring about the suffering of desire. Out of that awareness, which is your meditation, order will arise of its own accord.

The Tyranny of Hope

HAPPINESS PROJECTED INTO THE FUTURE is an illusion; hope is a powerful projection that guides us out towards an imagined horizon. Desire is always one step ahead of you, holding the illusion of happiness out in front of you like a carrot on a stick for you to run towards. It is like running towards the horizon, always the horizon moves away from you at the same rate as you run towards it. So it is with desire, forever moving away from you at the same rate as you run towards it. Whatsoever you have achieved, desire has moved on; it is always one step ahead. Hope is projected desire, the illusion of happiness on the distant horizon. You are only deceived when you want something and the very fact that you hope so much leaves you blind and open to deception, deceived by your hoping and desiring mind.[2] Understand the futility of hope; understand that desire never leads to fulfilment and that it will always remain unfulfilled. Only when this understanding is deep and complete will you no longer desire and will fulfilment be yours. We are not advocating pessimism, but rather drawing attention to the bliss of the present moment. We live in either gratitude or desire. When you no longer desire, you are grateful for the present moment; Now is enough. Joy is found in what is immediate and close, not in distant hopes and dreams that draw you away from the thundering, pounding, beating, exponential bliss of the present moment. This moment of Now is the only moment; this is the moment of freedom. Tomorrow is a trap, yesterday is a prison. Now is the eternal moment; Now is the only moment of authentic fulfilment.

If we are fully satisfied with the present moment, tomorrow does not exist. Tomorrow is an abstract concept of linear time, yet for most

---

[2] This truth will become painfully clear in the forthcoming years as the deception behind the American executive is finally exposed to the world.

of us 'tomorrow' is the day when we will have our joys. Most of us live for the future, but the future is an illusion; it is only Now that is real. Understand that living for the future is a way of escaping, and much of the world is trying to escape the present moment. Now is what is real, not tomorrow; tomorrow is an idea that we have created. The one who is joyful is not escaping, he is not distracted by tomorrow, his attention is here in the present moment. His joy – like all joy – is happening Now. Life is Now.

Because of our hope, disappointment is inevitable. If you pin your happiness on a certain event happening and then that event fails to manifest, you feel destroyed. You may think that life needs hope to make it bearable, but hope is a prison and your life is unbearable because you are pinning your happiness on a cause. Would it not be better if your happiness could be without a cause? Happiness without cause, now that is freedom. But instead our desires get projected into the future and in the meantime we remain unfulfilled. Our hopes are the future projections of our desire; by understanding these hopes your chasing of desires will dissolve of its own accord. The factor driving how you previously defined yourself will be gone. No longer defining yourself by your desire, you will find fulfilment as you become acutely aware that the essence of you is not this narrow, chasing, desiring mind, but that it is already complete. You will uncover the inner state of Being which you had forgotten. When you see the truth of what desire brings, you can see the truth of how it defines your ego, your sense of 'you' and how it can trap you as you form attachments to your hopes and dreams of paradise.

Busy Little Bees

IT IS THE MIND THAT perceives and meets our sensations. Even when it is gratified, the mind, in its quest for continuance, has already decided what to engage with next. Once satisfied, another desire will always arise in the mind and so it continues for the rest of our lives. This perpetual search for new sensation exists because we are frightened of our inner emptiness, we are trying to escape this feeling of inner incompletion, and so the ego will always try to fill this emptiness, quench it or run away from it using stimulations that distract, suppress, substitute or conquer. Such occupations fill the mind and this is ultimately what the ego wants. All such occupations are the desires of the ego because they distract attention away from the empty inner state. Thus the ego is principally occupied with chasing down its desires like a busy little bee. These desires can take any number of diverse forms – like the desire to be holy or the desire to be a celebrity – but ultimately they are all occupations that maintain the momentum of the ego in order to keep itself busy; this is what the ego wants.

So we are driven by a mind that likes to stay busy, suppressing and distracting us from what we think is our deep dissatisfaction within. When your mind is occupied with illusions of the future, in your hopes for a better tomorrow you are actually operating from the past rather than from the stillness of the present moment. You are thus not open to the new because your idea of the future is drawn from the past. You are not here and now, you are not present in the realm of the new. When caught up in the past or the future, your mind is busy and distracted so you miss the here and now, you miss the freshness of reality. Missing out on what is now and what is new can continue unchecked for an entire lifetime and you can end up distracted from the very suchness and essence of the present moment for years, even decades; perhaps until your dying days. The essence of reality passes you by as you are caught up in your hoping, dreaming, distracted mind. You are living in a dream of your own making, not present in what is here, now and ultimately real. Maybe you desire riches. Whilst you seek wealth and you allow this search to dominate your life, you are distracted by the illusion of what you think wealth will bring you. You think that wealth will buy you freedom, but if your psychological, emotional and existential freedom are not understood, then the liberty that you think economic freedom will bring you can only ever be short-lived. Whilst this misunderstanding remains, your craving for economic freedom will continue, blinded by your own self-deception of what you believe that economic freedom brings. This neatly summarises the immaturity of the American Dream.

The Illusion of Fulfilment

WE ONLY DESIRE WHEN WE do not feel fulfilled. Obviously when we are fulfilled there is no wanting, needing or craving; nothing to fulfil. Most of us are conditioned to think that fulfilment is reached when everything that we have ever wanted is ours. We think that fulfilment will be ours when all of our desires have been satisfied and when all of our dreams have been achieved. To achieve fulfilment we focus solely on the satisfaction of our wants and our dreams, rarely questioning *why* it is that we want. The satisfaction of wants is the foundation upon which the entire capitalist system is built; the promotion of hope that is the backbone of the American Dream. This central economic principle, as identified by Adam Smith in the 18th century, is what western society is founded upon and what we as a society have accepted today without question. The goal of our economic system and thus our own conditioning – since we are society and society is us – is to find fulfilment through accumulation and possession. Assuming we are successful, we presume that in this there will be the ending of desire; at least this is the rationale in our minds. But when you look at the lives of millionaires and movie stars, how much fulfilment do you see? They are still striving for more, and in some cases self-destruction sets in. The destruction begins with accumulation. In your drive to possess assets, or perhaps fame, knowledge, ideas, virtue, you have made your mind narrow, dull and insensitive. There is isolation in the search for gratification, regardless of your taste or preference. Clearly we are not looking upon this problem of desire with any clarity. We are not questioning why it is that we want in the first place.

Our existing perception is based on our conditioning; we are advised that only when we have achieved financial security and the love of a life long partner will we be happy. We believe what advertising companies tell us about possessions making us happy. We end up chasing goals, engaging our focus on the bettering of our relationships, our jobs, our home and our immediate environment, but it is not long before we take our satisfactions for granted. There is a law of diminishing satisfaction within the human psyche. Why do millionaires keep striving for more? How many dollars do you need in the bank before it is enough? In a growing sign of global wealth inequities, the Forbes billionaire list now includes hundreds of names and yet kids in their millions in Africa, South America and Asia still do not have even the most basic of necessities. Such a situation can only be the product of the human ego. Many of the world's wealthiest businessmen are still trying to score the next deal, or they are finding new pleasure in the pride and vanity of renunciation. Regardless of accumulated wealth, the mind still seeks more and is extremely cunning in its presentation of what constitutes 'more'. Desire for sensation – money, power, the rush of the deal or even contribution to a worthy 'cause' – is never permanently satisfied; it is always fragmented into moments of sensation that arise and fall.

The more money, power and influence we achieve, the closer we think we will come to satisfying our desires. We believe that one day we can make pleasure sensation continuous and permanent. Our world suffers disproportionate wealth inequities because of a handful of people and companies, and their acute need for the continuity of pleasure. The roots of this inequity, however, go deeper than the immature minds of the wealthy few. It begins with the way we are conditioned – by our education, by the media – to be ambitious, to achieve, to compare ourselves with others. Is there freedom in competition, measurement, conformity and imitation or is there only conflict? Is your child free to discover who he really is or must he adjust to become just another cog in the machinery of our monstrous and corrupt society; which you have accepted as inevitable and which exists and is maintained because you have never questioned the nature of competition and ambition? You do not see the conflict and antagonism these principles entail. You exist and live in accordance to an illusion, passing this legacy onto future generations. Any illusion created by the mind is rarely correctly identified by the mind. Everyone around you is engaged in the same illusion, so society deems the illusion 'normal'.

> "It is no measure of health to be well adjusted to a profoundly sick society."
>
> *J. Krishnamurti*

You want peace, you want a more even distribution of wealth and yet you remain ambitious. You think that without your ambition, your constant struggle, you will fail and that unless everyone around you shares the same realisation your downfall will be inevitable. And so the system is maintained, isn't it? It's easy to project the problems of the world onto a minority few, those seeking their own ideas of fulfilment through the accumulation of massive wealth and political control, but then you support the very system which you say is corrupt by sending your child to the best school so that he can perform, prosper and be happy – in his shiny and respectable job. You do your best to give your child a head-start in the economic race. See how you have projected your idea of fulfilment onto your child? You are not concerned with helping your child be free of his or her own conditioning, instead you are concerned that he be qualified, respectable, upstanding and socially acceptable. You demand that he conform to your ideals and beliefs, you turn him into an object of your own vanity. And then you assert that something needs to be done about the millions starving in Africa, when it is you who is upholding the current system. Our ideas of respectability and success are all phoney. Your hypocrisy blinds you, but you'll only see it once you feel a guarantee that all will be secure, or that your family can stop struggling. Your fear dictates your action and then you wonder why there is no peace or justice in this world.

It does not matter how successful one becomes in terms of money, power, status or fame; if our minds remain immature we will always want more, as is the case for many of the world's richest people. The more we accumulate, the starker the contrast between our outer riches and our inner poverty becomes, and the starker is our discontinuous feeling of satisfaction. When we are rich we can see our inner feeling of dissatisfaction much more clearly than before. Reality is stark for the rich man who, having 'made it' financially and accumulated all there is that can be accumulated on the outside, can easily see just how poorly his inner consciousness has developed. A great vacuum appears. In the words of the Bible, Man cannot live by bread alone. Material wealth can never bring fulfilment.

Consider the wealthy businessman. In the process of 'making it', the ambitious man delayed his happiness for a future moment of happiness he believed would be his, once his goals were achieved. Only now, once he has arrived, does he fully realise that the destination is not what he hoped it would be; so poor is his sense of fulfilment at the destination that now he says the journey was the best part. Look at the absurdity of the statement above; the journey was time that he sacrificed – in a period of distraction from the present moment – for the illusion of satisfaction in a future moment. The rich man is declaring that the interval of time during which he sacrificed his whole life in the past, in exchange for happiness in the future, was actually the best part. This is ridiculous! Even with the benefit of hindsight, few of the most ambitious and outwardly successful people realise the extent of their own delusion. Ambition occurs when you are dissatisfied with the present moment; to say that an ambitious period of dissatisfaction was your greatest period of satisfaction only demonstrates the extent of the delusion.

Attachment to Desire

> Sutra 347: "O slave of desire float upon the stream. Little spider, stick to your web. Or else abandon your sorrows for the way."
> *Buddha*

IF WE DESIRE WEALTH AND turn our attention to this with single focus, there is a good possibility that we will achieve it. Recognise though that in doing this we will be spinning a web for ourselves, a web based on the projected desires of what we think wealth will bring us. This web can trap us as we become consumed by our projections, always looking to the future and dreaming of what the future may bring. We may indeed look to the future or look to the past but in doing so we are trapping ourselves with projections and conditions for happiness of our own making; rarely is attention present in the here and now. We do this because we are looking outside of ourselves for fulfilment.

According to the square box principle, we make statements such as *"When I turn the corner and I attain Object A,"* (for example, a new car) *"Then I will be happy."* In the process of making this kind of mental statement to ourselves we are doing two things. Firstly, we are denying happiness now for future happiness at a later stage. We are stepping away from the moment of Now (which is blissful) to delay our sense of happiness at a later stage. We are blinded by the illusion of fulfilment through the acquisition or attainment of certain things, like owning consumer Object A. What we are in effect doing is cutting ourselves off from our connection with the state of Being in exchange for attachment to an illusion, such as the idea that Object A will bring us fulfilment. So in effect we are distracted from real fulfilment now for the idea of fulfilment in the future. Absurd, isn't it?

Secondly, we have externalised our happiness onto object A in a specific moment in time. Object A has become an ideal, distorted because of the emphasis we place on acquiring it in order to be happy. We are setting ourselves up for frustration through our striving for Object A – we may not even be successful acquiring it and thus we feel a sense of disappointment, or if we do manage to acquire Object A, we will be disappointed because in our desire for it we have blown its attributes out of proportion. Our desire has distorted what satisfaction we think Object A will give us, and the actual satisfaction attained cannot match up. At best Object A gives us a kind of fleeting, transient pleasure; far removed from the notion of permanent pleasure that we had built up in our minds. Because the ego is constantly looking for new and better sensations, it is not long before we start to desire a new object – Object B. You will know this from your own life experience.

Look into yourself. When you reach your goal, you may enjoy it for a while but that 'while' never lasts long. Soon you feel as arid as you did before achieving your mind's desire; in fact in many cases you now feel even worse, as is so often the case for the rich man. At least when your mind had something to do, something to strive for, then it was occupied and therefore distracted from the empty inner state which it so violently fears. The earlier drive for satisfactory sensation helped to mask your inner emptiness; now you have achieved your previous desires and you feel lost because your mind is no longer occupied and distracted. The inner emptiness, now unmasked, is much closer and much more noticeable, which makes you uncomfortable.

In response, your mind starts seeking a new sensation. It is reacting, and in reaction the mind is never truly free. The mind can rest for a while, but the nature of the mind is that it always wants to be occupied, to mask that inner emptiness so feared by the ego. Observe this in yourself. We cannot go on holiday without our newspapers, books and magazines. At home it does not take long for us to take new possessions for granted; this is because the mind always seeks occupation. It seeks occupation to escape inner emptiness; an inner emptiness that it has named, termed and labelled and therefore does not understand.

Possession and the accumulation of material wealth have their own intrinsic problems. We are never satisfied with all of the many things that we own – our home, the car, the wardrobe full of clothes – so we constantly try to improve them or change them. Despite not being satisfied, we also form attachments to our possessions. We crave and cling in the same moment, which makes no sense at all; in between our clinging for what we have and our craving for what we don't, we remain unhappy and unsatisfied. Most of our time is taken up in striving for objects of desire and then becoming attached to what we own. Our satisfaction with possessions is short lived and our gratitude brief; it is not long before we slip back into desire. We worry about losing or damaging our assets, we worry about maintaining a certain standard of living. In our worry and attachment we fail to realise that the items that we possess, or the lifestyles that we lead, are in fact possessing us. If we draw our sense of happiness from owning certain assets or living a certain lifestyle, then the assets to which we have become attached, or the lifestyle to which we have become accustomed, will eventually imprison us. We have become attached to our desires. We are clinging to what we have and yet still desire what we don't. This is the process of self-imprisonment, of karma. Our desires and attachment to material wealth have become so prominent in modern society that in 2008, when faced with two wars in the Middle East (where thousands have lost – and continue to lose – their lives), the voters of the American presidential election chose the economy as their top election priority, rather than taking the opportunity to reach out to the world in love, compassion and peace. This is the web we have spun for ourselves, as described by Buddha in Sutra 347 above.

Think carefully about what grasping does to you. Does it make you dull or sensitive? Does it widen or narrow your attention? Think about the moment leading up to a purchase; does the anticipation bring you a sense of freedom or do you feel that you will be upset if you do not acquire the object of your desire? We grasp and crave external objects thinking that they will provide lasting satisfaction, yet any satisfaction we gain is only ever short-lived. All we have done is to create idols in our minds; we have lost all sense of proportion. A deeper understanding of the nature of craving or, more specifically, of the entity that craves (that being you and the nature of your identifications) is a far better way to release ourselves from the trap of craving. Cravings, like addictions, can take us over, thus narrowing our attention. We can easily distort the object of our desire, blowing out of all proportion the attractiveness of this piece of jewellery or that person who we have become infatuated with. Such an object or person can never live up to the dreams or expectations that we place on them; expectations that are no more than an image we have created in our minds. We are fooling ourselves because our desiring mind has prevented us from seeing the real truth; we are no longer aware of the true nature of the object of our desire, or of desire itself. Desire exists only in relation to something. That something may change but desire is still the same. There is only one desire, though in its different manifestations and objects it may appear to multiply, even contradict itself. This singular desire is you; it is not separate from you. What you see will always be your version of what you see; an idea of your own creation, not what is truly seen. You are seeing only what you wish to see, you are hearing only what you would like to hear. The truth of 'what is' has not changed, only your perception has changed. Disappointment and self-deception are therefore inevitable.

Understand this about desire: what is desired may vary, but desire itself is always the same. The nature of desire never changes. There may be a sensation that you want satisfied – maybe you fancy an ice cream, and through your efforts you find an ice-cream man and the craving is satisfied. Then you move on to the next sensation that you want satisfied. Desire itself has not changed, only what is desired changes. It does not matter what sensation is satisfied, the nature of the mind is a state of constant dissatisfaction. The nature of the mind is the search for novelty, the nature of the mind is to desire. The mind likes to stay occupied and desire is the perfect mechanism for it to stay occupied, because desire can never be fulfilled. Desire is the continuity mechanism of the ego, and is inherent to selfhood. Look at your life. Whenever you attain a desired sensation, very soon you have a new set of goals, you desire a different sensation and the process starts all over again. What is desired may have changed but the nature of desire is still the same. It is very important that we understand this.

Understand that the more assets you own, the more likely it is that you will become possessed by them. Meanwhile those who are not wealthy are often 'possessed' with the need to become wealthy. If it is not wealth it may be something else – the desire to be holy, the desire to be an important scientist, the desire for recognition – whatever form it takes, it is still desire and it still spins a web to trap us. To be happy is to be happy Now, without cause or condition. So drop all desire projections and drop all dreams of the future, these are not helping you. If you chase the objects of your desire you will end up continuously dissatisfied, and if you examine your life carefully you will find that this is how you have spent most of your time: dissatisfied and frustrated. And isn't hate a form of frustration? Don't we become aggressive when thwarted? Unless this cycle is understood, a vicious circle of continuous, difficult-to-pinpoint dissatisfaction will continue until your dying day. Desire and fulfilment do not sit together; desire and frustration on the other hand most certainly do. Your liberation comes when these relationships are deeply understood. To be truly fulfilled, understand desire. With understanding, desire will dissolve effortlessly without you having to take any action. No webs, nothing to trap you, all effortless.

Continuous Dissatisfaction

WE LIVE EITHER IN GRATITUDE or in desire. If we are in desire, then how grateful are we for what already is? To desire is to state that we are dissatisfied with the present moment, that there is something missing that we seek to fill, that there is a source of discomfort within us that we wish to ease. You desire only when you are not fulfilled. How then can desire ever be fulfilled? Can we really fulfil our desires, or is this against the nature of the concept of desire within Truth? Let's find out.

If you observe desire you will see that it always remains unfulfilled. Desire cannot be fulfilled; it has never been fulfilled in the past, it will never be fulfilled now nor will it ever be fulfilled in the future. No desire has ever been truly satisfied, for it is in the definition of desire that there can be no fulfilment; not being fulfilled is part of the intrinsic nature of desire. Desire IS when fulfilment IS NOT. How can you fulfil that which is defined by the concept of not being fulfilled in the present moment? How can you fulfil that which is defined by the concept of dissatisfaction with the present moment, where this dissatisfaction is continuous? Now if desire IS when fulfilment IS NOT, then we can also say that fulfilment IS when desire IS NOT. You are fulfilled only when not desiring. Fulfilment is not the satisfaction of desire because no desire has ever been satisfied, fulfilment IS only when desire is not; this is the nature of fulfilment. We have seen that the drive for fulfilment is rooted in our fear of isolation (Chapter 5, *Your True Nature*), but we can also understand fulfilment in relation to desire. Fulfilment is complete and total satisfaction with the present moment, it is to be completely and utterly content here and now. In such a moment – in the bliss of the present – there is no desire. So desire and fulfilment cannot be together at the same time, there is either one or the other. But we don't see this, and we think that desire leads to fulfilment. Because of our identifications with certain sensations (our desires), so begins the duality of the observer and the observed, the experiencer and the experienced. This duality acts as a filter, clouding our ability to see what IS with any clarity. We think that desire leads to fulfilment because we cannot see desire clearly. Because of our identifications, which create the observer / observed duality, we are caught up in the whole process of the ego and we do not appreciate how there is fundamentally no seer, no 'I', no 'you', no 'observer'; that there is only seeing, only observation. Cast your mind back to our earlier discussion of anger and the way in which we identify with anger. It is the same with desire. Anger will never change, nor will desire; it is how we interact and identify that can change. A mind caught up in the illusion of duality thinks that desire is somehow the same and also separate from the 'I' and that the 'I' can do something about that desire. In Truth, however, there is no separation for the observer is the observed. There is no 'you' separate from desire, there is only desire. There can only be fulfilment when this has been understood.

We are each capable of seeing the intrinsic nature of the entity that is desire, but most of us do not appreciate the gift of seeing. We choose not to see ourselves as the actor of choice or preference, instead we sacrifice our whole lives trying to fulfil our desires. We scrimp and save for the home of our dreams, we want to own this house, nothing else matters and we pour all of our energy into acquiring it; we put our lives on hold in the name of this desire. When we finally purchase the house, the process does not end there. We then spend years decorating it and filling it with nice furniture and furnishings. When we finally finish, how long does the satisfaction stay with us before that empty, unsettling feeling of looking for an unknown something returns? After a year or two you want a new house, a better house and so the treadmill starts all over again. Soon we are looking for our next occupation as we slave inside the continuity mechanism of the ego, busy little bees working to keep the ego occupied so that we do not feel lost, so that we do not have to face the misunderstood emptiness within. Please do not misunderstand what is being said here. We are not advising against having a home or making it pleasant, we are saying it is how you *perceive* this home and in what way you understand the reason *why* you desire that home that determines your freedom. If you think that meeting your desires will bring you to fulfilment, then you will never be free. If you are in desire, then you will stay trapped, desiring. Nothing will change because desire will never be fulfilled; desire will remain as desire.

Desire: Accept or Reject?

REALISE THAT IF YOU DESIRE then you will always remain unfulfilled. See its hollow nature and see how futile it is to follow it blindly. In such a realisation, desire begins to dissolve as the primary driving force of your life. When you understand that desire will never satisfy you, that it will always remain unfulfilled, only then will you transcend it. You cannot transcend desire through suppression, denial or distraction; only through understanding. You gain awareness and thus understanding of desire neither by accepting nor rejecting desire, but by merely observing the process that drives it, which is the self. If you remain a watcher of this process, somehow separate and distinct, if you are no longer cooperating with desire and have disengaged, then there is still a seeker who seeks. Desire has simply transfigured. See how cunning the mind is at creating new occupations for itself. The mind is once again looking to achieve. It is the instrument of its own choosing and is self-censoring; it is caught in its own net of thought. To disengage is a choice. You cannot choose not to desire for choice itself is desire. Desire cannot cease through effort, for if you are seeking, censoring, willing something to happen, then desire is still pedalling. You cannot bring about the ending of desire through will or action. All will and action must cease. Without the action of will, the maker of effort, the self is not and the timeless comes into being. Observation alone is enough.

Repression or denial, as practised by certain ascetics, never weeds out the root of desire. You cannot be transformed if you repress, you may become an ascetic but still your dreams and hopes of fulfilment remain. If you try to repress desire, then you have cooperated with desire and the problem of desire is still there, only now in a different form. Desire has turned into denial and repression, which are another form of desire – desire for the outcome of what happens when you no longer desire. You are still fighting with your desire and this battle is a conflict which reinforces the ego. Strict ascetic practice fails to address this problem. Suppression, repression and denial indicate positively that your desires still possess you; it may not look that way but your desire is simply turned on its head. You are still in conflict and contradiction, and no happiness is ever found through inner conflict.

Across the ages many have tried to overcome desire through distraction, suppression or conquering in the hope of breaking free of it, but such activity can only ever lead to frustration and sorrow. Remember that all distractions, suppressions or attempts to conquer desire are themselves forms of desire of another kind. You only undertake such measures because of the future satisfaction that you think such activities will bring you. So to desire the ending of desire is nothing but absurd, reinforcing the very process – the very continuity mechanism of ego – that needs to cease. Likewise if you accept desire, you will forever be chasing a pot of gold at the base of a rainbow as you indulge in one desire, become unsatisfied, and then indulge in the next. Your desires and hopes will always be projected in front of you, and if you run towards that future, then you are running towards a rainbow on the horizon. No matter how fast you run, you will never catch it and genuine fulfilment will always remain beyond your reach.

Inner Integrity

AS WE KEEP EMPHASISING, WE cannot be free of the trappings of desire if we do not understand desire. By simply observing desire, looking into the causes or the problems of desire and watching what desire is actually constructed of, we gain potential insight into freedom. Desire is a movement, a process, a continuity of thought that is attached to the craving for experience. Break that continuity and desire ceases because desire cannot exist without the presence of continuous thought. But you cannot break that continuity of thought through action because such action itself is the reaction to thought by thought. All thought must cease, but you cannot tell thought to cease because that would be thought controlling thought. Simply watch the movements of thought. Observe desire without view, judgement or identification and then the nature of desire will reveal itself to you. Above all be true to yourself, open and honest in your observations. Notice if you are looking for something in what you are doing; admit if there is an objective or a goal in your watching. If you find that in your observation you are hoping for some kind of achievement, then you are not simply watching and are instead still engaged, even at a subtle level. Are you controlling yourself, are you back in the realms of the controller and the controlled? If you are controlling, even if just a tiny bit, be ruthlessly honest with yourself; something is wrong and more understanding is needed.

For example: you can disengage, you can no longer cooperate with your desire and if you catch it early enough its power will dissolve without much effort. It is much easier not to engage whilst desire remains a flicker in one's mind, but is this genuine understanding of desire? The action of choosing not to co-operate is still action. Any kind of choice is an action. What is not an action is when choice is not and awareness is choiceless, when awareness is aware without choice in any direction. (We will come back to a more detailed understanding of choiceless awareness later.) Now if there is action, then there is still a conflict and thus tension – however small and however controlled. Lose mindfulness and this little flame of desire can flare up into an uncontrollable fire that fully consumes you, causing you to behave unconsciously. Is this the complete understanding of desire or is this the suppression of desire, putting it aside without truly understanding it? This is what many gurus teach, but it is still choice and if there is choice involved then their teaching is mistaken. Catching desire early is still suppression, it is simply suppression that is quick off the mark and thus a little easier to achieve. It is no use catching desire early, thinking that this is what is implied in the understanding of desire. The problem is still there, albeit in a more subtle way. Your observation will only ever be astute in this way if you are deeply honest with yourself.

Where there is this inner integrity you will never go astray, for with integrity comes freedom. Freedom, joy and integrity come hand in hand. Only by asking yourself why you desire, and being brutally honest with yourself, will you ever be free. With integrity, you will realise that if you have an idea in your mind as to what will bring you fulfilment then you have already decided what it is that you are seeking. And if you have chosen in this way then you have already stepped back into desire, you have already stimulated a movement of thought or an action. What is required is a complete break from all action. When you are deeply honest, you will notice that you seek fulfilment through the attaining or receiving of a certain thing, through an action to gain in some way. Either you must gain, or you strive to efface yourself with a view to gain by stripping away layers of the ego. You desire because you lack humility and you lack humility because you are not being honest with yourself. You desire because your mind is immature, your mind is caught up in the idea of gain. Why is gain so important? What is wrong with what already is? The mature mind, free from desire, sees and is grateful for what IS. All of this relates to an inner issue of insecurity and lack of self-love and forgiveness, as you exchange clarity and gratitude for your ideal of 'what should be'. You are seeking fulfilment in the first place because you do not love and accept yourself for what you are, right now. It is the seeking of fulfilment based upon a lack of self-love, causing the conflict of change that is the very process of desire. You are seeking fulfilment, without realising that fulfilment is beyond seeking. With integrity and clarity you can understand this, and come to realise that fulfilment IS when desire IS NOT.

Watch desire with integrity and humility and then desire will drop of its own accord. Nothing else is needed. Let go of these false hopes of happiness and your far-off focus will automatically dissolve as your attention returns to the here and now. Now you are free from the self-imposed cages that you have built for yourself as criteria for happiness. You have broken away from the misguided idea of conditional happiness; the usual *'I must be this,'* or *'I must have that.'* Freedom and joy are without condition. Freedom – and thus joy – has always been right here next to you, but you have been too busy looking for it in scriptures or in books, chasing your desires or getting caught up in systems. See that your search for fulfilment is itself just another desire distracting you from the present moment; see the whole notion of looking for fulfilment to be the nonsense that it is. If you are looking for fulfilment, you will never be fulfilled. Fulfilment IS when you no longer look for it. In releasing the search, you realise that the future is not real, that it is a concept in your mind. You realise that the future is a concept made up of your desires, your fears, your projections and your aversions. In this moment of clarity, all of your desires will dissolve completely and in this moment there is genuine freedom away from this great illusion that we all hold, the apparent freedom of choice of the self.

chapter 11

Desire: A Deeper Look

Continuity & Freedom

NOW WE ARE BEGINNING TO understand why we desire and we have a greater understanding of who or what is the entity that actually desires; all part of our greater understanding of the process of the self. To reiterate what has been said: when we like a sensation our mind decides that it wants more and so there is will behind our action to seek the favoured sensation again. When there is this craving for further sensation, sensation and thought are working hand in hand, attached together. This movement of thought towards satisfying the favoured sensation is desire. What is desired may be satisfied, at least momentarily, but – as we saw in the previous chapter – desire itself is never satisfied. Desire IS when fulfilment is not; we desire because we are not fulfilled, and all of this is the action of the ego. It is the ego that desires and the very nature of ego is that it cannot be fulfilled, which is why we describe the ego as introjected desire. To be fulfilled is to be utterly content here and now, but the ego is never present in the here and now, it is instead caught up in psychological time in its distracting identifications, memories, dreams, hopes and projections. Why?

It is the inherent wish of the ego to escape from the present moment because the present moment is the only moment when the ego is not. The ego may seek fulfilment, but it is only in the present moment – which the ego cannot ever know and in which the ego cannot exist – that there is fulfilment. Thought does not see this, what it sees is that it must always defend itself against the moment of its own ending. It thus takes shape as the ego and fights to survive, and that means avoiding the present moment of here and now by busying itself with activities. In the present moment there is the ending of both attachment to the past and desire for the future, and this equates to the ending of the ego. This is why the ego mind asserts that the present moment is never enough – because it is afraid for its own continuity, and because thought has misunderstood true fulfilment.

The ego mind is caught up in wanting *more*; distracted by this idea there is thus no authentic gratitude or fulfilment. True gratitude, like joy, is not a condition in which the analyser is separate from the thing he analyses, declaring himself to be grateful (or joyful). True gratitude only is when thought realises that the analyser and analysed are together, that they are one. There is just pure gratitude – no sense of 'I am grateful'. So when we say 'a mind that is not grateful cannot be fulfilled', we are referring to the ground state of pure gratitude and nothing else. But we don't know this state, we only know 'I am grateful' with the analyser and analysed as separate entities; grateful for X, Y or Z as a state of psychological satisfaction. What is clear is that the mind is still caught up in the illusions of X, Y or Z; illusions of fulfilment that actually cause the mind to desire in the first place. We get caught up in our own psychological time; ideas of past and future. There is thus no real or authentic present moment awareness of 'what is' with any great clarity. The mind's understanding of fulfilment is distracted and blurred by chasing after its desires; desires which are all created, sustained and nourished by the very same mind. All attention is therefore distracted and fragmented. The ego mind is caught in its own cycle and there is illusion and deception in this cycle. In the book *Question Mark* we discussed seeing 'what is' with clarity – what is known as Vipassana – as the way of freedom. The way of freedom is seeing the 'what is', or exactness, of desire and fulfilment as they actually are. Fulfilment is when desire is not; and if desire is constructed of thought that has taken shape as the ego, then fulfilment must be when the ego is not. *Fulfilment is a non-ego state.* There is no such thing as a mind that is aware of its own fulfilment, in the same way that there is no such thing as a mind aware of its own freedom. A mind that thinks like this cannot ever be free; it can trick itself into believing that it is free, but that of course is only a self-deception. It is only the ego mind that is not fulfilled, only the ego mind that truly desires.

This brings us to a discussion about the true nature of the continuity mechanism of the ego. Thought thinks about a sensation – for example, the taste of chocolate or ice cream – and the mind decides that it wants it. Once this sensation – the taste of chocolate, or whatever – is attained, the mind turns its attention to the next sensation and so craving starts all over again. Who or what is making these decisions about what thought, or ego, wants in this process of desire? The 'decider' – or the experiencer or thinker – is the aspect of thought that you think of as 'you'. This aspect of thought has taken it upon itself to create a sense of permanence in a world of impermanence – that being a world of arising and falling sensation and a world of arising and falling thought. Why? This aspect of thought is trying to create for itself the notion of continuity in the form of a permanent thinker because it sees the inherent transience of its own nature, and what is transient is considered uncertain. The ego is trying to make itself permanent because it sees that its own nature – as a process rather than a thing – is actually impermanent. Can you see what is happening? This is the continuity mechanism of your ego, trying tooth and nail to make itself more permanent with more momentum, for it has no other choice but to do this. It is seeking security through permanence and defending itself against its own ending. It sees the present moment not as the moment of fulfilment but as the moment of its own ending, and so it desires in order to create psychological time, keep attention distracted and therefore fragmented. This is very different from the holistic engagement of pure awareness with the present moment. The present moment is pure awareness; thought is time. Do please think this out for yourself. All thought arises and falls and so without permanence, what is there? If life is a realm of endless arising and falling sensation, then unless some form of continuity is introduced into the equation there is no constancy anywhere for a permanent thinker to exist. Without this continuity mechanism, the ego would not be able to exist in the way that it does.

Selfhood requires a degree of permanence otherwise we might as well have the memory of a goldfish. The self requires memories, tastes, preferences and so on – a minimum level of identification – for it to function as an independent aspect of consciousness. Unless an aspect of thought – that being the thinker or the experiencer which we call the ego self – sets about creating some form of continuity, then the ego cannot exist, for all thought arises and falls. The ego is an aspect of thought within consciousness that has created a degree of continuity and permanence for itself. If it did not do this, if there was not a minimum level of identification taking place, then the ego simply could not function and it would cease to be. Without some form of continuity or permanent thinker, you would live in a perpetual moment of Now without any reference to memory. Nor would the psychological future exist because, without memory, it could not be constructed as thought. On a practical level in our day to day lives, things would grind to a halt; you would not be able to meet someone tomorrow for a coffee; you couldn't make or keep appointments. So clearly there is a minimum level of choice and identification undertaken by the ego for the ego to function; this is the stuff of basic necessity.

Of course where there is necessity there is no choice, but we can deal with this. We each understand that for us to be alive today to even question the world, certain necessities and choices must be taken, or must have been taken already. We can rationalise basic survival function and put it in its place. But a lot of what the ego does is beyond basic necessity. Desiring luxury consumer goods is not a necessity, and nor is dreaming of success or living through an image of oneself. A minimum level of identification may be necessary for a pragmatic life, but not the lengths we go to in order to assert our ego selves. The ego may like to create a legacy for itself by leaving a mark in history, or in genetic history (which is what most of us do), or the ego may like its identifications to be reinforced by adoration or praise. Whatever it is – and it can come out in a million different ways – the key point is this: an entity that is trying to make itself permanent through choosing to seek constant sensation in order to maintain its own momentum, is not really exercising freedom of choice. If the ego is making choices in accordance to its desire to maintain itself and reinforce its own momentum, then how free are those choices really? If the direction of your choice is determined by your ego, and the ego is always wanting and desiring the same, fundamental thing (self-preservation and security), then there is no freedom in your choice.

The fundamental desire of the ego is self-preservation and this can range from the subtle to the overt. We need to know the nature of this process, inside out, if we are to be free. We must understand what IS when the ego is not; the ending of all judgment, condemnation, identification and all the rest that comes with ego, particularly choice. In this understanding we can step beyond all of the usual conflicts and contradictions that blur our vision of reality, bringing us greater clarity of understanding. This Buddha recognised in his Noble Truths. He said that there is a degree of imprisonment, and therefore suffering, that is inherent for all aspects of consciousness, which we call the ego self. There is no such thing as freedom and therefore joy (which is fulfilment and the ending of desire) until the non-ego state; this is the death or ending of the ego. This happens in total and complete awareness, in what some masters call emptiness, where there is joy, freedom and space without boundary. In this emptiness there is nothing but pure attention – no choosing, no direction, just total freedom. This emptiness is positive because there is total joy, bliss and abandon. Until then you will desire, albeit overtly or subtly. What we are discussing here are the desires which arise from the ego in order to prevent its annihilation. When these desires end – through the understanding of their very structure – so does the ego, and it is to be expected that the ego will always wish to avoid whatever threatens its security. The ego will always create movement against anything that threatens its own momentum.

So any action, any choice dictated by the ego for the purpose of preserving the ego, is not freedom, it is slavery. Look at it clearly, this is what is happening. The choice of the ego is not freedom nor is the search for fulfilment free if we do not understand the nature of fulfilment. This search is desire; if we are caught up in illusions as to what fulfilment is, then the apparently 'free' choices undertaken are based upon illusions and delusions. How then can we say that our choice is truly free? To have 'free will' – and we mean to be really free – we must understand what drives every aspect of the process of the ego; our desire, our will, our fear, our identifications. This includes the understanding of these aspects' shape, source and determinants. We must regularly question whether our desires can ever be fulfilled. Can we be fulfilled through desire or is fulfilment 'what is' when we no longer desire? We must question whether there is such a thing as fulfilment that is the product of the mind, or is fulfilment something that is beyond the mind? These are the questions we have been discussing in the preceding chapters, and they are questions which I recommend you return to every now and then, particularly if you feel that life can get a little off balance. Now we will take our analysis a little deeper, into what happens when there is the death of the ego.

Cause or No Cause, that is the Question

THERE IS NO SUCH THING as fulfilment that belongs to the mind; the ego mind is never fulfilled, and it is from what is not fulfilled that desire arises. Of course there can be gratitude or happiness in the feeling of completion, but understand that these are emotional or psychological characteristics that come with fulfilment, they are not causes of fulfilment. Authentic fulfilment can never be caused, it can only ever be uncaused, just as authentic joy and freedom are uncaused. To be authentic they must be lasting and free of dependence. If your joy or your freedom is caused and you remove the cause, then you lose your joy or your freedom. Now if this is the case, was your joy or your freedom authentic? That which is conditional is not truly free or authentic. We have seen that joy and freedom are the same, and we know that they are only true and authentic when there is no dependency. They must be without cause, without origin. Think about it: how can freedom be dependent upon anything? Absurd! If freedom was dependent upon something then it would not be freedom. Freedom can only be freedom if it is not dependent upon anything. Freedom can only ever be total, whole, indivisible; never partial. Freedom can only ever be dependent on the absence of dependency[1].

This also applies to fulfilment; it is not the product of thought because any fulfilment arising from thought – such as the feeling of satisfaction derived when a particular desired sensation is momentarily achieved – would be caused and therefore not authentic. All projections distract the mind away from the present moment of here and now – where we understand there to be fulfilment – to desires which exist in some future moment in time. The pursuit of a projection is a form of self-worship and in the worship of oneself, truth cannot be. We are ignorant of authentic fulfilment; we think fulfilment has a cause. This is, of course, a projection of self and so it must be enclosing in its very nature. Remember that fulfilment, like joy and

---

[1] This is one of the universe's strange little paradoxes.

freedom, has no cause; it must be independent of all projections. It rests only within Being and Being simply IS in the present moment. This Being is always uncaused; it is beyond effort, beyond volition. In effort there is agitation not tranquillity. Effort denies understanding. Effort creates a path, which then makes Truth exclusive. Truth is non-exclusive and it cannot be divided.

You only notice the desire to be fulfilled when there is the sensation that something inside is missing. What needs to be fulfilled? Something is missing and you are seeking to fill it. You desire a chocolate cake, you desire a car or a house, you desire to stay occupied. If you investigate this sensation, if you look into yourself with honesty, you will see that you only seek fulfilment when you sense a form of incompleteness inside. There is this void, this stark inner empty feeling and you are seeking to fill it. Remember the inner, empty, incomplete state discussed in the chapter, 'Your True Nature'; it is consciousness of the self without activity. Is that not loneliness? So fundamentally we desire in order to escape our inner feeling of loneliness. This insight into understanding desire leads us to investigate why we make moves to escape our feelings of inner loneliness. We are getting closer to the real root of desire and, in this new understanding, closer to the essence of what Buddha is saying.

We may temporarily fill this loneliness with one sensation or another, but as soon as the sensation ends, the lonely incomplete state returns. Naturally we want to return to the sensation that we like – the cake, the chocolate, a cigarette, alcohol or sex; you know all of the addictions that we each have. The lonely inner state is a creation of the mind because the mind misunderstands the fundamental truth of Being; the truth of its empty awareness and the freedom that is that awareness. The mind is scared of inner Being because inner Being is not of the mind. The mind does not understand this pure inner emptiness and, because it misunderstands, it is forever running away from it. In reaction to its ignorance, it forms ideas about it and then calls it 'loneliness'. It then tries to seek fulfilment through various pleasures in an attempt to create continuous sensation to cover up this inner loneliness. This is what is really happening. We desire because there is a root fear of ego annihilation and loneliness; we desire for the sake of ego continuity and preoccupation. You can say that we desire because we are bored or indifferent or curious or whatever, but at the root lie these twin fears of ego annihilation and loneliness. We desire because we are ignorant of what it is to just Be.

As we have seen earlier, the path of the ego is always isolating in nature. The drive towards our idea of fulfilment is an isolating process as we go about seeking our own unique ideas of fulfilment, thus separating ourselves from others. This is why marriages break apart and relationships fail; we each go about our search for fulfilment in our own unique way because what our egos desire can only ever be different. These ego-led desires may be the same for a while but they are rarely the same years into the future. If you can live freely where there is the ending of ego then all relationships work, but if you are caught up in only seeking satisfaction in accordance to the desires of your ego, then your relationships are more likely to break down. Most relationships fail because one or both partners' egos strive to dominate, and thus cause separation.

Your ego wants pleasure, my ego wants security and so it possesses, it gets jealous; this is separating in nature. Your ego tries to achieve, it lays down criteria for fulfilment and where there are criteria for fulfilment then you are locked up inside the notion of conditional happiness, and your own desires. This is an isolating process because you are driven by your own conditions and thus your own motivations. Think about how potentially isolated you could become in the future, all in the name of an idea of fulfilment which you carry in your mind (and which we know can only ever be illusory). This is what happens if you have not deeply understood how isolating the process of the ego really can be, if you let the desires of your ego go unbridled. The conditions you set for yourself, the ambition, the 'what should be' of the ego at whatever level, make up an unforgiving, remorseless and mercilessly separating force.

The misunderstanding lies in the failure by thought to see that fulfilment through action is an illusion and that the ego exists in that action; that the conflict towards 'what should be' is the very basis of the ego. The more we strive to be fulfilled, the more the ego feels lonely and thus the more isolated it becomes; the problem is aggravated.

Greater isolation induces even greater efforts to seek fulfilment, and so the cycle continues. There is no genuine fulfilment that is the product of the mind because fulfilment is when desire is not; fulfilment is when the mind is not. Fulfilment is Being and Being is not understood by the mind. Being is 'no mind'.

The self, the 'I', may think that it is fulfilled in a transitory moment, but when that moment has passed there is always the drive for the next source of fulfilment. The very fact that it is looking for the next fulfilment means that thought has misunderstood what fulfilment is. If we are still busy looking for the next thing, chasing horizons, then we are not really fulfilled. For a brief moment we may feel fulfilled, there may be the abandonment of the self in pleasure for a few seconds or even a few minutes, there may be the stepping into pleasure sensation and feeling lost within that sensation for a brief interval (the feeling of being nowhere and everywhere, where there is no centre); there may indeed be this stepping into Being, but then it will pass as thought kicks back in. Once this happens, we are back once again to chasing our next feeling of bliss.

We don't see this bliss as the abandonment of the self, we don't see that the self only exists inside the conflict to change; instead we see fulfilment as something that can be achieved permanently through action. We believe that, if we struggle enough, there can be permanent satisfaction of whatever the mind has decided will make us feel fulfilled. But the mind can never fulfil, only the heart fulfils because the heart is already fulfilled. Seeking fulfilment through a product of your thought can continue for the rest of your life. All such activity is a continuing and self-isolating process of thought, where there is this sense of never feeling quite complete. We always want more and the perpetual dissatisfaction always remains, never fulfilled. As any addict will attest, we are left chasing this sense of completeness, which the mind in its reaction to sensation can never bring.

Complete Sensation

WHAT IS THIS COMPLETENESS THAT we seek? It is the pinnacle of bliss and in that pinnacle there is the utter abandonment of the 'me'; there is the surrender and release of the self. There is the ending, the death, of the ego. Think of a sensation that feels nice; let's think of a sexual sensation as an example. Why does it feel nice? What is going on? When such a sensation is taken to its furthest reaches, to utter bliss and abandon, it can lead to the dissolving of the 'me', the melting of the 'me' into the bliss of existence, into nowhere and everywhere, into nirvana, into exponential orgasm. We are returning to a primordial state. Ultimately we desire to abandon the 'me' and return to a primordial state, because we want the total and utter bliss where there is no 'me'. As soon as thought enters and says, *'This is nice, this is pleasure,'* it has started to label and to remember, and then the bliss will cease. You have turned off the tap.

The 'me' is lonely, the 'me' is isolated and feels incomplete. It wishes to escape from this loneliness and incompleteness into wholeness. Wholeness is the absence of the 'me', but the ego does not want to see this because therein lies its own ending. So instead it seeks completeness or wholeness in the totality of the 'me' (in absolute power, absolute domination, and so forth), but this totality of the 'me' can never elicit an integrated state of being, it can only fragment. What gives strength to the 'me' is memory and where there is memory there is thought and that which thought thinks about; a thinker and its thought. This is psychological fragmentation, which is separation. The way of the 'me' is the way of isolation and its consequence is the striving for greater power to compensate that isolation. Any path undertaken in the name of the 'me' can only lead to what is not integrated, to what is psychologically broken up and therefore corrupt and sorrowful. Desire is the conscious movement of thought to find bliss, but is bliss even knowable by thought? Can the known ever find the unknown – thought being the known? And this search for bliss, the direction towards a gratifying external or internal sensation purports thought evermore; driving the very process of ego. This is the contradictory nature of ego; its apparent strength being actually weakness. Its very existence negates freedom. Our desire springs from a feeling of incompleteness, expressed in action towards the illusion of completeness in our mind. Desire is the movement, the conflict, the action to change, the effort, the controlling, the censoring, the choosing, the act of volition or will; it is our suppression or the domination towards 'what should be' (as we struggle to reach the ultimate pleasures, our desired bliss). The self is conflict; it is the struggle to become *more*. Conflict is the very process of the self. The self exists in this disorder and in this disorder there is immense suffering.

The absence of the 'me', on the other hand, is beauty, virtue, love and compassion. It is the very bliss of existence. Desire is the conscious movement of thought to find absolute bliss, but bliss rests in the non-ego state rather than in an ego state. In understanding and observing that the conflict towards 'what should be' is the disorder of the ego, there is the ending of effort; in seeing the truth of this fact there is the ending of our censoring and choosing, or our action of will to change or control. There is complete inaction. All conflict ceases and there is the ending of ego. When the ego is not, when there is inaction, there is freedom from desire and the beginning of bliss, contrary to the demands and motives of the ego. This inaction, or non-action, comes not as an action or a movement but from the stillness of observation; observation of this fact with clarity. It begins with non-identification. There can be freedom from desire but not freedom from *what* you desire. Freedom from what you desire is a reaction, an identification. Desire and identification *are* ego. Freedom *from* ... is a form of resistance. A mind conscious of being free from something is never free. There is a thinker analysing an idea of freedom, which can never *be* freedom. Freedom is when the thinker is not. When all search, all effort, struggle, will, censoring and choosing have come to an end.

Non-Identification

WHEN WE HAVE AN EXPERIENCING of a sensation and identify with it, we are observing and feeling the sensation in a distorted way. We tend to think that the sensation is the same as the observer but also somehow different from the observer, and so the dualism between the observer and observed comes into play. We know this identification process to be the essence of ego. The ego is the division between the observer and observed, and the conflict that ensues. When one can observe 'what is' as sensation without identifying with that sensation, like trying to be free of it or trying to subjugate it, then this dualism between the observer and observed comes to an end. Observing rather than identifying with sensation allows the ending of this dualism of its own accord, ending the ego. There is no separation, no division; the observer is the observed. Now there is the observation or feeling of sensation without identification with that sensation; there is only sensation and seeing the true nature of that sensation. In seeing its truth, there is freedom. This is the key to the ending of the 'me' and the suffering that accompanies it; in the non-identification with sensation there is the ending of the process of the self.

Let's present this again using different terminology. Desire is born out of the memory and/or association of the mind with pleasure sensation. The memory of pleasure and pain sustains and nourishes desire, or aversion. These memories may divide desire into different values, giving the impression of many forms of desire, but in reality there is only one desire. What you desire varies, but your relationship to these variations as desire is essentially the same. It is important to understand this otherwise you will forever chase these values, and think they are all different desires, according to your mood, taste or current preference. You may chase X and avoid Y in one moment and then avoid X and chase Y the next. You *are* these movements, many of which exist in opposing directions and all of which are based in conflict. The conflict towards 'what should be' at any and whatever level is you. What needs to be understood is the source of this conflict. This cannot be done as the observer observing the observed, since the observer *is* the observed. The analyser of desire is himself not separate from desire and he analyses in order to overcome and defeat desire; another form of desire. Understand that whenever there is desire, the conflict to change, this is not nor will it ever be separate from you. Then you won't be caught in the illusion of being able to defeat desire and you won't create another conflict for yourself. Instead, awareness of this truth as and when desire arises will bring about the natural dissolution of the will of the chooser, the censor, the maker of effort, which is the experiencer / thinker. When there is the realisation that the observer is the observed, the experiencer the experienced, the conflict of desire will cease.

The master key is to understand the nature of the identification process with sensation. It is to understand that when you are caught up in your desire for more, then there is not the seeing or the feeling or the hearing of 'what is' in the here and now. In desire and identification there is only partial attention to what is happening because the mind is split up in the contradiction between 'what is' and 'what should be'; there is not total sensitivity to what is happening in the present moment. When you are no longer caught up in desire, in the idea of 'more', then there can be awareness of 'what is' rather than conscious identification with 'more'. It is then possible for there to be the complete and total attention of the senses in the present moment. And in the observation of sensation, without identification with that sensation, there is the seeing of it as it actually is. In seeing the essence of a thing, there is freedom. What we are discussing is not attention with a thinker at the centre interpreting the sensation and thus forming reactions, this is instead pure awareness of sensation, with no thinker at all. In this non-identification with sensation there is the ending of the process of the self and in the ending of the self there is only sensation; there is thus no desire for sensation nor for ideas of 'more', there is only sensation. If we can simply observe, where there is only sensation, only sensitivity and nothing else, then there can be complete freedom. In this sensitivity of pure awareness we are able to unlock the door of reality.

> "If you touch one thing with deep awareness, you touch everything."
>
> *Thich Nhat Hanh*

So we are discussing complete sensitivity to everything where there is total attention and thus immense energy; where there is the feeling of sensation without a reaction to sensation in the form of identification such as a choice, prejudice or preference. Instead, there is only the holistic awareness of all the senses. In such holistic awareness there is sensitivity and this sensitivity can forever increase for it is limitless and there are absolutely no boundaries. We are discussing a moment where there can be awareness of sensation that is without effort, where there is complete sensitivity with your whole being as opposed to the need to choose or identify with a particular sensation. Such a choice or expression of preference – the identification process – requires directed attention and thus energy. The holistic sensitivity that we are discussing is a total break away from the mechanical identifications of the past. These past identifications have become so dull over time that we have responded to this dullness by desiring new sensations, always in the hope of breaking away from the indifference and insensitivity that we feel in relation to our regular, routine sensations. This is why we desire. We desire because we want to feel, we want to experience, we want sensitivity. Whereas if you look at how you feel, how you experience and the nature of your sensitivity, that is where your freedom lies.

Now sensitive, you are truly open to the new. Your meeting with reality rests within opening yourself to what is fresh and new. Reality is gentle like a flower; to open the door and meet with it, to feel the enormity of it, there must be equivalent gentleness, openness and sensitivity. There must be the complete, utter and total surrender of the self, which means the ending of all identification. This means total attention to all senses – not a scattered attention when there is an observer at the centre choosing, censoring, deciding and focusing attention, but a total attention where there is no centre and no self to choose and identify. There is only attention and awareness of the senses. All senses. This is true freedom. This is meditation.

True freedom is not found in the choices made by a centre, arising out of the conflict of the self. True freedom is the choicelessness when the self is not; it lies in the death of the self and the flowering of sensation, without thought entering into the fold. In complete union and relationship with the senses, in surrendering to them, releasing yourself to them, imbibing them and being them; in observing their ISness such that there is only sensitivity, all senses are alive, alert and awake. They are blossoming in a way that is beyond description in words. There is the total awakening and flowering of the senses into 'what is', into Truth, into the life force of all energy. There is the attention of all senses and one is awake, fully and joyfully consuming sensations.

There is total awareness of all that is in your vicinity, expanding outwards into existence itself. What we are discussing here is the bliss of meditation. In this bliss desire is not; desire is irrelevant. Understand therefore that the self does not find the bliss that we seek; bliss is a state the self cannot give. The self is ultimately preoccupied with returning to a state of bliss; all fragments of conscious awareness are being pulled and driven to return to what is not an ego-state, to what is existence. But this pull is grossly distorted by the conflict of the ego. The return to the bliss of existence is the driving force behind all aspects of consciousness; it is this bliss that has been called by many 'divine'.

Pure, clear attention is this life force. In the death of the self there is absolute attention, there is energy, there is life and love itself. In this choiceless attention (the choiceless awareness to which we referred earlier) whatsoever happens, happens. There is complete freedom, freedom from any direction (for direction is now irrelevant). There are no boundaries, limits or frontiers, there is only space; a vast, limitless space of blissful awareness. Freedom, and thus joy and fulfilment, IS when there is no longer identification, judgment or the act of choosing. This is so because all movements by the self in a direction can only fragment attention, lessen sensitivity and break down that great contact with existence. With this breakdown, in the movement of the self, your supply of bliss dissolves. You desire because you are not in bliss, so when in bliss there is no desire.

So desire[2] is the movement of the self towards greater bliss. This is what we are all doing or trying to do, is it not? Bliss, as we have established, is a non-ego state. How is it then that an ego state, a self, strives for a condition that is characteristic of a non-ego state, of what is not a self? Let us think through this apparent contradiction. The self is striving to be what is characteristic of what is not a self, but the self does not see or understand this and, in its misunderstanding, its activity is actually more separating, reinforcing and isolating. The self has misunderstood what fulfilment is, thinking that it is a product

---

[2] The etymology of the word desire means, 'without the stars / without the cosmos': meaning 'without the bliss of existence'.

of the mind. Now if you can understand this, then you have the key to understanding desire. There is a way of Being that is blissful and euphoric, and this Being is when the self is not, when mind or identification with sensation are not. This Being is the choiceless awareness of all sensation, which is a moment where there is no centre present that is recognising sensation as being separate in terms of the observer and observed, but where there is only sensation. This is central to understanding the kernel of what Buddha is saying. There is a way of Being that is blissful and euphoric and this Being is when the self is not.

Remember, if you force sensation to make it greater, better or louder, then there is an enforcer, a censor. There is a duality and sensitivity is lost. If you demand it, want it or need it, your sensitivity with reality is cut. Sensitivity is not something that arises from choice, sensitivity arises from what is choiceless and what is choiceless is always aware and open to all, without direction or motive. In sensitivity you will find that reality will come and dance with you, she will mirror you, she will pour herself into you and your whole field of consciousness will melt and merge deeper into itself. Go deep enough and you will see that there is no outside consciousness or inner consciousness, there is only consciousness; you have just forgotten it. There is no outside reality or inner reality, there is only one reality, and you will remember and return to it.

A Warning Shot

WHEN WE STEP BEYOND DESIRE we are able to gratefully accept whatever happens. In gratitude there is delight, there is total contentment in the present and there is freedom. In gratitude there is no tension or agenda or will to change. There is instead the total openness of one's being in the present moment without the desire to change 'what is' into 'what should be'. There is complete love for oneself and all that IS. Now you are in tune with the Tao, and there is no more karma holding you onto the dream. There is a change of vibration; there is contact with existence. But if you are dropping desires purely because you want to become egoless, because this is the state masters have reported is necessary to see the underlying truth of existence, then your search will be futile. You are still in desire, you are still in a subtle ego state; in fact, you are effacing and practising a form of self-worship. Your effort to be humble is, in truth, vanity. Remember that existence is a non-ego state, so contact with existence is to merge with existence. Any sense of desire which remains in our actions is an ego state, however subtle. Only when desire is not, when the mind that seeks to achieve, that thinks in terms of a result and is therefore divided and exclusive, only when such a mind has come to an end is there contact with existence and the arising of Truth.

> "He who wishes to awake consumes his desires joyfully."
> *Buddha*

Heaven is here and now; it is in every flower, every tree, every dewdrop and every birdsong that you ignore, too distracted on the treadmill of desire. This treadmill distracts you from life; it does not bring you closer to it. You say you have no choice, but it is not just the choices you make about *what* you desire, it is the very fact that you desire at all which traps you. You only choose because you are not clear. You are not happy with the present moment, you are caught up in time and you are caught up in mind. The fact that you desire takes you away from Now into ideas of 'what should be' in the future; into ideas of fulfilment and wholeness tomorrow. In your choices about tomorrow you are dreaming of a better life, hoping that one day fulfilment will be yours. Perhaps you hope for fulfilment in retirement, by which time you are old and tired; maybe then, at the end of your life, you will finally realise that tomorrow never comes and that choice is not freedom. Your whole life you have been sacrificing the present moment of here and now for a better future, caught up in the illusion that is tomorrow. Only now is real, not tomorrow; tomorrow is a fiction that your mind has created, tomorrow is desire that is a product of your mind. Desire takes you away from life, away from real contentment; which is not mere satisfaction but rather the seeing of things as they are and therefore being free of them. Desire is a distraction into mind because the mind is unclear; the distortions between mind and Truth are still present.[3] Surely it is better to be clear by understanding your relationship to the many aspects of life, like attachment or psychological dependency, so that you are not asleep and distracted into mind? So that you are, instead, awake and joyful, alert to what is here and now, where there is life.

As long as you are hoping for a better future you are many steps away from the gift of existence right here, right now. Existence is here, now. Now is enough, now is more than enough, now is wonderful. Freedom rests always in one step; not two steps, not four steps, not 100 steps. Freedom rests in the first and last step; they are the same step. This step is so close and yet so far as we step over it everyday, looking outwards blinded by the illusion of fulfilment in the future. The person who is wise knows that fulfilment is now, that contentment is here, and they are joyful at whatsoever is happening right now. There is no cause, there is no dependency; only what is here, what is now, what is life.

Wanting Nothing

> "Even in the empty forest he finds joy because he wants nothing."
>
> *Buddha,* Dhammapada verse 99

LIFE IS THE ULTIMATE GIFT but we don't see it as a gift because we are asleep to its joys. We step away from the blissful state of presence, but this state is ever present wherever you are, no matter where you go. The bliss of the here and now is not found in India or in Tibet or at the foot of the Himalayas, it is right here, right now, with you and within you. The here and now is always here and now. In the present moment of here and now there is no future and no past, and there is thus no desire. A joyful life is a simple life and where there is no desire, there

---

[3] There is no such thing as distraction in an enlightened mind, for every moment is embraced for what it is. We are distracted and impatient only when we think there is something to be gained, when we lack humility.

is fulfilment. It is not a life that is imprisoned by ideas of its own making such as the need to be pure or worthy, or to possess knowledge or live with conditions that are a call of duty. How much freedom do you see in duty? It is a life where the greatest service to the self is to be free of the self and be free from the need of want, gain or goal. In wanting nothing there is no desire, there is no disorder, there is no sorrow; there is only contentment. Even in the empty forest, even when consciousness is void of the most simple of pleasures, there is still joy because there is immense freedom in wanting nothing. When desire is not, there is absolute bliss.

Liberation is joy without cause, it is a serenity felt in the heart. Sitting under a tree, listening to the birds sing, enjoying the sounds of a nearby stream; such simplicity away from the desires of the ego has innocence and grace. Innocence is the genuine appreciation of the quality of existence prior to intellectualisation or categorisation by the ego mind. It is the existential realisation of the wonders of life and nature. It is the way of the heart; no past, no future, only now. Adopting such simplicity opens the heart and nurtures wisdom, and in wanting nothing you are wise and you are mature.

We are joyful to be alive, we are grateful for every moment life throws at us and so everyday we feel blessed. Our joy is not dependent on outside pleasures because instead there is freedom from the search for pleasure, freedom from the choices that are dictated by the ego, and freedom from the associated disappointments and frustrations. This freedom is blissful because all freedom is blissful. Bliss is not pleasure; bliss IS when freedom IS whereas pleasure is a remembrance, pleasure is an idea, an image that thought has created around a certain sensation. Desire is the reaction of the mind in relation to that created image; desire is the chasing of shaped thought as pleasure. What shapes, what creates an image is the identification process.

There is immense joy, freedom and peace in wanting nothing. Ultimately all we really need is the air we breathe, our health, sustenance, shelter and freedom. And in this freedom there is laughter, love, joy and serenity. Remember when we are born we arrive with nothing, when we die we leave with nothing; all these things in between – our jobs, our status, our cars, our wardrobes full of clothes – are all transitory elements that do not last, they are all part of the dream that we will have to let go of eventually. There is no need to let them go literally, so long as you understand deeply that nothing is yours. Know that this life is a dream and that one day it will end, and you will find a whole new quality to life emerges. The only thing that is truly yours is your consciousness; it is your only true treasure, so nurture it in meditation, in watchfulness, in mindfulness, in awareness.

We pour money and time into our houses and our cars; we expend a great deal of effort on our exterior selves in the form of hairdressing, the latest fashions, accessories, ipods and phones. But do we understand our inner Being? The greatest asset of life is our inner Truth, not our outer fabrications. The only nourishment each of us needs is Truth. Then there is freedom from psychological time, freedom from the ego, freedom from desire.

chapter 12

Meekness is Most Powerful

"Society is me and I am society."

Society has been structured in response to the desires of the individual. The macro psychology of a society is built upon the micro psychology of each person within it. We are society and society is us; we are separated only in scale as fractals of conditioned behaviour. Our idea that society is something separate from us is fundamentally flawed. The motivations that exist at the level of the individual go on to form the general layout and structure of a society and, in response, society conditions each of us and our behaviour. For example, if a society has been built upon ambition, such as in certain modern societies where the idea of never quitting has become a virtue, then its structure will be very different to that which has been built upon valuing a simple and quiet life. It is important for us to realise that if there is to be a radical transformation in our society, then we must look not only at the question of how society has conditioned our beliefs, our fears and our desires, but also at how together we form the aggregate macro psychology of a society. In western culture, many of us live in an aggressive, dog-eat-dog world that is deeply rooted in the fears of the individual, where the conditioning of the individual is also the product of their society. There is an interdependent relationship between society and the individual, and it is important that we recognise the nature of that interdependence. Perhaps with greater understanding we will be able to reverse our complete dependency on government to solve problems, and begin to solve the problems of individuals at the level of the individual. We may well find this to be more effective.

Those who seek power do so for a very specific reason. There is no love if one is caught up in ambition, and the corridors of power are filled with ambitious people. A politician has no virtue unless he is willing to expose the true nature of the political system – which is intimately tied to a deeply immoral fractional reserve and cartel banking system (who owns the Fed?). The rhetoric of Obama or Vince Cable may appeal but their empty words have not exposed the system as it is. Their personal ambition is still present and clear to see. Neither statesman is any less corrupt than your local gangster. Corruption and deception are the inherent nature of government, and so dependency upon government can only ever result in fear, misery and suffering.

If we are dependent upon government and that government knows no love (as trillions are poured annually into the industrial military and disaster capitalism complexes, rather than into real education or charity), then that is a sure path to tyranny and oppression – as can be seen in America today. An oppressed society is a society which lives in fear, and many today even fear their own government[1]. If we are to live in a world of freedom not tyranny, then we must solve the problems of the individual at the level of the individual.

> "If you are happy at the expense of another man's happiness, you are forever bound."
>
> *Buddha*

Being happy at the expense of another's happiness entails competition. All competition, comparison, measurement or the necessity for personal success and achievement are rooted in fear. The competitive spirit has been bred into us from an early age – within families, at school, college, university and then at work. Our competitiveness is encouraged because it serves the monstrous economic system in which we live. We are conditioned to believe that we should be happy if we have beaten someone in the game of life, when we come first. But who, or what, does this serve? Such competitiveness serves to possess, to dominate, to seek power and wealth, but not to love. Is this intelligence at work? An economic system founded upon greed and fear is not intelligent, it is a disease, and that which is founded upon fear will eventually implode. Ego happiness is an illusionary happiness which we know in truth to be a prison. There is really no need to be happy at the expense of another; your idea of gain at the expense of another only demonstrates your misunderstanding of what is freedom and what is fulfilment. All that you need you already have, bliss is available at any moment. When you are free from the trappings of

---

[1] If you investigate the activities of government and that government questions whether you are a patriot, simply highlight that patriotism knows no love. The Patriot Act is not an act of freedom, it is an act of tyranny.

desire, you will no longer be bound by the compelling desire for external pleasures at the exclusion of others.

Individuals' desires are an expression of their hope for a better future, and in this future we each wish to maximise our gratifying sensations as best we can. Our search for fulfilment begins with a projection of where we perceive fulfilment to be found – in success. The joys of childhood are sacrificed for the grades needed for a better education. Instead of playing, exploring the wonder of nature and being allowed to enjoy the beauty of imaginative play, we make our children study excessively so that they can get ahead. There is no introduction to the wonder and freedom of meditation, no encouragement to get in touch with their inner Being, instead competition between school children reigns supreme and this activity is the driving force for even our most innocent minds. Soon begin the contradictions and tensions (and thus the psychological disorder) within the minds of our children as they are caught up in the fear state of assessment and 'what should be' in order to meet the approval of their parents, teachers and friends. Acceptance and love appear conditional (it does not matter whether they are or not, it is how they appear that is important for the child), and because disapproval signals pain and a deep, inner fear of potential abandonment inside the mind of a child, so begins the striving activity of the child to deny such sensation. Extra layers of ego form early for the child – layers of ego which are isolating in nature – and so his innocent nature is foreshortened and polluted in response to his exposure to stress. As we subjugate the free spirit of our children using various punishments and incentives in an effort to make them conform, the innocence and innate wisdom that is normal within the mind of a child is lost, or rather exchanged, for a life of conformity, dependency and ambition. As we now know, this leads only to psychological suffering, with the inevitable result of future generations dependent upon pharmaceuticals to ease that suffering[2]. Our children are taught little that is truly useful at school. How much of what you learnt at school has been useful in your adult life? Not

---

[2] See the movie *Generation RX*. Observe how many kids in America are today hooked on Ritalin and Prozac.

a lot. Yet the indoctrination of children at a young age into a life of submission to the rules of society is useful for the elite few who wish to dominate society, using the education system as one of its mechanisms.[3] Many key families financed, shaped and moulded some of our most respected educational institutions in the nineteenth century, thus setting the tone of what was to come in the twentieth century (this practice is reflected in the contemporary formation of 'academies' within state sector education). This legacy continues today, stretching into our media, our entertainment and virtually every corner of life. This discussion takes us beyond the remit of this book, but suffice to say that the extent and depth of the indoctrination within society can be measured in the distance between the innate wisdom of a child and how much we as adults project ourselves onto our children. The truth of this is clear enough.

Look at what happens. School indoctrinates our youngest, most impressionable minds and then our children grow up a little, they get a better education so that they can get a better job, buy a better house, be more socially acceptable, be more attractive for a potential partner by being successful and appealing within romantic assessment. Have you ever seen a speed dating event? I walked into one by accident a couple of months ago and it was like watching a sales team in operation. The idea that is set inside the minds of young people is to be able to soak up their pleasures in life by reaching predetermined goals of success and achievement, but they don't feel the joy of life because they are focusing too much on the future or on their self-image, trapped inside their projections of 'what should be'. So they graduate, they get a job, get a wife or husband and soon there are children. These new parents, whilst projecting themselves and their wishes onto their kids, then sacrifice the remainder of their lives to raise the finance to put their children through a decent education, and with these children the treadmill starts up for another generation. Meanwhile the

---

[3] 'Women's Lib' was actually financed by elites with another, more sinister agenda. Employment for women is of course a worthy cause, but what is not widely known is that it was also a mechanism to get children into school at a younger, more impressionable age.

parents are slaving at work to buy a plot of land that belongs to no one but Mother Nature, they slave to take the family away on holiday, to get away from the prison we call the office or to go shopping for fashion items and household goods which marketing companies have convinced them that they need, when really they don't. They fall for an image – a limbic system reward that is the creation of a product's marketing team – because their minds have become so dull, so mechanical, so locked up in routine, so indoctrinated, indifferent and therefore insensitive to the simple pleasures of life that even a shopping trip will give them a thrill. We desperately want to feel something – anything – because we are searching for something, some intensity, so even the temporary illusion of fulfilment from retail therapy feels like an escape from the trap of the treadmill of society. In this desperation we are missing the gift of existence, stuck in mind-numbing work, the 9 to 5 routine, where pushing little pieces of paper around a desk for a company brings nothing in return other than an illusion of some financial freedom and the destruction of the planet's beauty and resources. Taking twenty days' holiday per year is not living. You get up, go to work, pay the mortgage, have dinner, watch TV, ignore the wife, ignore the husband, no sex, go to bed… and you do this for forty years! Meanwhile in the back of your mind, you are thinking, *'There must be more to life than this!'* This is the great distraction from existence, from life itself, and a child could have told you this in a single moment, but you have hushed him up instead. You have told the child that 'fun' is for later, when work is finished and you can afford to indulge. The child says, *"Play now Dad, not later!"*

The shocking part of this story is that in the back of our minds, we all recognise the truth of this situation, but we are so fearful of our own freedom that we ignore it and instead comply with the rules of society. You live your whole life without authenticity, in the anxiety of what will become of you if you break out of the mould. As we have seen elsewhere, your entire life has been dictated by fear.

Conditioned Desire

WE HAVE SAID THAT ALL competition, comparison, measurement or the necessity for personal success and achievement are rooted in fear, but fear of what? It is the fear of assessment by others. What is our state of apprehension caused by, why do we feel so anxious? We each feel a subconscious fear that if we do not meet the expectations of others, then we will be abandoned, we will be alone. As we have seen, it is this deep fear of loneliness and the anxiety which accompanies it that drives nearly all human behaviour, including what we desire and what we wish to avert.

We have said that the essence of freedom is to know one's absolute correctness, but because we do not feel this inside, because we do not know the correctness of our fundamental nature, we are forever caught up in the notion of aspiration. There is a feeling of insufficiency which we are looking to change and the mechanism which we employ for this task is the seeking of permanent satisfaction through sensation. We each search for the sensation of success in our respective fields so that we can feel good about ourselves; we want a position of authority over others because the feeling that we draw from this is one of power, which masks our insufficiency. We wish to be admired and respected by our peers because when we are, we feel empowered. We require many satisfactions to feel good about ourselves and when we feel good about ourselves, we feel secure in the illusion that we will not be abandoned. Empowerment through such activity is of course a complete nonsense.

The self feels that it needs to assert power, no matter how acute or how subtle, because to not do so creates the possibility of rejection and abandonment. What this means of course is that the self feels deeply powerless. Inside you feel thoroughly inadequate, you feel tiny, small, worthless, useless, third rate and of course you don't admit this to anyone because in your admission you fear that others will abandon you. Rather than face these deep feelings within, you project yourself outwards in demonstrations of bravado, success, achievement, confidence, self-worth and success to your friends and colleagues. You assert your persona in the belief that by demonstrating some power your deep fear of inadequacy will disappear. You believe that the trappings of success – a big house, a luxury car, the respect of peers, the wielding of power and authority, the recognition of others – will lead to fulfilment in the assuaging of your fears. All of this self consciousness is no more than a method for you to demonstrate one of your primal instincts. It is an isolating process; the more self conscious you are, the more you feel the need to keep up appearances and the more isolated you become.

Your craving for position and authority and your desire for admiration by others are no more than public demonstrations that you do not know who you are and that you are still being driven by your primal fears. You desire certain things out of fear; your desire is a process of denial as well as of fulfilment. When we look at the natural world, there is always a pecking order amongst any group of animals. At the top is the alpha male asserting his authority over those beneath him, his action drives forward his message that what he says, or rather what he grunts, goes. He is aggressive in order to secure the top position within the community and he seeks that position of power in order to assert his preservation and continuity. In this assertion he feels a certain primal satisfaction, driven by the force of 'survival of the fittest' in the evolutionary process. He feels better about himself, more secure. Human society has its own way of struggling with the same forces and processes. Our activities reflect the fact that the selfish gene is still very much a part of our genetic make-up, although many deny this in the name of being 'civilised'.

Those who seek money and power only do so because underneath they feel the need to assert power; a need to assert the self in some aspirational way. Understand that this is not much different from a graffiti artist spraying his name on a road underpass in an attempt to declare a sense of self-permanence, using his graffiti name to declare *'I was here'*. Both actions are actions of self assertion; means by which the self asserts its own existence in an attempt to make that existence more permanent. The self is so frightened of being a nobody, it is so frightened of the inner empty state, that it will undertake all kinds of (often aggressive) behaviour in order to assert itself. Our deep desire for the permanence of the self has infiltrated the very core of our society so deeply that we have even made it respectable for those who are successful to be treated as model citizens for the rest of us to aspire to. You are a successful businessman and you have been driven by ambition your whole life, you have in effect been a lifelong slave to your inner fear of insufficiency, and now you are upheld by the establishment as an upstanding moral individual. This sense of values is fundamentally warped.

True Power

THOSE WHO SEEK POWER DO not possess it. They seek because they have a point to prove, either to themselves or to others. When there is no point to prove, then you are powerful. If you are powerful then there is no need to seek power. Why seek that which you have already? We usually think of power in terms of the individual – how much money or how much influence they have. This is not power, this is being possessed by the drive for power and in this they demonstrate that they are powerless. Political, economic or social power is the only power that the ego knows, but it is these trappings of the ego that make people poor. Dictators are poor because they are not overflowing with love. They are seeking political power because it reinforces their perception of ego continuance, and they try to prove something through their achievements – historical greatness and a legacy so that city squares can be named after them. What is it all for? What is the value of being remembered by one or two future generations, none of whom will truly know or care for you? A life of ambition is a life of struggle, conflict and disharmony, for what exactly? If you want to be extraordinary, you are very ordinary; everyone wants to be extraordinary. Remember that the ego can only ever move in the direction of self-preservation; what else is there for the self beyond the will for continuous existence? It knows that it is a concept of thought; a fictitious entity constructed only out of layers of identifications, desires, beliefs, memories, projections, values, fears, attachments, and so forth, and so it is bound to desire its own permanence.

By searching for power, fame and fortune you are denying yourself true power. In seeking you are no longer in harmony and cooperation with existence, you are held instead in tension, conflict, contradiction and thus disorder. You are back in desire and this desire locks you out of your true power, which is to BE one's truth. In seeking you are far removed from Being, far removed from love. Only when we are blossoming with the delight and joy of our own Being are we powerful, are we love. Stepping into existence is the way. You only have to surrender and your desires are gone, then there is gratitude and harmony because there is no longer contradiction. There is order and there is fulfilment. Only when you have totally surrendered are you powerful; unlike ordinary power, which can be taken from us at any moment, nobody can take your empowerment away from you because it is what you already are. In total surrender, you are invincible; you are love. Only when you are overflowing with love can you share it, but you have to possess it first to give it. You cannot truly practice compassion until you are bursting with compassion. Your vibration changes and this becomes infectious for those around you; you are a magnet. There is a subconscious transference of energy from existence through you to others. This is what Jesus was doing, so overflowing with compassion that it rained down upon everyone he met. His vibration was so high that people were drawn to him.

"One who is in accord with the way is great."

Buddha

To be in accord with existence, be in total harmony with existence. If you open your heart to existence your energy will be boundless. This is what it means to be meek. You may be noticed or you may go unnoticed by history, but this is irrelevant for a heart and mind that is open.

Buddha said, *"Meekness is most powerful, for it harbours no evil thoughts, and moreover it is restful and full of strength."* Jesus said, *"Blessed are the meek, for they shall inherit the earth."*

Only when you have fully surrendered are you truly empowered. Only in meekness is there the rediscovery of the power of inner Being and, since it draws from within, it can never be taken away. Like love, it is yours and always yours and you are then invincible. You are overflowing with love, with power, and it can be shared freely; always undivided and unlimited. Lao-Tze, Jesus and Buddha all understood this deeply.

The story of Jesus is the best known metaphorical, or perhaps actual, manifestation of this concept in recorded history. He had surrendered so profoundly that he was in love with the universe, with existence itself. He had merged so deeply into existence that his own desire for physical liberation became meaningless. He understood that there is no such thing as personal salvation, which is exclusive; there is only the salvation of the human mind. A human being who does not feel deeply responsible for the mind of humanity as a whole is both shallow and petty. He will never discover Truth, he will only discover what he is, which is enclosed. He may try to become intelligent, erudite or clever but he will still remain petty, narrow and limited. Acknowledgement of one's own pettiness rather than one's effort to be free of pettiness (which is a form of running away) is the first sign of greatness. Jesus merged with the whole so profoundly that he was no longer separate from the whole. In the same way, you truly conquer when you merge with the whole because the whole has no opposition; there is no 'other' with which to be in conflict. All is one and the whole is power. The message of our masters teaches humanity that you cannot defeat that which has already fully surrendered, because there is no ego to defeat. When totally egoless, then and only then is there true liberation. This was the message Jesus learnt from Buddha, and went on to demonstrate in a more physical context. The message of his life was not to save us from our sins in the way we think of today, but a message of liberation which few truly understand. You are NOT, existence IS. Meekness is the non-existence of the 'I' and the ISness of existence. Bliss and Truth arise from meekness, from inner existence when the 'I' has gone and only existence IS. Sensitivity to existence increases with the dropping of the 'I'.

Human Insensitivity

HOWEVER, WE FIND IT DIFFICULT to drop the 'I'. We crave success because success brings with it certain satisfactions – an element of notoriety, people wanting your attention all the time – and the ego enjoys these satisfactions because they distract you from your aching sorrows and anxieties of being insufficient and unworthy. To have status gives you a sense of importance, reinforcing your sense of self in a satisfactory manner and giving you a pleasant psychological sensation. You also desire status, power and reputation because you have been conditioned to think this way. You have been indoctrinated since childhood to succeed so that you don't end up a failure, so that you don't end up alienated and abandoned, so that you are accepted. What is the effect of this indoctrination, over time?

Your ambition distracts you from the present moment and from your inner freedom as you get caught up in meeting the criteria you have set for yourself and the criteria others have imposed upon you. Your feelings of completeness and acceptance are now wholly conditional. The trap of 'what should be' continually confines your sense of freedom and so you feel inwardly restricted and consistently insecure. When boxed into a corner like this your instinctual response to your fear is to be aggressive. Aggression helps you balance your fear and as such it is a form of desire because it is a mechanism to deny that fear. This learned aggression is the product of the society in which we live; the product of a lifetime of fear. Fear causes us to lose all sensitivity. We get so used to feeling fear, so used to being told what to do by the superstructure of our society, that we fail to realise that our outlook on life has become increasingly automated, insular and banal. The more we conform, the more afraid we become of breaking out of the norm, and the greyer and duller life becomes. Nature no longer holds such majesty for you and you no longer have the energy for life that you enjoyed when you were young. In this trap of ambition, aggression and fear, you lack vitality, openness and freshness. Your lack of vitality is not exclusively caused by your body; physical tiredness of course exists but in general the body always has some energy. (In an emergency the energy is there; you can be falling asleep, but if your house is on fire you will still find the energy to run.) Your lethargy is caused by your thoughts, and when you recognise the potential for change, as you did when you were younger, that itself is energising. So fear is making you insensitive and this insensitivity is not satisfying. You go to the museum and you feel nothing, you go for a walk in the park and you feel nothing; life seems void of any intensity, it is mediocre, lifeless and boring. *Same shit, different day,* as they say.

So of course we want change, we want some excitement. Life is dull, life is boring and we want to feel something, to feel some intensity before we die. We express this in desire. We have become insensitive and indifferent to many of life's sensations and so we are forever seeking newer, better and more exciting sensations in order to gain some sense of satisfaction. We seek distraction from the perpetual state of dissatisfaction which is always there, lurking around inside, creeping up on us. If you become insensitive to life, then life becomes a form of suffering because you do not feel that you are living; your pursuit of pleasure is therefore nothing other than a desire to escape from pain.

"How is it possible that life has come to this? How can it be that I feel so indifferent?"

Let's think of an example. You fall for a girl or a boy, and for the first few months you cannot keep your hands off each other. Sex is sensational and every time you see them you admire the way they walk, the way they talk, their eyes, smile, the way they wear their clothes. The movement of her hips is dazzling; the look in his eyes is irresistible. The years pass and you no longer see these fine details, no longer are you looking with eyes that are fresh and open; now you look at your partner through eyes that have argued with them, eyes that have been upset, eyes that have been comforted, eyes with a history. Do you still see that person, and only that person, without your mind and your thoughts interfering? Or are you now seeing an image of that person which has been constructed in your mind as a result of interfering thought? Your eyes are looking now with the filters of a shared history, of knowledge and memories, and you are therefore no longer seeing with clarity. This is when the rot sinks in. The connection and sharing of truth together is no longer in unison like before. You have become increasingly indifferent to mutual pleasures, meals together, holidays together, time together. The tracksuit is always on, you take each other for granted, sex is no longer sensational. Through habit you have become indifferent, you have become insensitive. This insensitivity, in relationships and in all aspects of life, blinkers your ability to see 'what is'. You habitually filter 'what is' with your interfering thought, which distorts your vision. Your inability to observe with clarity, your loss of the art of observation, has caused you to become insensitive to life itself. Your thoughts are always interfering.

This example illustrates the danger of allowing habitual thought to interfere with what you see. The result of watching something with reservation and judgement in this way is that you no longer see the essence of your observation, and this breeds indifference and insensitivity.

Regaining Sensitivity

THERE IS AN INTERVAL BETWEEN sensation and thought, or the identification of thought, which we have called pre-intellectual awareness. There is an interval of watching the essence of a thing without thought or judgement, without desire, where there is the seeing of a thing without distortion or interference. If you can observe the movement of pleasure within your mind, you will notice that pleasure does not exist in the observation of a thing, but arrives in thought after observation of that thing, when thought says to itself, '*How lovely that is!*' Why does thought come into the equation? Why does memory need to interfere, distracting us from the suchness of a thing? Why can't we look at something without the distorting mind interfering to create an image of what is seen? The reason is that you have been conditioned to think this way. You have been conditioned into habitual thinking, naming, categorising and thus distorting what it is that you see.

We are conditioned to solve our psychological problems through effort. We believe effort is required to save ourselves from stagnation. However, what may be appropriate to solve our technical or technological problems is not necessarily appropriate when it comes to our psychological problems. To solve human psychological problems is it not important to understand the root of these problems, so that they can be eradicated completely, rather than concentrate effort on how to solve a particular problem? If we are always looking for a solution, the mind is not capable of being still and tranquil enough to see the problem in its entirety. And without seeing the exactness of a problem, the problem as it really is, it is not possible to truly understand it and be free of it. The understanding of a problem is not found in its apparent solution, it is found in the problem itself. *Why does it arise? What are its causes and complexities?* A question has the answer within itself. The answer is not found outside the question. Look at your questions as they are, don't look outside them. When the solution is more important than the problem itself, when we are more concerned with an answer, we don't see the problem as it really is. But when we experience the truth of a thing without distortion, then we are free of it. For it is Truth that liberates; not our effort to overcome, solve or suppress. Effort without understanding is merely the felling of the branches of a problematic tree; it does not go to the root of that problem, to the very structure and trunk of the tree.

It is important therefore to understand why effort comes into being. Why, when presented with a truth we don't see it as it is and be finished with it, but rather create an idea about it and then act on that idea. The idea is inevitably more concerned with the overcoming of a problem than it is with the actual problem itself; we want to feel better, do we not? The idea causes us not to act in response to the truth of a thing but rather create an abstraction out of it, to postpone it and to deal with it later, over time. Freedom is now, in understanding. It is not a thing to be achieved over time through effort.

Effort, desire, volition or will are the mind's responses to ideas that it has created around a certain problem. For example, we may intellectually understand that attachment is corruption and yet we go on forming attachments in daily life. If we really understood the corroding nature of attachment we would not be able to do it. We would be finished with it. Even though intellectually we may know that attachment is corruption, the very fact that we are still attached or attaching means that we have not understood this fact clearly. Our intellectual understanding is superficial and ultimately meaningless. Either we see Truth completely, without distortion, or we do not see

Truth at all. Intellectual understanding is nothing other than a registration, a memory; it is not real understanding.

The cause of all of this dysfunction is in the psyche. The ego is the result of time, of memory, knowledge, experience, and it can only think in terms of a result. Its very nature is to think in terms of achievement; always calculating from the field of the known. The ego seeks security through beliefs, attachments, ideas and ideals, and so when presented with a truth that threatens its security it will do whatever it can to avoid any uncertainty. When the ego is deeply disturbed, caught in uncertainty, it will always move in the direction of certainty. This movement from uncertainty to certainty is the movement of fear. So its typical response to a disturbing truth is to create an idea around that truth in order to avoid facing it directly; the ego avoids 'what is' and so will inevitably fear 'what might be'. The creation of an idea causes fear; fear is the ignorance of 'what is' and ignorance is caused by the idea. Ideas distort. The ego avoids facing that which threatens its very structure – which is its idea of permanence and safety.

The ego is a momentum and so when anything threatens the very structure of that momentum – its desires, fears, attachments, beliefs and so on – its habitual response is to create something to reinforce momentum. That something is the idea around a certain fact and the desire to solve the problem of that fact over time. The ego is seeking a result, it is seeking security and because it is more preoccupied with its own security than it is with seeing the essence of a thing, the result can only be something corrosive and corrupting – attachment. We seek security and that denies us the ability to see the truth each and every moment; the search for a result prevents us from understanding the very structure of a thing, from understanding, in this case, the nature of attachment.

True discovery – or the discovery of Truth – is a gift. It is a gift which cannot be without stillness, without passive observation. But we cannot observe passively, we tend to observe only through self-minded filters. The mind watches and records in order to achieve. The accretion of knowledge is part of the process of becoming, and in becoming *something* we feel secure. The mind, in its search for security, has trained itself to always record. If you are locked up in these mechanical routines, if there is the tension associated with psychological progress or the drive for freedom, then true discovery cannot be. The mind can watch without recording, which means to watch without the need for a result or a solution. This ability to watch without the creation of an idea is meekness, it is to be free of the self's natural drive for security.

In meekness there can be love, there can be virtue, there can be space for the understanding of one's own mind; an understanding which is itself freedom. Understanding does not bring one to freedom, as if freedom is something separate. Understanding is freedom. Effort is not freedom because effort implies restriction, concentration, the narrowing down of the mind. Effort implies activity, movement and agitation. There is no tranquillity or serenity. Virtue is not an ideal to be conformed to. Virtue is to see things clearly. Virtue is Vipassana observation. A mind that isn't still cannot see. Do please see the truth of this fact. The ability to watch without effort, without the struggle to become, is the abnegation of the 'me' and such abnegation is meekness. Here alone is there the freedom that only Truth can bring.

If thought can rest in a moment of pure observation, the mind can regain its sensitivity, regain its art of listening, its art of looking. In this way, the mind can step beyond the confines of habitual thinking, beyond the craving for security, beyond the habitual preferences which breed indifference, beyond the subsequent mindless pursuit of new pleasures. If we explore this possibility in our own minds, we regain the potential to overcome our conditioning.

The alternative of course is that we remain with our current way of thinking, locked up in time-bound patterns of thought: the cycle of experience, memory, knowledge, thought, reaction and then the next experience. When caught in such a cycle, we are narrowing our perception of Truth. We remain in the trap of our habitual behaviours, but within habit arises indifference, dullness and insensitivity. The mindless pursuit of pleasure over time breeds indifference and misery. By looking at desire, we can see that it is the continuity of thought that is attached to the craving for experience. When that continuity is broken or dismantled, desire ceases because desire cannot exist without the presence of continuous thought. A sensitive mind has watched the whole process of pleasure, of achievement, and seen that pleasure and the quest for pleasure can only be supported and thus made continuous by thought. Such an astute and sensitive mind is operating on a new level of intelligence.

You cannot defeat a person who is beyond the desires of the ego. He wishes for nothing, there is nothing to conquer, he is not looking to gain. He already IS. His freedom already IS because he is free of his desiring mind. He is beyond ego and whatever is beyond ego will be in harmony with reality. You cannot defeat a person who has no wish to succeed, he will not respond to any carrot you present him with. You cannot defeat such a person, you cannot threaten him and you cannot whip him with a stick. He is the embodiment of liberation, he has already stepped beyond the boundaries of that which can be imprisoned – the ego – and that which is the jailer – desire. Total liberation is beyond ego. When there is no ego, there is nothing left to conquer, coerce or defeat because by surrendering so completely, one has already accepted defeat. There is nowhere left to go. When your back is up against the wall, an aggressor cannot push you back any further. As soon as he can no longer push, it is he who is defeated, not you. In complete and utter surrender there is no fear. The power of others is only possible because of our cooperation; if you no longer cooperate, no dictator or tyrannical statesman will ever rise again. Free from conditioning, you are your own master, freed from the trap of desire and aggression, of ambition and fear. Open to Truth, and truly powerful.

chapter 13

Love & Forgiveness

> "See, how she leans her cheek upon her hand!
> O that I were a glove upon that hand,
> that I might touch that cheek!"
> *William Shakespeare,* Romeo and Juliet, 2.2

THE LOVE WE READ ABOUT in our literature, such as in the plays of Shakespeare, is portrayed as desire and temptation; love that is as much intense as it is exclusive. This love can be the sweetest of things, it can be the very breath of life, but it can also be our greatest torture for Cupid's arrow is blind and shows no mercy. In the scene that we most remember from Shakespeare's greatest work on love, as Romeo lies dead after drinking poison, Juliet laments the loss of her love and in utter despair stabs herself with the dagger from his sheath. It is from stories and artistic portrayals such as this that we form ideals in our mind as to what love should be. We then carry these ideals out into the real world, into our lives.

According to these ideals, romantic love is shaped by desire and this desire is exclusive. We love a particular person, we are mesmerised by their beauty and their grace. We notice all of their qualities and are charmed by their every word, thrilled by their every action. The object of our desire becomes everything to us, such that we cannot conceive of life without them.

According to this ideal of love, the loved one is the very food of our survival and nothing else matters; if we were to lose them, we'd surely die. This love is a fusion, a meeting of two centres. The intensity that we hope we will one day feel represents an escape from mediocrity and so we see it as the very substance of life itself. If we experience such intensity in our first love, we wonder how we could ever live without such a feeling again. What would be the point of continuing to live without love – it would be like living without breath? In the minds of these romantic idealists, a life without love would be futile.

Not everyone subscribes to such romantic ideals, and many people have become cynical about romance. However, many of us live with the expectation of meeting our soul mate or 'other half' and then living happily ever after: an ideal which is providential. When 'in love', we cannot contemplate life without that other person. Love is literally life and death. Your head is spinning, you are love-struck, walking on the clouds, twisted and fuzzy in the company of your loved one. You become lost in a whirlwind of passion. This is our ideal of romantic love, and it is far removed from the reality of most relationships today. Notice that even here, in our ideals, our love is for one and not for many; our passion is as much selective as it is exclusive. It is unique to our lover and no one else; not dissimilar in a way to how our love is unique to blood family and close friends. This is how we conceive love; this is our conditioning.

Now is love passion or is passion the activity of the ego? We can be passionate about an object, an objective, an ideal or a person; we can be emotionally overwhelmed by any one of these things, but is this love or is this sensation? This is what we are going to find out, in order to understand what love is. Is love compassion or are passion and compassion just characteristics of what it is to love? What is the relationship between passion and compassion? The prefix 'com' in Latin means *with* or *together;* add this prefix and passion can no longer be selective like it is in our romantic ideals, for compassion means passion for all. Compassion is inclusive, not exclusive and selective like passion. If we are to come upon true love – and by this we mean the love that does not exist merely as an idea in our mind, but is based upon a genuine love of existence – then there must be compassion, there must be passion for all. This is the love that our masters speak of. It is neither selective nor is it exclusive.

How can you say that you love if that love is exclusive? For most of us, love is something that is reserved for those who are close to us, those who we cherish and hold dear in our hearts. If you love certain people and hate others, like those who make you feel uncomfortable about yourself and thus disturb you, then you have made your love exclusive. Is true love exclusive, or does love know no separation? Are there many loves, are there different types of love or is there just one true love?

Enemies & Equanimity

NOTICE THE REACTION THAT OTHER people can provoke in you. Maybe someone insults you and you are offended or maybe you strongly disagree with someone; we tend to translate these reactions as dislike. Why do you dislike that person? Someone has created a reaction within you because you have allowed them to create a reaction within you; they have stimulated a disturbance of your ego. It is you who is still unconscious, it is you who reacted (still caught up in the image that you have of yourself). Equally, someone may hold views that contradict your own, and because you are identified and attached to your views – identifications that can form the very foundation of your identity – their views shake your sense of self. You are shaken because you are forced to re-evaluate and question who you are, which is bound to happen at some point in your life, particularly if your sense of self is derived from your beliefs, values, judgements and opinions. If you identify with your values and beliefs then it is inevitable that you will disagree with others and you are bound to meet individuals who shake your identity. Are you going to dislike them all? If you dislike another simply because they disagree with you, is love possible?

Think for a moment about what is really happening in such a scenario. Is it the fault of another for disagreeing with you or even insulting you? Do you have the right to hate someone because their views do not fit with your own or because you are offended? It is you who has taken offence because it is you who has failed to understand the process of the ego.

You have missed an opportunity to learn and your sense of self has lead to feelings of dislike or even hatred, because it feels threatened. This projection of the self is the work of the ego, which fears being undermined. Your dislike is merely a response to that fear and has nothing to do with the other person. What their view is, or what their opinion is, is their business not yours; you have only made it your business because the image that you have formed of yourself has been offended. The ego, which is the product of its identifications, is concerned with the image that exists in its mind, it is thus looking for this image to be reinforced, restored or repaired whenever and wherever possible and so it is concerned only about itself. The ego is preoccupied with reinforcing its own existence. This is why you hate, this is why you dislike others, this is why you say 'sorry' when you don't really mean it; they are merely reactions of your ego rebuilding, reinforcing or restoring itself. There is no room for love in this ego activity. Can you not see this as a lesson to understand your own vanity? If there is only concern about oneself, then love is not. Look into yourself, if you have an enemy then this suggests that you are not concerned about the other, but only about the image that you have of yourself (an image which gives you certain satisfactions). If you are only interested in yourself then you cannot love. Now if this is true for each of us, and the sad truth is that it is, then it is no wonder that human history is a history of conflict and suffering.

So whenever someone offends you and you respond with anger or hatred, note that it is a reaction of your ego and the identification process that is 'you'. Until you can understand this process, you are enslaved by your own thoughts. The idea of an enemy or foe, the very function of dislike or hatred, is a reaction derived from the ego designed to reinforce its sense of identity. If this process is true of you, then your idea of love will also be a product of the mind; something that reinforces your sense of identity. You will only 'love' those who reinforce you, and buoy your self image. This may begin with your spouse or your family, but it soon extends outwards to your friends or even those who are within your 'movement'. You love only those who strengthen your sense of identity; those who are on your side, never strangers, never those to whom you feel indifference. If this is so, how can you say that your love is love? Your love is no more than self-love; love for your own ego.

What about people who we dislike just a little bit, do we love them? What about strangers? If we are brutally honest with ourselves then no, we don't really love them. We may be charitable on occasion, we may put out an olive branch for someone we don't usually get on with, but what we do is ultimately for our own satisfaction. Maybe we want to feel like we have done something good today, maybe we are looking for an easy life. If this is the case then your olive branch or your donation – your so called act of love – is really an act for your own self-gratification. You have made love an act of pleasure sensation, and this is not love. Why is it difficult to treat a stranger in the street with the same good intention and care as we would our close friends? The very fact that we are selective and exclusive when it comes to distributing our good intentions suggests a motive. Motive, much like devotion, acts with a view to receive and if you have to receive then it is not love. Is your loving intention truly loving? Are you free of the need to receive? Be honest. The answer is no because you have walked past the beggar on the street, callous, cold and indifferent as you are. If there is freedom from the need to receive, there's freedom from the idea of intention altogether. In this freedom, loving action becomes an automatic response to all. You feel responsible for humanity as a whole, unable to walk past the beggar in the street, unable to watch another suffer and do nothing. You become passionate about all of the injustices in the world: the open prison of Gaza, the privatized war in Iraq, the ubiquitous political deception or the pure evil that is capitalism – and your passion is selfless, universal. You act. You respond. You forget partisan politics and tribal loyalty, and you bypass corrupt NGOs to help the needy, direct into the other's hand, looking into their eyes with a real, selfless love.[1]

Why is it so difficult to be unbiased towards the people around you? On what basis is someone your friend, enemy or a stranger? We are constantly judging people by their appearances or attitudes. When we look upon someone we form a judgement which influences the way we behave towards that person. Issues of race are based on such prejudices. In these moments of judgement, all we are doing is holding up a mirror to our ego self and seeing a reflection of our own beliefs and values. We are defined by our views, beliefs, opinions and judgements. Always we are operating from the self.

A man is begging, hungry, and you want to help him. Why do you want to help him? Perhaps it will make you feel good to buy him a

---

[1] An investigation by the BBC has found just 5 per cent of the money raised by Live Aid and Band Aid actually made it to the victims of famine in Ethiopia. Instead, the millions of dollars of international aid intended to buy food for starving Ethiopians was used by rebel groups to buy weapons. Source: ABC News

sandwich. Look into yourself and be completely honest. If your actions are driven by some form of satisfaction, then it is not love. Even psychological satisfaction is a form of pleasure sensation, a form of self-gain. This may sound cynical but it is not at all; it is merely observance of the fact with brutal honesty. If you buy the man a sandwich and he then throws it back at you cursing, asking for money instead, you judge him. Look into yourself and see why you are responding in this way; look inside and question why the image that you have of yourself has been disturbed. If your compassion for the man is conditional on how he chooses to spend his time or his money then you are not loving; your compassion is false, your compassion is cultivated, your compassion has condition and purpose. Love forgives regardless of whether a person is growing or not growing. Their growth and happiness will most likely occur naturally in the presence of loving action but it is not a precondition for love. There are no conditions of growth within love; love is without condition. But the majority of us love with motive and within motive there are always conditions.

When you walk through a busy city it may seem as though everybody is angry. Yet if you were to stop the nearest person and go with them for a coffee, it is very likely that they are just as friendly and warm as you are. Strangers are met, at best, with indifference. Why are we so indifferent, why can't we love those we do not know? Strangers on the street have done neither good nor bad to us, but the love we feel is a product of the mind and comes with specific criteria attached. We love those who are amiable, dependable, respectable, unaffected, but not those who are fickle, inconsistent or unreliable. We have laid down criteria for our care and affection. Strangers are only strangers because we do not yet know them, but should knowing them even be a condition for love? And the idea that everyone is angry, or no-one can be trusted, is a false perception, a distortion resulting from your judgement. Strangers could become friends if you took the time to find out. But can you see them without your criteria? Honestly? It is a very difficult thing to do.

We tend to categorise people in terms of 'friends' and 'enemies' depending on whether they share or oppose our beliefs and values; whether they have been kind or unkind in the past. These categorisations always depend on the nature of our own identification process; namely what we like or dislike, what offends us and what flatters us. It is actually a reflection of our own vanity. We love only those who gratify or those with whom we can identify. Many of us define ourselves by the friends or enemies that we have. For example, our current enemy may have been someone we once loved very much, it may be an ex-partner or a friend with whom we once had an argument and then the ego boundaries shot up and now the issue remains unresolved. Such situations can even devolve into a form of hatred; particularly if you are identified with your pride or your rage and have allowed the situation to escalate. Now is the problem with the other or is it with your own ego? If you say it is the other you say that because your ego has been bruised. This is why your enemy is rarely someone unknown to you. It is only possible to have enemies if you are identified with the image that you have of yourself, if you have yet to understand how that identification process functions.[2]

Unconditional Love

UNCONDITIONAL LOVE IS TO TRULY and deeply comprehend, welcome and forgive another in the presence of their views, opinions, mistakes or judgements. They may insult you, they may beat you with a stick, they may bring upon you the most abhorrent of things; the person who is wise knows that these are the activities of an unconscious mind, being carried out by a person who is asleep. Asleep, we don't know what we're doing; we have no clarity, hypnotised by our own ego. When hypnotised by the ego we are incapable of love, and we usually perceive this to be more visible in others than we do in ourselves.

Any activity of the ego – its justifications, condemnations, views, opinions, judgements, conclusions, projections, expectations, or anxieties, desires and attachments which occur at a conscious or

---

[2] In Tibet, they say that the greatest service someone can do for your soul development is to be your enemy. As you will come to realise, your enemy is another aspect of 'you', teaching you not to be identified with the image that you have of yourself.

sub-conscious level – renders love impossible. Wherever the mechanism of the 'me' is still present, and as long as these processes and activities of the self continue unabated, you will never know what it is to love. Love is when all of the processes of the ego cease. There is no possibility of love whilst any of these activities are in motion because the ego is not, nor will it ever be, love. By hating, disliking or judging others, or by reserving your love for the few and not the many, you have made your love exclusive, satisfying the desires and fears of the ego. You are caught up in the motions of the ego. You are neither love nor are you freedom; you are instead reinforcing the self. This describes much of the world today.

But true, unconditional love is a state of Being where you do not need such a response to feel good, since you are goodness already. Love needs no reason. Love IS without cause. Love is compassion without wanting anything in return. There is no purpose behind love, no motive in an act of love and no reason for your activity at all. You give your help freely, asking nothing in return. You don't need any form of psychological 'pat on the back'; to love is to never require anything in return. Anything else, any form of return, is sensation and gratification, and would be like equating satisfying sex to true love. Equating love with sensation is to make love a thing of the mind, and this is what most of us do. We donate, we feel good in response and we think that this is love.

Look at what humanity is like. We love only those with whom we share common values – our countrymen, our fellow team supporters or our local church group – and we do not love those who are different – the supporters of the rival team or the attendees of the mosque down the road. If we love only those who are just like us, or similar in many respects, then our so-called love is a reflection of our own identifications. The fact that we love some people and not others is purely a reflection of the self; it is the ego reinforcing its own identity. If we could love those who shake our foundations, rather than treating these individuals as the focal point of our hate, then there is the possibility of unconditional love. Instead, we have made love into something that is exclusive to those who meet specific criteria, something that is the product of our beliefs, our values, our opinions and our ideas; something that brings us satisfaction. We have attached certain criteria to our love and have made love a product of the mind. Surely this cannot be love?

Is love thought or the product of thought? When you give someone a hug, is thought running through your mind in the opening moments of that hug or are you just hugging? Do you have to be thinking about how much you love the person whom you are hugging for there to be love, or can love BE without the function of thought? Is love the product of thought, or is love something that is independent of thought? Look into yourself, and you will find that when and where there is love, thought need not be functioning. Love is independent of thought and therefore need not be the product of thought, like a psychological sensation. Whenever thought is dominant, love is barely seen; we are not saying that love is not or is no longer, we are simply saying that love is hidden. Love is always there, it is eternal, it is the essence of 'all that is'; love can either BE or be hidden, and it is hidden for most of us. The way of goodness does not depend upon imported virtue but on understanding that which hides the love within you. It is the ego which hides this love within its distorting layers. Is virtue a positive ideal, a layer of the ego, or is virtue the capacity to see the nature of darkness and be free of it? Virtue begins in observation without distortion.

What is certain is that love is independent of thought. Love is more prominent when the mind is quiet. Thought may come into play before an event, after an event or even during an event, but that thought is sensation. It is thought as emotion or pleasure, it is thought responding from memory, it is not love. Love exists independently of the function of thought. There is love when the mind is free of fragmentation and duality. Love IS when thought is not. We are not saying that thought is the opposite of love, not at all; we are simply saying that thought need not be functioning for love to BE. And remember, the essence of you is not thought. Perhaps then the words of our historical masters are true: the essence of you is love. Love is equilibrium within, it is 'what is' when there is order within the mind. Love is whole, non-dual, indivisible and universal; it is never selective or exclusive like the love of our romantic ideals. Love exists like a flame within each and every one of us; it starts and there is no end. Love is eternal. It is inclusive and unconditional.

Love in the 21st Century

SEX AND THE CULTURE OF youth and beauty have become hugely important in 21st century culture. It is amazing to observe just how many of us confuse sex with love. Many find that during sex we abandon ourselves for a moment and in that abandonment there is the ending of the 'me'. Sex is a way of escaping; sex is a way of forgetting ourselves and because most of us do not know Being outside of the mode of the self, we value sex as the most precious of things. In sex we are escaping from ourselves and so this is our only real breath of freedom. Freedom is like breath; go without it and you wither and die. Look at what happens to someone without freedom. They are miserable, already dead. We crave freedom because our essence is freedom, and this is why we value anything that gives us a glimpse of that essence.

As we have seen, the vast majority of our daily activities – including everything that we do at work, socially and in our spiritual or political lives – serve to reinforce and expand the self. It is the self that decides what to strive for, what to become, how to behave, what to desire, how to achieve gratification. The self is this fragmentation of the enforcer and the enforced. Conversely in sex there is this moment where, unless you are playing some form of kinky mind domination game as the master rather than the slave, there is complete self-forgetfulness. You lose yourself, you abandon yourself and for a moment you feel free. In the moment of orgasm there is the complete absence of the self; that is why you orgasm. Our self-forgetfulness is a moment of authentic freedom, and for many of us it is the only moment of true freedom in our lives, no matter how long or how brief that may be. Despite spending much of our time and effort reinforcing the self, we crave this moment when the self is not.

It is our only moment of freedom, and it has become the most important thing in the world. We desire it and make it this big thing upon which we build our entire culture. We make it an ideal, we make it a problem; we glorify sex because orgasm is our only glimpse of real freedom. Yet ironically we have become slaves to sex, we have become slaves to a moment of freedom. See how absurd this is! In this craving and slavery, you are no longer free.[3]

Sex may look and feel like love, but love is when the absence of the self happens through genuine understanding. If the pseudo nature of the self is not understood, then we can easily confuse sex with love, we can easily confuse the momentary abandonment of the 'me' with love as so many people do all over the world. Men leave their wives for mistresses only to find that what they thought was love is in fact only a transitory moment of self-abandonment. The majority of us think love is sensation, we think love is the reaction of the mind to sensation, yet all sensation is transitory. How can love be transitory? Love is indivisible; it is eternal, total, never partial or temporary. If your love has ever been temporary – you once loved in the past and now your love is no longer – then it was not love in the first place. Your love was the product of the mind; it was a reaction of the mind to sensation.

Sex is a way of momentarily forgetting the self, and without realising it we crave sex because we are clinging to the repetition of the bliss, freedom and joy that comes with self-forgetfulness. This is in stark contrast to the daily activity of the self which reinforces the 'me' in every way; a process that we know to be isolating in nature. If we equate the self-forgetfulness of sex with love, without understanding what is taking place, then we are easily confused into thinking that we know and have experienced love. Only when there is deep understanding of the process of the self, with its barriers to love in the form of identifications, attachments, dependencies, desires and fears, is there the possibility of love.

---

[3] This is true of any area of life, including the spiritual search. This is why Truth belongs to no path, no sect, no religion or doctrine. Truth is above and beyond all 'isms' because Truth, which is love, is freedom.

Love & Fear

PERHAPS YOU WISH TO AVOID feeling lonely and you use your relationship as a distraction away from your fear of the empty inner state. The ego will always seek to escape its deep fear of loneliness and insufficiency and it will trick you into thinking that through romance, through security and dependence upon another, these fears can be alleviated. Of course there is nothing wrong with romance, romance is a beautiful thing. Just don't use romance as a mechanism to alleviate your fears, otherwise it is bound to turn ugly.

Whilst in a relationship you may be able to suppress your fears for a while, or distract yourself so long as your attachment goes undisturbed, but if you rely on your relationship the foundation of your security will always be shaky. It will be dependent upon a cause and therefore unstable. To be safe you may seek out a partner who is dependable, constant, devoted or loyal but when the source of your security or attachment is removed, there is bound to be misery. This threat will always be there in the back of your mind, and everything that you do subsequently in your marriage or in your romance will be rooted in the fear of loss. You will never overcome your fear of the empty inner state, of being left abandoned and alone if you are – in your jealous action – constantly seeking to protect yourself (which is an escape). Are these the actions of love, or are they reactions to fear?

Think of all that we associate with the experience of 'love' – alongside company, mutual interests, sharing and companionship we also have the movement of thought for pleasure sensation, sexual sensation, desire, jealousy, attachment and dependency. Most of us, particularly those in anaclitic relationships, know love through control, manipulation, possession, conflict, exploitation and domination of the other. We know love when our partner is away because suddenly we feel isolated and lonely. It seems that for most of us, 'love' has become closely associated with sensation. When we are jealous, possessive or dominating, what is taking place in these moments is that the ego is reacting to a threat to its security. In the face of such threats we, in reaction, seek our ideal of love; an ideal that is determined by the ego. The ego wants comfort, company, security and adventure and so we seek love with expectations of whatever that love should entail. When we don't get what we want we are hurt, angry, sometimes even aggressive. We have made love conditional, laying down criteria for our love as though it was some kind of bargaining deal. Love is not an exchange. There is no motive in love.

We all seek love, we have all had glimpses of love and we form ideas around love based on the past, on what we have read, experienced or on what we have heard. From this idea in our minds we decide that we want it, and set about our search for love in our own particular fashion. But if we are deeply honest with ourselves, we don't know what that love truly is. Can thought ever truly know love? Is love something that the mind can truly understand or is it a state of Being that is beyond the mind? Of course we may know who or what we love, but we can never truly know, psychologically, what love is. Try it and you are guaranteed to fail. We can be earnest and determined about the object of our love, but such movements of thought are desire, not love. We can only ever BE love because love is a state of Being, it is neither a state of thought nor something that the mind can know, describe or label. At the very best, thought can describe the characteristics of loving behaviour but it can never describe love itself.

We desire, crave and seek love because we think that when we find it there will be fulfilment; a fairytale ending that is fated, almost providential. We think that by having a partner, by being in relationship with another, we will find completion. We use romance or interpersonal relationship (thinking that these are the extent of love) as a mechanism to reach our goal. We have made love into a utility, a tool with which to guarantee our fulfilment – or at least, so we think. Can love be used as a tool in the search for fulfilment or is fulfilment something that is by itself when you are love? If love is what you fundamentally are, then perhaps it is our search for love that is acting as a barrier to love?

When we seek love, it is the ego that is seeking, trying to find safety and security. As we know, the nature of ego activity is always isolating and separating and this is true also of its search for love; it is bound to be self-enclosing. Deep-rooted feelings behind our search for permanent love, like the alleviation of our deep fears of loneliness or abandonment, can be expressed in a multitude of subtle ways. Your insecurity and fear that your partner might leave you cause you to indirectly start restricting their movements; perhaps you start questioning them about who they are seeing when they go out. We know possession, jealousy, manipulation and domination are all born out of fear, and these are typical reactions of the human mind when it comes to what we think of as love. If we are to come upon the truth of love, all these ego-based fears must cease; the ego is to be understood completely. There are no shortcuts.

Perhaps you have recognised the flaw of possessiveness, and realised that you cannot love if you deny the freedom of another. The problem is, if the nature of fear is not understood, if there is not the realisation that the ego is conflict, then you'll be adhering to the way of doing things that you've decided is correct, without ending the conflict of ego. The mind will remain fragmented. Yes it is true that when your partner is free to grow and understand what makes them joyful for themselves, with you or without you, there is love. And it is true that as soon as you restrict them you do not love them; you cannot possess what is inherently free – neither another, nor love. But don't make this into an ideal because as soon as you do you will not be able to see the true nature of ego as conflict; conflict caused by your ideal, by 'what should be', which is fear. Your ideal will distort understanding because any movement towards an ideal is conflict. You may desire to continue to evolve as separate, unique individuals while also growing as a couple or you may not wish to be with someone who inhibits personal growth and aspiration, but if you do not understand how desire, growth and aspiration are also part of the ego's idea of becoming, love is not possible. Love is only possible in aloneness, in being happy alone; when one is free to be without any adjustment, which means to have understood the processes of the ego. Then you won't project your ideal of love onto another, trying to overcome or suppress your fear through action. Only when fear has been understood are you ready to be with another. Then there will be no dependency in your relationship.

The self-enclosing activities of the ego – its various movements to overcome fear – are the barriers to love that must cease. How can there be love in moments of anxiety, or attachment or the search for gratification when what is clearly visible is fear? Fear indicates an absence of love, an absence of light, and something must be blocking that light for it to be hidden. What blocks is the activity of the fear-orientated ego self, seeking its desires and aversions.

If I am dependent on someone then of course I will get jealous and possessive because I fear losing that person. All attachment is suffering. All attachment inevitably leads to corruption because all attachment is rooted in the fear of loss. The reason for being attached in the first place is that without the person to whom I am attached, I feel insufficient and lonely. There is the anxiety of loss and because there is this dependency, I have no freedom. To protect myself from hurt, I will try to manipulate my partner so that I am not left alone and abandoned. I can only get hurt because I do not know the freedom of the essence of my Being, which is the empty inner state. I can get hurt because I have identified with the image that I have inwardly formed of myself; an image which, when I break it right down, is that of a single, isolated and insignificant individual. No matter how vain or humble I may appear to be on the surface – I could be the king of the world or a beggar on the streets – inwardly I feel separate from existence and unhappy to be alone, so my base psychological and emotional state will always be fear. This is true of most people today.

Fear derives from our sense of separation from existence. It is the feeling that comes with isolation, when there is no contact with the being of another, your inner Being or the Being of existence. Everything that I do either consciously or sub-consciously, ranging from the formation of certain beliefs to virtually all of my daily activity, will be designed to reinforce the image that I have of myself because this image is all that I have; it is the only mechanism that I can conceive to alleviate my deep fears within – fears which never seem to go away.

I must protect this image of myself, I must preserve it and because I have placed so much emphasis on it, the very placing of this emphasis makes it extremely fragile. Thus, I become very defensive. My self-image is easily dented and as a result I find it difficult to love, because the alleviation of my fears will always be my priority. I must begin by looking into not *what* I fear but into the nature of fear itself. Perhaps then I might come upon this wonder of love all by myself. If I can face anxieties head on with awareness, once I understand them it is easy to transmute and release them. In such alertness there is a sense of integration and wholeness within, there is forgiveness and self love without any of the justifications devised by the self. There is no longer contradiction and fragmentation in my mind; there is order, the foundation of all effortless virtue. I am indivisible, free of conflict, and only then, truly individual. And if there is to be love, I must first be individual.

In the case of possessiveness in relationships, there is contradiction and tension inside me because I fear the loneliness of life without my partner. This attachment is part of my identification process, trapping me in my own enslaving thoughts, from which I cannot seem to break free. I want to break free, not from the interpersonal relationship necessarily but from my attachment to that relationship (hence the contradiction in my mind), only now I have to be careful not to get attached to the method of freeing myself from attachment. If I am attached to the method that frees me from attachment then I have only swapped one attachment for another, which is why living according to ideals or through the systems and methods of gurus and religions can be so counter-productive. To know why I am attached, I must know why my action is rooted in fear in the first place, and in order to know this I must face all of my fears head on. I must watch these fears in meditation rather than try to escape or overcome them. In watching the problem the problem reveals itself. I cannot learn if I am forever trying to move away from a problem. Ask, *what is the source of this disturbance?* Not, *how do I solve the problem?* There must be self-knowledge because without this knowledge, everything that I do, including all of my choices, will be rooted in fear. I will never know the freedom and forgiveness of love.

Love as Utility

TO WHAT EXTENT ARE OUR human relationships more of an arrangement than an expression of love? When we say 'arrangement', we are referring to the kinds of relationships preferred by the ego because they reinforce the ego in some way, helping it in its joint aims of self-preservation and self-gratification. Whenever ego is involved, your relationships serve the interests of the ego and you have them because of what they can bring you – be that security, convenience, comfort, pleasure, companionship or any one of a whole host of sensations which alleviate your fears or give you pleasure. These are the types of relationships that we have today – arrangements that may involve house sharing, where both partners tire themselves out at work all day striving for whatever their ambition is and then come home demanding to be loved. We want to feel something, we demand pleasure, stimulation, conversation, company; we make many demands of our partners. When things go wrong, we might say, "*My partner does not love me,*" or ask, "*Why does my partner not do this for me?*" We are making love into a bargaining tool, something to be demanded. If we want love, then we do not possess love. We only possess that which we can give away freely. And because we are not love we rely on the other, always wanting, always looking for something from the relationship. When you love your child you never ask for anything in return, why then do we place such demands and expectations on a partner? Understand that you demand because you are not fulfilled and you are looking to the other for your fulfilment. In such a relationship, the partners are using each other, which is one degree away from exploitation. And we call this 'love'.

You are dependent on the other for a sense of completion and when that completion is denied, you naturally feel upset, hurt and angry. Is this love or is this dependence? Can you not be complete in your own aloneness? If you are dependent upon each other and this is what is sustaining the relationship, if you are using each other to escape the insecurities and insufficiencies that you feel inside, such as your inner loneliness or your fear of abandonment, then you are together in order to alleviate these fears. If you are together out of fear, petrified of being lonely, then you do not know what it means to be related; to have relationship with another and be in harmony with that other without the projections of your ego interfering. We are not discussing an infantile relationship with the image of another formed within memory, adjusted by knowledge – which is always incomplete and therefore corrupting in nature. We are discussing something much more remarkable: the ability to see what is 'actual' when it comes to another and for this to be free from knowledge, free from the past, free from our projections – like our ideas about what a relationship 'should' be. Normally such ideas are imported from trashy magazines or holy books and not worth the paper they are printed on. Right relationship is to be related without dependency, without any self-centred activities such as the need to escape your fears or your wish to gratify. Love comes into being when there is complete freedom from the self-projected desires and fears of the ego. We are then able to meet others with empathy and compassion; a deep harmony and communion without ever demanding that our narcissistic needs be met. The problem of human power struggle, from the subtle to the overt, is subsequently removed. Then we can live in peace, free from psychological conflict.

In some cases we use relationships with others as a mechanism for the fulfilment of certain desires. Maybe you have relationship because you have formed an image of yourself and without this identification you would feel incomplete, lost and lonely. Maybe your relationship strengthens the image that you have of yourself – a rich man with a trophy wife, or a devoted partner and parent. Whatever your self-image may be – 'I am successful,' 'I am a failure,' 'I am lucky,' or 'Why does it always happen to me?' – it will be based upon identifications that have built up over time. If you are using your relationship to reinforce these identifications, whether consciously or even subconsciously, then you are seeking gratification in your own way and you are looking to the relationship as a mechanism for this gratification. You are using your relationship as a means to strengthen and reinforce your sense of identity. Is this love or is the ego reinforcing itself as a process and in that process making itself more secure and permanent?

I have an image of you and by being with you I feel gratified; you have an image of me and by being with me you feel gratified. If this is true, as it is of many relationships, then our relationship is a relationship of mutual gratification. Now what is related? Are you really related to what is the essence of my Being, or are you related to images that you have formed around me? The truth is that most couples are in love not with each other, but with the image that they have formed of each other in their minds. These images are held and made possible because of the ego's drive to self-preserve, secure or gain. In the creation of an image the ego generates further momentum for itself, a mechanism of preservation in terms of continuity. It also likes to generate an image so that it can draw pleasure. The ego creates the image in order to avoid being disturbed. This is why we say love is blind. Do you really know your partner or do you only know the created image? They are images which are not fundamentally real, images that meet certain criteria of psychological satisfaction. We then put all of this together and call it love. This is how most of us know love. The truth is, love has no criteria, but the images we hold onto meet many criteria. The result can only lead to misery, deception and corruption, for the relationship will inevitably turn sour as the truth of the imaging process makes itself known.

Love cannot flower in the presence of what is fundamentally not real. You may present an image of yourself and feel the need to keep up appearances, but then authentic relationship is not possible. Equally by holding an image of another you are not seeing that other, you are seeing a set of ideas around them which you have formed in the mind, or which have been purposefully presented to you in order to win favour. In the face of such distortions, how can love be possible? Such a relationship is rooted in both falsity and fear, and once you go down this well trodden road, you will both soon be trying to manipulate each other through the adjustment of the image that you portray. You do this in order to gain power and then possess the other so that you can make them *yours*, so that your ego can relax – like in a marriage contract.

The ego seeks to possess because the ego does not like to be disturbed and it defines a disturbance as anything that threatens its security. Through our justifications, condemnations, judgements, opinions and conclusions, perhaps presented in the form of ideals, beliefs or marriage values, the ego will seek to prevent a disturbance. It is this desire not to be disturbed that causes us to avoid 'what is' which, in this case, is the danger of possession. We may see our efforts as freedom *from* the problem when in reality what is really happening is the continuation of our avoidance to understand the true nature of the problem, which is possession. Freedom *from* something is not freedom. To be free from something, the ego must first identify and then cultivate resistance. It sees what it would like to see, which is *"Rest, you are married, you are safe"* not 'what is' or 'what is actual' – this being the falsity and absurdity of possession. How can one see and understand 'what is' in the face of such distortions? When not clear the fear of 'what might be' is inevitable, there will always be conflict around it and wherever there is conflict there is no freedom. Yet for most of us we consider this normal. Most of us call this 'love'.

If you have made your love conditional or, let's turn this around, if you have felt that you must meet certain criteria in order to win love, then there is the ache of fear of not living up to the image that you have presented of yourself, and so there is all the fuss and sorrow of striving to meet expectations. There is fear, but we call it love. Where there is love there are no images, there are no judgements and there are no criteria; as soon as these enter the frame the whole relationship turns ugly – just look at the face of divorce to see that this is true.

Are we discussing a relationship of gratification, where you are gratified and your partner is gratified, where the relationship has continuity because this gratification is mutual, or are we discussing a relationship that has nothing to do with sensation or the search for sensation? If a relationship has continuity because it is mutually beneficial, like most relationships today, then you are using each other. This is not dissimilar to a business arrangement, a relationship of mere convenience. Relationships based on mutual gratification are not authentic. They can be fun and exciting but let's not pretend that they are real. What is real is to have genuine interest and care in another as they are, not as we necessarily want them to be. Genuine interest in another, without that interest having to lead to something or go somewhere. Surely this is a sign of something authentic, something real? Today most relationships are based on motive, goal, convenience or agenda and this is why so many of us feel isolated and disconnected from each other. We feel the need for psychological strokes – a pat on the head for the ego. We each seek gratifying sensation whenever an opportunity presents itself, attempting to relieve our loneliness. But this search in itself is isolating, divisive and separating in nature, both from one other and from existence itself.

Where there is a relationship based only upon the stimulation of sensation, we get used to the sensations that the relationship brings, and then we form expectations. This sows the seed of habit and indifference within the mind and what follows is the wholesale corruption of indifference and insensitivity. Insensitivity, as we know, is the ending of intelligence. Indifference signals possession, where you start to take each other for granted and the novelty of the relationship begins to fade. This will most likely continue until there is a threat to your possession, until there is the potential of a disruption or disturbance – perhaps someone else takes an interest in your partner, or one of you begins to look outside of the relationship to spice things up. Look into life, look into the many poor relationships of today, and of course such demands, urges and eventual outcomes are inevitable. In reaction you manipulate the other, you are jealous, you feel threatened and then all of the power games between couples begin. This is a reaction which stems from your fear. How can any of this be love? How can love ever be reaction or be contained within indifference or fear? Love knows no exploitation, no usage, and no dependency upon another. Love is never born out of fear, love has no fear within it; love is indivisible, whole and can never be fragmented. There is no hate in love, there is no fear in love; there is only love and love IS when all the things of the mind are not. Until the freedom of aloneness is deeply understood (as discussed in the earlier chapter, *Your True Nature*) we will never know what it means to love. Until then, all of our relationships will be based in fear, based upon utility and the mutual usage of one another.

There are many consequences of building relationships upon utility. What happens when the sensations that we desire out of our relationship cease? If we have made love physical pleasure, what happens when that pleasure is denied? A new mother is less interested in sex after the birth of her child, and so for the husband there may be resentment and frustration, both potentially leading to anger. When pleasure sensation is denied in the animal kingdom there is aggression; witness the alpha male fight for food or the most fertile mate.

We humans are not much different, not underneath. We disguise this with all of our social graces, etiquette, and so forth, but when our gratifications are truly denied, there is often frustration, tension and the potential for resentment and aggression. You will be surprised to learn just how many men have expectations of sex in their relationships of love. Is that love? Surely not.

If the relationship that you call love is really a relationship to secure favoured sensations, you are related for purposes of utility, for what the relationship can bring you. You have reduced love to sensation, to a product of the mind. But love is not something that is the product of the mind, nor is it something that the mind can truly understand. We have said that thought need not be functioning for love to be. By all means think about who or what you love; write ballads, write poems and paint pictures, but these are merely words or mechanisms of description; they are never the actual. The naming of love does not change, improve our understanding or have any bearing on what love actually is. Yes it is lovely to describe love within our arts, and the richness of description can elicit the removal of barriers between you and that which is love, but this description can never actually BE love. How can the description truly be the described if love is a state of Being? No description of Being can ever substitute or actually be that Being. Further to this, all description is limited by language, which is why art often does a better job at describing love than words can. At best, art can assist in the ending of the barriers between the thinking you and what is love by catalysing the ending of thinking, and thus the ceasing of the distorting self such that there is the absence of the 'me'. It is through the negation of that which divides and separates – the barriers created by the ego – that we come upon this thing called love. That which divides and separates is the continuity mechanism of the ego, and to come to love we must understand this mechanism deeply.

The projections of the ego – in the form of desires, fears, expectations and beliefs – always fragment a person inside, breaking apart the harmony of one's true intelligence; the intelligence which comes into operation when the heart and mind speak as one. Our ambitions, jealousies, attachments and greed act as barriers between the heart and the mind, and in the absence of heart-mind intelligence each of us goes about our daily activities pursuing our own personal goals and achievements. This is normal for us today, this is how we have been conditioned as a society and we accept it blindly without ever really thinking about it. How can there be an authentic relationship with another if you are driven in this way? And if you are not related, how then can there be love? As long as our interpersonal relationships are neither deep nor authentic, then wider relationships between groups of people, countries and religions are always going to be characterised by conflict.

To Be Related

TO BE RELATED MEANS TO be in complete and total communion with the essence of another, rather than with the image or the knowledge that you have of that other in your memory. Knowledge, as memory, is past. Knowledge operates out of the past and today knowledge seems to be the very basis of modern relationship. Knowledge is always incomplete and since there is no complete knowledge it must rest within the shadow of ignorance. What is incomplete will always generate conflict. When we relate we seem to relate from the past, from what is incomplete. *I am English and you are French: I am Hindu and you are Muslim: I am better than you because I have been educated rightly and you have not: You are from a good family and they think of me as common because my father was absent*: all that nonsense. Can there be love when we operate this way, from the past? Surely the past obscures and distorts what is 'actual' right now; that the tramp you ignore is a fellow human being, part of the group consciousness that is humanity. See how the past creates images and false ideas in the mind, ideas of comparison in the form of a feeling of superiority over others.[4] We are intellectual and still the problems of the world persist, as we fill our heads with false ideas to disguise our ignorance. Look at

---

[4] An idea, incidentally, that is most certainly true of the Bluebloods who secretly rule this Earth – but that is another story.

the mess we have made of it so far; comparison[5] which is the cause of the war, and the sickening and corrupt culture of capitalism that we have embraced. Ours is a culture that has no love within it at all.

To be related, there must be no distortion in your communication, and it is the past that distorts. These distortions arise from the ego's pursuit of fulfilment; the seeking of certain pleasures and the avoidance of pain. The pursuit of fulfilment rests inside our every desire, our every fear, hope, projection, belief, attachment and aversion. It is this very activity, driving every aspect of our behaviour, which is always isolating in nature, denying us authentic relationship with both ourselves and others and acting as a barrier to love.

Relationship is only possible when there is complete openness, integrity and humility with yourself and others. Where there is such openness, you are able to face deep fears within with a clarity and precision that you have never known before. In a sense, there is complete vulnerability; everything is open, you are naked, you are laid bare like an open book. He who has surrendered himself completely, where his back is against the wall and there is nowhere left to go, becomes invincible in his vulnerability. As we discussed in the previous chapter, it is in complete surrender, which Buddha and Jesus called meekness, that you become most powerful. In the death of the ego, in the ending of psychological time, in the total surrender and vulnerability of everything about you, you are love. Your vulnerability is momentary only in the sense of what disturbs the ego, but just as the ego is a nonsense, so too is any idea of vulnerability. They are mere ideas that exist in your mind. Understand that you have nothing to lose and that in your nakedness, where there is nothing left but your Being, you can return to freedom and to love. You are no longer capable of being hurt, there is no image that can be shattered, no reputation to preserve, no ego that needs feeding; you are free of all that nonsense. When it comes to the moment of your death, when you truly understand that even your fragile body is no more than a simple bag of skin, you can enter death

---

[5] Comparison exists because we have put all of our faith in the intellect, in knowledge.

with enthusiasm, excited by the adventure of what it is to die. You are truly free; authentically beyond all fear.

To come to love you must drop the ego, for the ego mind will always wish to maintain its own security and protect against anything that disturbs its momentum. When there is no mind, when all fear has been put onto the table and you are there and you are vulnerable, what exactly have you got to lose? Understand that it is only the ego that is capable of feeling a sense of loss; understand the falsity of this process which forms the momentum of the ego. In this understanding you will automatically become unaffected by it and completely free of it. What have you to lose really that is not part of the image that you have formed of yourself?

Our relationships tend to be founded upon actions that are self-orientated, like our pleasures and gains, and so our relationships have become relationships of usage; they have become mechanisms to feed the ego. If you are related to another with a view to reaching an objective, if your relationship is a means to gain something, then you are using that relationship to achieve a goal. Wherever there is a goal there is ambition, there is comparison, there is measurement to go beyond yourself or others; there is a lack of dignity and respect for both yourself and others and the conflict to change 'what is' about yourself.

Perhaps you feel the need to prove to yourself that you are extraordinary, which means excelling socially, at work, at sport or in some other field. If you fail, then you may feel that you have let yourself down. Your sense of self is greater when things are going well, but as soon as life becomes a little arduous you view this as a personal failure. *'I am not enough'*. *'Others will only love and accept me if I excel.'* This may not be a conscious statement, but if ambition and comparison are the driving activity of your life then you are subconsciously telling yourself that love is conditional. This can be so deeply rooted that it goes unnoticed for years. You set yourself targets, you become competitive, you seek success and wish to change many things about yourself, all because you are fearful. Unless you can forgive yourself of all such tensions within, they remain inside as fear. How then is love possible when everything about you is rooted in fear?

The point to consider is this: usage of another can never be love because all usage is rooted in fear. The fact that you are using another – just as you use a job or a title – to reinforce your sense of self, indicates that you are driven by the wish to change what currently is. You are striving because you still feel insufficient inside. Always there is 'what should be' in your activities; you are driven by fear.

A Meditation

Please meditate with the following:

> Total integration = Total Forgiveness = Self Love.
> 'That Which IS' is totally integrated.
> 'That Which IS' forgives itself completely.
> 'That Which IS' is Pure Love.

THERE CANNOT BE LOVE WHERE there is desire or the search for gratification, because you are then caught in the trap of adjustment; you are caught up in the chasing of 'what should be' rather than fully comprehending 'what is', as it is. Understanding is only ever complete and truly integrated when there is no self-orientation; the self binds our understanding. Loves knows no bondage, only freedom, and this understanding is free from the projections of the ego. With love there is no struggle to change, there is no need for adjustment of what you already are or what already is; there is thus never any comparison or measurement against another. Love can only be when you know and comprehend your absolute correctness in this, the present moment. Otherwise you will always wish to adjust yourself, you will always wish to make yourself better, and these activities are all rooted in fear. Fear can never be love. There is no fear within love, there is only love within love. In adjustment you will always be caught up in the idea of success and achievement, you will always be caught up in the trap of 'what should be', even in relation to your spiritual development. Love is not nor will it ever be a product of the mind, love only IS when the process and the mechanics of the mind cease. Love IS where there is a quality of stillness in the mind, not a quietude that is enforced.

Enforced quietude is a contradiction in terms; in subjugation the controller is himself also the controlled.

We need not worry about how to love or how to find love, we need only concern ourselves with what hinders love because love comes into being when all barriers to love are removed. These barriers are created by you; they are created by the thinking aspect of 'you' that you think is 'you'. The ego is the barrier to love; the 'me' aspect with all of its movements is what hinders and blocks out love. Know that this idea of 'you' that you have formed in your mind is not real, for the ego is a false entity. Only the love within is fundamentally real. This love is whole and indivisible, free, unlimited, unbound and eternal. It is life, it is existence; your existence and all that is. Love without condition comes about with self-knowledge and temperance of the self, not through reaction but through self-awareness. It comes with understanding the mechanism of the self at every moment in our lives – in every step, in every word, in every communication – and the resulting freedom from the constant adjustment towards 'what should be' – a condition disguised as an ideal that we create in our minds. It is only in the present moment, in the moment of 'what is', that unconditional love is possible.

Our understanding of virtue, too, is coloured by ideas of 'what should be'. 'What should be' is a distraction from 'what is'. It is a creation of the ego. 'What should be' is a self-projection, just like when we compare, measure, judge, condemn, justify, resist, suppress, repress, sublimate, cultivate, control or discipline ourselves against 'what is'. We have even made virtue, in the form of control and conforming to patterns, yet another form of self-projection. Virtue-as-self-projection is actually the antithesis of true virtue. It tethers the mind and reduces its swiftness and pliability to see and understand 'what is'. A mind tethered cannot understand 'what is', for always its field of discovery is limited by the distortions of its beliefs, opinions and judgements; most of which are notably about the self. 'What is' can only be understood in the present. All distractions exist in time, they exist in the conflict of the opposites; the 'me' and whatever the 'me' thinks about and desires to change. There are no distractions in the present moment.

Love belongs to the present moment. Where love is, there are no movements of attachment, jealousy, envy or fear; the mind is no longer caught up in its beliefs, its views or its judgements. Love is a state of being that is characterised by the ending of striving, where there are no particular quests for new sensation. Love IS when the demanding, desiring, ambitious mind is not; love IS when there is the ending of the need to change. Love comes into being when there are no urges to move away from the present moment. Where there is love there are no further expectations of this moment, nor is there any concern or worry about the past or the future. Love IS when fulfilment IS, and fulfilment is when all the ambition, striving, desires and fears of the mind cease. All such activity derives from a lack of contact with existence; love happens when there is contact with existence.

If you think that love is the product of the mind, then you have attached certain criteria to love and have made your love conditional. How can love ever be conditional? Love doesn't have a cause. Love only IS when there is complete and total acceptance of 'what is'[6]; when there is total forgiveness of both oneself and others without any idea of changing yourself or these others into 'what should be'. Love is to truly accept yourself (and others) in the presence of your own (and others') mistakes. As we have seen, blaming yourself and not forgiving yourself is the biggest sin against the self and it prevents you from growing. If you blame yourself, you will always remain stuck. If you forgive yourself by understanding and integrating your mistakes, then there is the gift of more self love, more wisdom of oneself, more integration and thus growth. The way to Truth is to be true to oneself, free of all the justifications of the self, and in this truth there can be self-knowledge.

What you don't integrate will always keep coming back at you, until you have learnt and understood. This is why the human theatre of

---

[6] We do not mean, by this, acceptance in terms of a justification by oneself or of oneself or of the world around you; thought declaring that *this is fine* or *satisfactory*. In love, the self is free of the need to accept itself or even affirm itself because the very nature of the self is understood clearly. In understanding that the self is a false process, self-affirmation and self-acceptance are not relevant. We must be wary of the process of justification.

life has been constructed the way that it has, with the earth as the stage and the solar system as the pulleys and levers above that stage. This is why at varying and differing stages in our lives, we each endure and go through archetypal events, energies and situations – like those that are characterised within our ancient myths – in what are called astrological transits and progressions. These myths and maps were known extensively across Europe and beyond before the Christian era; subsequent intervention by the Vatican quashed this ancient knowledge.

Understand and forgive yourself and others, nothing else is needed. The 'forgiveness of sins' that Jesus speaks of in his teachings is the integration and forgiveness of mistakes against the self; it is the clarity of love that leads to understanding of the self, which means to be free of the process of self-adjustment. You must love that which you wish to understand. Know that religious traditions have hijacked the teachings of Jesus and twisted them by promoting forgiveness on one hand and denial and guilt on the other. This is trickery; guilt comes not from the inside but is imported from the outside and where there is guilt there is compulsion. Where there is guilt there is no freedom, no love and thus no understanding. If your love contains the desire to change yourself or another because you feel that you 'ought to' or 'should', then there is no acceptance of 'what is'; there is no forgiveness of oneself or others, and so love is not possible. This acceptance of 'what is' should never be a justification. The acceptance of oneself should never imply worthiness. Worthiness is identification. Why give, or feel the need to give, value to what is a false process, the ego? What role do self-affirmation and self-acceptance play when the pseudo nature of the ego is understood? In understanding, you will be free of the need to build a foundation of love from your own inner resources. One cannot cultivate love; what entity is cultivating that compassion? Love is to be free of the idea of *becoming*. The ego can never release the ego. Love is to be completely free of the idea of a centre, where there is no self, only existence, only meekness; where compassion is a natural action free from cultivation. You cannot cultivate what already is. What you are fundamentally is love, it is the ego that is the force of separation. Only when the ego is fully understood does the ego naturally go into abeyance, and our inner essence shines.

Free yourself of this toxic idea of loving oneself first so that you are free to love others later. Self-love and compassion are not separate; to suggest otherwise implies that love can be exclusive at first before it becomes inclusive later. Love is only ever inclusive, at the beginning and the end. Where there is self-love free of identification or self-projection, the term *self-love* becomes somewhat moot: there is only love. Then you will evolve, free of the need to evolve.

To Come to Love

TO COME TO LOVE THERE must be astuteness and self-knowledge, there must[7] be right relationship. There cannot be love if you are filled with jealousy, anxiety, possessiveness, attachment or expectation. All such movements are founded upon fear, even your desires derive from your fear of the empty inner state; they are all the product of the ego seeking its own fulfilment. Wherever there are any such movements, they are bound to be isolating and can never bring togetherness like love. For love to be, all there is to do is simply BE. This is not a compulsion – you cannot be compelled to BE, it is not possible. Live beyond any ideas of 'what should be', beyond any idea of insufficiency. Embrace your aloneness to become free of all past influence, and therefore all dependency. Love of course has no dependency because all dependency is fear. To come to love you must know yourself deeply, you must know what thwarts love; you must know the mechanism of the ego, the nature of the mind.

In love there is the complete absence of the 'me', there is a stillness of mind and it comes into being when all of the distorting activity of the mind ceases. It happens when there are no longer expectations or demands for a particular sensation; it happens when the mind is no longer projecting its desires or caught up chasing its hidden urges. Corruption begins when thought works for itself, its own security and gain. Thought is vagrant by nature, always looking for a home.

---

[7] It is wise to be mindful about our use of words such as *need* or *must*. The problem with such words is that they encourage patterns and a way of living that must be adhered to; this is the foundation of dogma.

Love comes into being when there is order in the mind, when the mind is able to see such contradictions within itself and step beyond its own dualistic considerations of 'what should be'. Order is a quality of stillness within the mind, not a quality of stillness that is brought about through chanting or some other mechanical discipline designed to numb down the mind. It is a stillness that brings absolute clarity and insight into the nature of the conflicts and contradictions within the mind.

To come to love, there must be meekness. Meekness is when existence IS and the 'I' is not; there must be humility if there is to be love. Love never looks to gain or achieve; it is the processes of the self which form the great barrier between us and existence. The cause of all of our fear is our sense of separation and isolation from existence. It is the ego, with its separating thought movements, that divides us from what is real.

Thought Divides

IT IS OFTEN SAID THAT thought and ideas can bring people together, but do they really? A group of people may gather together but that group will inevitably oppose another group. Ideas divide and separate, they do not unify. Does the ego permit a union of ideas or do ideas always, in the end, fragment? You may join a political party, you may share common values and this sharing can bring people together. You may be a conservative or a liberal, you may be a communist in China or a democrat in the United States; whenever you share common ideas with your peers it will look, at first glance, as though there is unity. This may be sustainable in the short run, but what about the long run? Let us look closer at the example of political parties. Across a range of topics many members may agree on certain basic principles, but probe deep enough and extend the range of topics far enough and eventually all elements within a political party will fragment; there will always be sub groups that wish to splinter off for they are bound to disagree over something. There will be varying and differing views on abortion, euthanasia, crime, immigration, drugs, economic policy, foreign policy and so on and so forth. Each member will have a different version of the perfect social ideal in their minds and there will be no end to the range of views or opinions, or to the wish to impose those opinions. This is particularly true amongst individuals who are acutely attached to their ideas and opinions, as many politicians are.

Now if fragmentation is true for one party or one religion, or any group of people for that matter, then it will be true for the next. Where there are common and shared values, the group is united on the surface; probe deep enough and eventually the splinters and fractures within a group will be revealed. There may be new unity and strength from disagreement and the subsequent negotiation within a group, but this inevitably leads to just another layer of identification. No matter how unified a group becomes there will always be another group in opposition. Identification will always be a fracturing process, despite providing the ego with an illusory sense of belonging. Nationalities can be united yet humanity remains divided. No matter which way we look at this, the identifications of the ego will always in the end separate; it is its very nature to isolate. Ideas and ideals segregate because they are constructed from the images, opinions, beliefs, judgements and values of the ego. The ego will always be the factor of division.

If the total agreement of ideas is not possible for even the closest of couples, it will certainly not be possible at the macro level of society. Of course any social or political movement can be held together by coercion, but then there is no freedom. Fear can unite a society, as in the case of a mutual hated enemy during times of war, but such togetherness is neither sound nor stable. Nothing founded upon fear is stable. Love is the only sustainable way to bring people together, whereas ideas inevitably splinter and separate. Fragmentation is therefore inescapable. A *good, old fashioned war* or – the technique of today – a false flag terrorist attack; these government tricks may bring people together for a while but ultimately all ideas separate. There can never be a fundamentally sound unification of people through the process of thought. You just need to probe deep enough and you will always find a point of weakness, where ideas divide the group or that group from another. Fragmentation is unavoidable because we humans do not know our true nature, which is psychological fragmentation, and each of us is bound to identify with our beliefs and ideas at some level. It is this identification which will always, in the long run, divide and separate.

You know what people are like; whenever a person's identifications are particularly strong that person is neither free nor embracing of others. Such a person is not open to the new, he is like a closed book. How then can he love? You cannot love if you hold beliefs and then try to impose those beliefs on others. Love is not possible in the presence of belief because belief is the reaction of the mind to the pursuit of fulfilment. You hold a belief because by holding that belief it gives a certain psychological sensation; that sensation must be satisfying for you in some way (even if it is self-defeating) otherwise you would not hold that belief. So you hold beliefs because they provide you with gratifying psychological sensations. Love is only possible when the mind no longer projects itself, when there is no longer the pursuit of this sensation or that sensation – pursuits which are dictated by the ego. Love is only possible when the ego ceases its search for fulfilment; it is only possible when the ego is not, when we no longer identify with belief.

A mind caught up in belief, including religious belief, cannot love. If you are caught up in a sect or a movement, living your life according to fixed beliefs which form a map for living, then there is disorder within the mind because of the conflict of adjustment and the fear of not achieving your goal. All expectations, searching, desiring, craving, striving and fearing must cease if there is to be love. The only genuine moments of love in your life have been moments of fulfilment and those moments have only ever been when the desiring mind has ceased, even if only briefly. Look back and remember such moments – hugging a loved one, cuddling your partner, playing silly games, mucking about – when nothing else was needed, wanted or demanded. The present moment was absolutely enough.

Sharing & Unity

WHEN LOVE *IS* THERE IS a connection. There is a communion with all that is around you and you are in contact with your inner Being. You no longer feel separated, isolated or lonely because love brings people together, it unites; never has it been known for love to divide and separate – not if that love was authentic. If your love has been divisive then it was not love, it was a product of the mind. Love is togetherness, sharing, a union of essences; the essence of your Being with the essence of another. This is possible because where there is love there is absence of the self with all of its urges, demands, expectations and fears; an absence of the ego's isolating processes. Where there is love there is the ending of all striving; the ending of the many movements of the mind that divide and separate.

There is relationship in love; a deep sharing of Truth and understanding. In order to share understanding there must be the art of listening, the art of observation where you are seeing the nature of a fact without your distorting, interfering mind projecting itself outwards. If you share a view – of a beautiful waterfall, perhaps – without any interpretation drawing from memory or conditioning that is past, then there is the flowering of the essence of that which is seen – the essence of the waterfall – which is beauty. Only then is sharing truly sharing, and to share is an act of love. Beauty IS when you are not, sharing IS when you are not. All sharing is an act of love and if you are love, you cannot help but share that love.

To share love you have to have love in the first place, you must be overflowing with love. Right Samadhi, which is what we are describing, is to be overflowing with love and it is only possible when there is a deep compassion, care and affection for all life, a direct contact with existence. Love is Death; the death of the ego. This is what is truly divine, not your church or temple or holy book. This love is neither imported nor cultivated, nor can it exist in a book, it is an essence that is when the 'me' aspect that is your centre – which you think of as 'you' – finally ceases. It is the bright flame inside that is forever yours and burns increasingly brightly when you give that flame away freely; in your every word, in your every step, in your every act. Only when you give love do you truly possess love; love is your only true possession, everything else is illusion.

Love That Which You Wish to Understand

IN ORDER TO UNDERSTAND AND observe with clarity, our observation – whether of a fact, an emotion or an external object – must be free from all view, naming and judgement. When the observer is no longer and there is only observation, it is possible for there to be an authentic communion with a fact and thus understanding of that fact. Just because you may have categorised a flower, as a botanist would, this does not mean that your understanding of that flower is any deeper. So to understand a fact there must be observation of that fact and for this to be clear then there must be the absence of the distorting 'me'. To know and understand an emotion like jealousy, for example, you have to observe jealousy without the distortion of the self; without the usual suppression, distraction or attempts to conquer which we impose upon ourselves. You must go into it deeply, fully, existentially; you must love the jealousy rather than deny it, and then there can be the authentic knowing of it deeply. You will see it for what it truly is. You will see where it leads, you will see all of the misery that comes with it. You will be able to step away from it without having to question how; all will happen of its own accord, effortlessly.

To understand a thing there must be a communion with that thing with absolute clarity, for if there is no communion then there is bound to be misunderstanding. To know a fact, you must love that fact and surrender to it completely so that you can imbibe it, drink it, be it and thus understand it. This is the way of wisdom. Wisdom arises through self-knowledge and love for all that you see, hear and feel; it arises when there is love for everything, even that which we consider to be negative. Without wisdom we deny our dark side and this is why we have failed as a society to go beyond ourselves. To know hate, you must go into it deeply, you must let the poison of it run through your veins. To give something to another you have to have it first; you have to be full of hate if you are to throw that hate onto another – I recommend you do this experiment at home alone. Try it now, be full of hate and see where it leads. Soak up all of what hate represents and you will see clearly what hate is and the misery that it brings. You will understand that to hate you have to poison yourself, you have to harm yourself and when you know what this is deeply, then for you it will be impossible to hate. You won't need to think about how not to hate, you will never hate again because you will know where hate leads. The only reason why hate exists in contemporary society is because we do not truly know the level of misery that hate brings. We are asleep to its poison and it is because we are asleep – and subsequently deny ever understanding these darker aspects within ourselves – that the world we live in is corrupt.

What we are saying is that you must love a thing to understand it, whatever that thing may be. This is where there is potential for change in our society. Any revolution without love can only ever be cosmetic. As we demonstrated with regards to the empty state and the problems of loneliness that we have formed around it – ideas that have been driving virtually all of our sub-conscious behaviour for centuries – if we love and embrace that empty state then we will be able to know and understand it. When you know it and you know the freedom of it, your old idea of loneliness and the resulting problems of attachment, possession, dependency and desire will all cease. Then you can love freely without attachment or dependency; then the world will be unrecognisable and truly wonderful.

This deep relationship between love and understanding applies not only to you, me and to everyone in society, it also applies to existence itself. This is how existence operates within itself; it loves every aspect of itself and therefore understands every aspect of itself. Can you see that for existence to know itself, to truly understand itself, it must conceptually love itself? Existence is built upon love; it has to be, otherwise Truth could not know itself. Love is 'what is' in the present moment – the only moment, the moment of eternity. Love is 'what is', it is existence. Love is ISness and whatever IS is love.

The Connection with Truth

WE COME TO LOVE WHERE there is the ending of that which blocks love. We cannot make this ending an action or a reaction, it will happen of its own accord when there is understanding of what divides and separates us from the freedom of our Being. To come upon love, we have to negate that which is not love (and not freedom) and what is not love is the movement of the self. The way to love, which the Buddha taught, is the negation of that which is not love. You need not worry about how to love, love comes into being spontaneously and immediately without you needing to think about it or find it. This love will flower of its own accord when all of the barriers which block love break down. Only out of the negation of what is not love do we come to love.

One cannot negate barriers to love through suppression, distraction, sublimation or conquering; true negation is only possible when there is understanding, when there is astuteness and sensitivity to the processes of the mind. There must be attention, sensitivity and alertness to the processes of the ego – what they are and why they are happening – not just occasionally but at every moment in life. A master who is awake possesses this astuteness of self-observation; he is clear and knows himself fully. At the Temple of Apollo at Adelphi – where Apollo represents the ego self – famously inscribed above the entrance were the words: '*Know thyself*'. We must know ourselves and be highly sensitive to this self-knowledge if we are to love and Be love.

Negating the barriers to love includes breaking down the self consciousness which so many of us carry into our interpersonal relationships and out into the world. You can be naked and no-one will ultimately care. No-one is out to get you; people are not interested in you, they are only ever truly interested in themselves. It is you, being self-centred, who thinks that people are bothered about you. If you are brutally honest with yourself, if you can put aside all your ideals of 'what should be' for just a moment – how you ought to behave, what you want to look like – and take a long, hard look at yourself with complete honesty, you will see that you are only really bothered about yourself. You may think of others from time to time, but these times are rare; most of the time your concern is only for yourself. We are not saying that this is right or wrong, we are merely observing the fact because to see this fact is useful. Once you see it accept it as true, in spite of your ideals, and then forgive yourself for it. Then you can go forward. Now if this self-centredness is true for you, then it will also be true for others. Accept that others are not really bothered about you, unless what you do or say disturbs their ego. And if they are only bothered about you in such scenarios, then why should you let this disturb you, or hinder your loving actions? Why should you be at all bothered about what others think?

If you can die to this daily, hourly, every second; if there can be the ending of all aspects of feeling self-conscious, then there can be love. If you can die to your pleasures and your dependencies, to your attachments and your ambitions, then you will know already that this is enough; you will know by now that you have forgiven yourself completely because you already feel your own freedom. In this freedom you are love and when you are love, everything you do will be loving. Your goodness will not be imported from morality, your goodness will arise naturally because you are goodness already. It will be your nature. If on the other hand you feel that you need to make a public demonstration of the ending of all self-orientated activities, as certain ascetic practitioners do, then are you really free? The very act of such a demonstration is itself a self-orientated activity. Freedom, and therefore love, lies in the death of all self-orientated activities. Whatsoever is free is love and whatsoever is love will always be free. Where there is immense freedom, joy and bliss lie in wait. Truth waits for you always, because she has all of the time in the world; waiting for you to die to yourself, to resurrect yourself at each and every moment, waiting for you to end your own movement of psychological time; then there is communion between you and existence, then there is love. If you want to know love and know reality then be real in everything you do, say and feel. No more personas, no more image or self perception, just the essence of you. Then you begin to know who you are and your individuality will shine. Your old personalities will drop but you will be happy and for the first time your individuality will emerge without fear. Now life will be a true joy because now you are finally free to be your true expression.

When you are true to yourself, goodness will follow you wherever you go; it comes with you because joy and virtue are your basic state. You need not worry about the morality of society. What we call 'wrongs' in society are subjective, but what we call 'mistakes' from happiness stem from a state of disturbance within the mind. When you are aware, goodness, happiness and harmony follow of their own accord; there is no need to think about 'being good' as goodness is only an effort if you are not clear. 'Being good' comes from morality, from the laws of society, but remember society itself is deeply corrupt: raping and polluting nature in the name of money whilst celebrating success, ego and competition. All morality is manmade and has to be enforced upon society through the rule of law, which is not freedom.

When you love, that which you do will always be good. Goodness arises from freedom within one's mind, from forgiveness of mistakes against the self. Authentic goodness never stems from the outside but is your natural state of Being when you truly understand your own mind. So be true to yourself regardless of everything and then you will begin to understand who and what you are. In this understanding you will come to know what is your essence. By conforming to all of the views of others and the norms of society, you are not being true to yourself. All understanding and release must come from you – not from the law, not from your peers or even your own internal rules; all of these stem from the outside.

Where there is love there is always freedom, and where there is freedom there is order. Where there is order, the contradiction of the duality of the self finally ends and virtue and goodness will happen of their own accord. This goodness is not cultivated or imported; it is what you already are when the barriers constructed by the self finally come down. Goodness and rightness of action are more than second nature, they are your primary nature. This goodness is not dependent upon anything; it happens without cause. In this goodness there is compassion for all. Such goodness, such love and compassion, is not exclusive to one tribe or one religion, to one beloved individual or to those who share your views; it is universal and extends to everyone and everything. Love is universal, it begins and never ends; it can never be selective or preferential. Like freedom, it is indivisible. There is no such thing as partial love; love that is partial comes with criteria attached to it, and is conditional rather than universal. This is as true of our ideals of romantic love as it is of religious practices which call themselves love – they come with criteria attached, so how can they be love?

To understand love you must understand the root activity of the ego which hinders love. When there is activity of the ego, activity designed to reinforce its own process, activity which is rooted in fear and self-survival, there cannot be love. Love is always present, ready to emerge and show itself in the instant when the barriers between you and 'what is' dissolve. These are the same barriers that exist between you and existence, between you and your inner Being; these are the barriers created and driven by the ego. When love is, there is nothing that separates you from existence, all barriers have dissolved. Existence is pure life, pure energy.

Coming to Love

TO COME TO LOVE YOU need not concern yourself with how to love, you need only concern yourself with what is blocking you from love, and what blocks you is 'you'. You – the dictates of your ego – are the barrier to love. These activities divide and separate, they move you further away from your Being towards greater isolation. All fear is disconnection from existence, it is a form of death. It is a state where you are no longer in contact with existence; this same existence which is your inner Being. It is the ego that is the foundation of fear because it is the ego that is conditioned to behave in a self-orientated manner. At school we are taught to be competitive, to get ahead; we are graded, examined and indoctrinated into comparing and measuring ourselves against others. Everything that we do in our drive for success, achievement and our own personal gratification does nothing but separate and increase our sense of isolation. Where there is this division, isolation and loneliness within, what we are left with is a feeling of inner insufficiency. We live in this fear because this is how we have built our world.

It is fear that hinders love, like clouds blocking a clear blue sky. Love is like that sky; it begins but never ceases and cannot be contained. Love is like the air; it cannot be trapped or it will grow stale. Love is freedom and you cannot trap freedom; as soon as you trap freedom it is no longer freedom. It is the same with love. As soon as you try to possess love in terms of it being exclusively yours, it is no longer love. You have to open up your windows to the air outside, air that is unbound, free and forever new. Love is always new and because it is new it belongs to the language of now – like freedom, joy, order, virtue and goodness. All these are beyond boundary, beyond limit and thus eternal. They are all facets of the same fundamental truth; they are all faces of love. Love is the only true eternity and we are that eternity. We just need to see this clearly. Eternity is the void of awareness, which is the womb of existence, the inner emptiness about which Buddha speaks. It may be hard for us to understand, but it is our primary nature.

Where there is love there is complete communion, without separation or isolation. There is the ending of thought as movement (which is time), the ending of that which divides and separates you from existence; there is the ending of all activity of the self. There is contact with existence and the breakdown of the observer and observed. There is the ending of perception itself, the death of the self. Where there is love, there is connection with Truth and the realisation that the essence of you is Truth.

chapter 14
Quality of Stillness

Ripples in a Midnight Pond

THE ANCIENT MAYANS WERE KEEN star gazers, with sophisticated knowledge of the constellations and the earth's precession wobble. They knew the exact days of the winter and summer solstices and their Earth-moon-sun calendar is nearly as accurate as our calendars today. What is not commonly known about the Mayans is that they used to study the stars not by looking upwards at the night sky but by looking downwards into pools of water that were perfectly still. These pools acted like mirrors to give the star gazers a perfect reflection of the night's sky. Now, think of one of these pools as your consciousness at rest. In stillness there is a total clarity of reflection within your consciousness, like that of a mirror reflecting perfectly all that is placed in front of it. The Mayans' pools reflected the night sky without any blurs or distortions of perception, and it is the same for a consciousness at rest. There is observation of 'what is' with absolute clarity, like a mirror of pure awareness reflecting perfectly whatever is seen. When there is no wind or vibration or disruption in any shape or form, then there are no tiny ripples distorting the reflections in the water. This quality of stillness is order, it is a mind that is meditative and much can be learned from it. Such a mind is undisturbed, balanced, integrated and whole. There are no tiny ripples wavering over the surface of the pool of your consciousness, no ripples of desire, fear or identification distorting the clarity of your awareness.

Pure, clear awareness is fragile, delicate and gentle. One little desire, one small disturbance and a water ripple can spread out across the entire pond, disturbing the clarity of reflections of the night sky. It is the clarity of reflection that is important as that clarity represents your pure consciousness. One ripple and now all is blurred and your ability to see has become distorted. Add another ripple and a new distortion begins; yet another ripple and the reflection distorts even further. The chitter chatter of the mind creates many distortions, which is why materialists, many rationalists and those who follow traditional religion always seem disturbed and a little tense; the pool of their consciousness is reflecting a confused night sky. In a still pond, a pond without the distortions of thought, there is a single, crystal clear reflection; just one Moon, one Venus, one Alpha Centauri. This stillness and purity of observation is your essence. It is the same stillness of reflection that the Mayans used to great effect in their astronomy and astrology.

All mental distortions are contained in wave interference patterns across the surface of the water. In a mind of disorder, there are a multitude of distortions running across your field of vision. The surface of the pond is no longer clear and there are distorted reflections everywhere. Only when the water of your consciousness is still, only when the pond is fully at rest will the surface image accurately reflect that which is Truth. Only when the mind is still, only when the mind is fully at rest will your awareness be fully aware of 'what is'. Only when the mind is non-dual, only when one side of the mind is not telling the other what to do, is there the effortless effort of pure attention. This is the meaning of meditation: the effortless effort of pure attention.

A non-dual consciousness is a consciousness with no desire or attachment, where the quality of reflection is pure and not contaminated by any activity of the mind. Desire is one form of distorting wind that blows ripples of water across the pond of your consciousness. So long as desire or any thoughts are remaining, there will always be ripples distorting the clarity and purity of your awareness. It is important to understand that this purity is possible at any moment, not necessarily after years of meditation, therapy or counselling. This purity of awareness is an immediate possibility for any and all of us, as long as that which distorts is removed. This happens not as an action by 'you' but freely, of its own accord. A mind of perfect order is the greatest gift that you can ever give to yourself. It is the gift of the purest quality of existence from existence; the gift of bliss.

It is no surprise that, given the busy nature of 21st century life and the whirlwind of activity going on inside our minds, we find it hard to understand, meet and commune with our essence. Because this communion never takes place, we fail to see and understand our sorrows and pains with any clarity. Imagine an alarm that has been ringing in the background for years, there is a wonderful feeling of relief when the alarm finally stops. For many of us the alarm is still ringing, so we endeavour to cover up our background suffering with more foreground noise. Life gets louder and louder and more stressful as we try to solve our problems with more activity, with more winds blowing bigger and faster ripples across the waters of our consciousness. This is modern life. This 'Samsaric' cycle of cause and effect ties us into psychological time, providing us with a perpetual distraction from exploring our inner space. As long as we continue to identify with the winds of the ego mind, we will never know the beauty and peace of our inherent inner stillness. We will never open the door to our inner perfection.

The active mind is a pool of water that has been disturbed by many thought ripples running across its surface. The capacity for such a mind to see with clarity is distorted. You are distracted from your fundamental essence, which is the stillness of your consciousness without thought; it is pure awareness, empty and silent. When you stop, sit still and meditate. When you can Be and be joyful, free from all waves of desire, then there is fulfilment. Fulfilment rests within a quality of stillness where no waves are rising and no ripples are being blown; your peace of mind rests within 'no mind'. The ease, bliss and magic of this moment of stillness is what you are returning to. In this moment there is joy without reason; now is enough, now is more than enough, now is blissful. Your inner contentment needs no reason. In order to come upon such a moment you must be gentle and patient, playful too. It comes when you are relaxed, not fighting with yourself; it comes when you can watch all that is happening free of all waves of interference across the water of your consciousness. So be free from expectation, because expectation is a mind that is looking for a result, a mind that is still locked up in desire and objective. Don't be impatient or greedy for results, don't try and grab existence otherwise you will fail. The contentment of this moment of stillness will only happen in the total abandonment of the 'me', in self-abnegation, in the total surrender and release of the self.

You Are Awareness

AWARENESS DOES NOT REPEAT THE desires of the ego. Awareness is just there, watching, witnessing, observing, listening, Being. Learning how to find greater clarity of awareness is the essence of all meditation. We can observe the mountains, the busy streets, the child in the sweet shop; it makes no difference what you observe, it is *how* you observe that is important. (The *how* of *no how*, if we are to be specific.) What is important is not the object that you are watching but the quality of your observation, the awareness of the moment. Observation is meditation. Does your observation have your complete and total attention? Are you awake and alert to whatever it is that is seen?

A meditative mind can watch the trees, the people in the streets or the cars on the road with absolute clarity, attention and alertness. There is energy in this watching, when it is clear of all constraint and all distortion. One is alert and awake to everything rather than moving through the day half asleep. To be awake is to be alive, bright, luminous, vital and full of energy, but most of us go through each day asleep to its simple joys. The art of meditation is to take you out of this sleep. It is to bring forward one's alertness and attention to everything – not by cultivating this alertness and attention (in the sense that they are lacking), but by removing all distractions and distortions which block awareness and attention from fully being. Remember that you cannot cultivate what is already perfect; your awareness and attention are unchangeable because these qualities are your true essence. What each of us can do is to see, ascertain and eliminate that which distorts our fundamental essence, pushing aside whatever distracts us from our inherent state of Being.

Meditation is a state of awareness and in awareness you can be walking, running, cycling or even crawling – it does not matter. What matters is that you are not half asleep and inattentive to whatever it is that is happening. The art of attention is the capacity to be alert and aware not only to all that is happening outside of you but also to all that is happening within. The art of attention is the art of meditation, the art of being aware. Awareness is not something that we go out and seize, it is something that we simply allow to be of its own accord. For awareness already is – only it is usually subdued behind the activities of your mind. As long as you are not asleep you are aware because awareness is your inherent state, but the sensitivity of that awareness can range from numb and dull to highly alert and extremely sensitive in more ways than you can ever imagine. Such sensitivity of awareness does not arise from concentration, which intensifies attention into a narrow and confined space. Quite the opposite is true; finely balanced and delicate sensitivity comes from deep relaxation and the openness and freedom that come with this relaxation. This is the relaxation that comes from understanding, where the ego is no longer capable of being hurt or disturbed. You can be relaxed at work, in a meeting, driving in traffic – whatever you're doing and wherever you are you can remain relaxed and 'tuned in'. As long as there is sensitivity within your Being, there can be effortless awareness and alertness in whatsoever you do. Bliss happens only when there is deep relaxation within and a total surrender of the self, including your desire for bliss; it does not prevent you from going about your daily business, but now you do this joyfully. It is a whole new way of living.

You are awareness, but in everyday life this awareness is spread out across so many things. You are distracted by this and that; you are, if you're honest, all over the place. Many of us are dominated by thoughts that send us chasing after this and that, tugging at us as though we were possessed. Remember that you are not your thoughts, and until there is the natural dissolving of thought within awareness you will remain a slave to your own mind. This problem has become so acute in contemporary Western society that many of us are unable to observe without freedom from the field of memory, without freedom from all the baggage that memory contains.

For example, can you observe and be free of all judgement? If this sounds simple enough, let's take a closer look. Someone is dressed most strangely and they are walking towards you – perhaps it is a man in a dress; yes let's assume that a 'trannie' with a beard is walking towards you. Where will this lead? Can you really see this person without any of your views, prejudices or ideas about what is socially acceptable interfering in your mind? This is a simple question. A man is wearing a dress, so what? As long as he is minding his own business, he cannot be said to be harming anyone or anything. You would be surprised at just how quick people are to judge something like this, and at how immature they can be. Try to live and let live, let out a little smile knowing that this man is happy expressing himself. Can you be unmoved or is your mind so narrow that you automatically think this man is a pervert? Examine yourself closely; can you observe and not be offended in any way? If you are offended, remember that it is you who has taken offence because you are identified with your views, and much learning is still needed. If it is human nature to judge in this way, then is pure observation without judgement or distortion even possible? This pure observation is where the 'me' – with all of its baggage and all of its memories – has been forgotten, such that there is only observation. If you are offended, shocked or disturbed by a transvestite walking towards you minding his own business then the 'me' is still present. Pure observation is where the observer is now irrelevant; there is only the observed. In such clarity one can observe another without distortion, judgment, view or prejudice. In such clarity the mind is meditative, capable of non-judgement and aware of what it is to love. If this clarity of pure observation is difficult for most of us in practice, then it is no wonder the world is the way it is today.

Intelligence is Freedom

INTELLIGENCE IS THE ABILITY TO respond to all of life's happenings without having to resort to a blueprint which tells you how to behave or what to do. Instead, you act in accordance to what is happening, free from the distortions and reactions of the mind. Your action is total because you act with clarity; instead of being dependent upon another or importing ideas about what to do from the outside, you are dependent only upon yourself. Meditation reasserts this intelligence, this ability to see the prison of your own thinking, enhancing your sensitivity and attention to everything. By 'everything' we mean not just the tones of what happens on the outside, but also the subtle tones that occur within. Intelligence cuts through all of the indoctrinations that you learnt at school, all of the imported nonsense from religions, politicians, traditions, media and society. It cuts through the distortions of the mind and sees 'what is', as it is. Intelligence sets you free from the traps that society has placed around you, it sets you free from the cages of thinking that you are using as barriers to protect yourself, without realising that these barriers are really your cages. You have imported all kinds of junk from the outside and this rests within your mind as ideas, beliefs, views and judgements which act as barriers between you and your inner Being; barriers in the form of memory and knowledge.

Memory is like a sponge, it mops up everything that it touches, not caring what that is – anything will do, as long as you escape your idea of empty loneliness within. The barriers of the mind block you from the freedom of understanding, while meditation takes you beyond these barriers into freedom; beyond the field of the known, beyond that which always imprisons.

Meditation breaks through memory, knowledge and all that is past, connecting you with that which is present. Meditation negates what is not real – that being the various prisons of thinking within the mind – to enable communion with that which is truly real, with your Being. Something must cut through the periphery if you are to break free into the real. Just look at what the periphery does: you create a prison for yourself when you are locked in the trap of self-consciousness, you create a prison of fear for yourself believing in heaven or damnation. These are prisons that rest only within the mind as creations of the mind. Because you lack courage and are too scared to embrace the new, you do not allow any real possibility for transformation; you are stuck in a prison created by the mind. The ego mind does not like change, it is apprehensive of any kind of disturbance; the mind paralyses your freedom and spontaneity. How then can you ever grow?

Intelligence is the ability to move away from psychological danger; it is to grow and this growth happens as a blossoming of your Being. As humans we blossom in meditation, releasing a sweet fragrance to the world when we open the heart. Mind alone is not enough – it may be intellectual and clever, but what is clever is not pure and clear. Just look at how we have built our world, a world where intellectuals and politicians have dictated policy. The heart is as clear as crystal waters and can always see, but the world lives according to the dictates of the mind and this is why it knows no love. Intelligence blossoms when the heart and the mind operate as one, and in this clarity intelligence is able to recognise the potential for growth, to recognise the fallibility of mind and the imprisoning nature of mind. It is able to discover the freedom of Being. Meditation reconnects you with your inner Being; the sky of awareness that is inherently free of the usual clouds of distortion.

Intelligence wells up within meditation because meditation uncovers and negates that which blocks intelligence; it uncovers all the junk and distortions of the mind. Meditation reconnects you to your Being – to your acuity, your insights, your intuition and your perceptiveness. Now there is beauty because now you are operating from freedom, freedom from the prison of the mind. Now there is integrity as you are operating from a mind in order, a mind without tension and contradiction, a mind that is not looking to gain, a mind of humility. You can clearly see the trap of the field of the known, and with this perceptiveness you are able to stand alone and be happy alone, free from all past conditioning and dependency, happy to be reliant only upon yourself. Most of all, the art of being alone is to be happy and delighted in that aloneness.

When 'you' – but not 'you' – when something still IS and it is not your mind, when awareness is watching all that is happening, all the activity that goes on but is no longer recording, for the first time in life there is freedom. Previously, you 'the observer' may have been looking inside at your emotions recording or looking outside at the garden recording that too, except now there is no longer even observation of these acts of looking, there is just looking. There is simply pure observation without the process of recording. This is not, as is commonly thought, a new, higher witness observing 'you' observing both the emotions and the garden; what some have called the observation of these acts of looking. A higher witness, or an Atman, is simply another form of observer, another 'I', another duality. Instead all of the sensory responses are firing, and when all the senses are fully engaged there is no 'I' present to record. It is simply observation of the whole movement of consciousness, the watching of everything without thought attached to this watching. The observer is the observed; there is just observation. There is no seer and nothing seen, only seeing. This pure observation is your essence. This is the quality of the meditative mind; it is awakened and has returned to its inherent state of clarity. Your essence witnesses all of life – its tensions, struggles and sufferings – and is free of it; in fact it has always been free of it, but you have spent your entire lifetime living in duality. Intelligence is freedom. Freedom happens when the 'you' – and its processes of recording – cease. Intelligence wells up out of your Being – a sentient Being of pure observation. Meditation is the way of Being, and out of meditation comes freedom from the enslavement of mind.

You are meditation; you are this awareness of Being. Meditation is not something that you go out and 'get' and then bolt onto yourself; it is not something that was missing before and now, having practiced this or that technique, you can add it onto yourself. Meditation does not work like that at all. You are born as awareness, you are born already Being – this is what you fundamentally are. You cannot change it, you are either aware or unaware, either awake or asleep. You are awareness, both conscious and unconscious. Meditation is no more than awareness of the real and the real is pure awareness; meditation is awareness, meditation is you, but not 'you' in the sense of you 'the observer'. Meditation is something that flowers within when you get more and more in touch with that which is already within. It blossoms from your Being, like a sweet fragrance that you release as you open up more and more – like a flower, opening itself up to the world as it expresses its Being and its very suchness. You have to understand this about meditation otherwise you will waste years, even decades, caught up following silly methods. Meditation is a growth out of 'what is'. It is awareness becoming more aware, purer and emptier as its distortions lessen.

The Art of Non-Doing

WE DON'T LIKE TO THINK of ourselves as slaves to our thoughts. Perhaps with willpower and discipline we can successfully conquer and suppress our judgements, attachments and desires, but as we have seen, suppression is not freedom. In suppression there remains a duality between one side of the mind and another, between the controller and the controlled, and it is the controlled aspect of the mind which usually dominates our attention. Only if our thoughts can cease and there is observation of the thought processes of the mind without an engagement with those thoughts or a translation through the filter of the past, can there be freedom from the mind. It is this discipline beyond discipline which meditation brings.

> "To think the thought that is unthinkable; to practice the deed that is not doing; to speak the speech that is inexpressible; and to be trained in the discipline which is beyond discipline."
>
> *Buddha*

This sutra should not be viewed as a statement, theory or 'ism', but as a description of a happening. You cannot *think* reality because reality is constantly changing, it is always in the process of making itself anew. Whatever you *think* can only create a world of conclusions, opinions, ideas, imaginations, theories and ideologies; a psychological world of thought which is just as valid as the next man's. In thinking there is thought and that which thought reflects upon or wishes to change. Thought takes it upon itself to create a centre, as the 'me', which then separates itself from thought in order to dominate and control that which it thinks about, as though it were a separate entity. It creates the idea of the 'me' as a coherent and structured centre, attributing to itself a sense of permanency and a periphery of thoughts emanating from that centre of permanency. There is division, duality and separation from what is actual, and this duality then dominates our lives. One part of the mind is always controlling another part of the mind, trying to control its reactions. Where there is a centre there is division; the fragmentation of one aspect of thought that has taken shape to control what is effectively just another aspect of thought. In this division there is inevitably conflict. Where there is division there is control and all control is conflict. But is this division, this duality actually real? Has thought, in creating a centre, created the illusion of this division? It is only the reactions that are real, not the controller of the reactions or the idea of a division. How can that which is not permanent – thought – attribute to itself a sense of permanency? Can you see this? Can you see that the 'me' is just thought and what it creates is also just thought? There is only thought. There is only reaction as desire, fear, anger, jealousy, frustration, loneliness and so on. The centre that you think is real, constant, fixed, is just thought; it is a concept.

One can only *know* reality, and by this we do not mean understanding it intellectually or placing it in the context of knowledge. The only way to know tenderness is to be tender. The only way to know curiosity is to be curious. Reality can only be known existentially and the only way to know reality is to be real, which means to be free of the psychological world of memory, experience and knowledge. Knowledge is useful but knowledge exists in time. The accumulation of knowledge is time and what is of time can never be timeless. Can the false ever inquire into the real; can only the real inquire into the false? There is only one way to come upon Truth and this is not through dependency on the psychological world but by understanding the nature of the psychological world. This is what meditation is all about. To *be* real one must inquire into the false. All falsity comes from thinking; there is never falsity in Being.

'*To practice the deed that is not doing*' is to practice the deed of non-doing. Non-doing is soft and feminine; it is the way of the Tao, and is effortless. Don't do anything at all. What will happen happens when we are non-doing, when awareness is watching whatsoever is happening rather than engaging with what thought thinks about what is happening; when watching is an effortless non-doing. Thoughts will always come and go and you cannot stop them with force. By and by, you will see that your thoughts are nothing to do with you, they come from somewhere else and that 'somewhere' is your personal dream which you've taken to be your life. By and by, you will find that all of this dissolves naturally as you no longer engage, as you move out of your personal dream into what is real, into what is universal; where all personal dreams are universal. This emptying process will continue until there are no more thoughts bobbing up and down on the sea of your consciousness and then one day reality, the universal that is your inner divinity, will well up from within. It is an illumination, the grace and beauty of which is immense and indescribable.

If you are meditating as the 'meditator', this illumination will escape you. Meditation as the meditator is an action, a 'doing'. The non-doing of true, illuminating meditation happens when you are sitting still, not doing and not thinking at all, just Being. In pure Being there is no 'you' present. You were waiting for something, you forget what you are waiting for and your mind just stops; perhaps it will happen then. You were watching wildlife, your mind has stopped defining that wildlife, now your heart is beating at one with the wildlife; perhaps it will happen then. You are lying on your back watching the clouds without thinking about the clouds, the birds or the trees at all, just thinking nothing; just thinking *the thought that is unthinkable*. Perhaps it will happen then.

Illumination can arise at any time. You may have to make an effort at first in order that there is then no longer any need for effort. You first have to understand the futility of effort. Your meditation may take a little discipline and involve some effort at the outset; you have to row a few strokes to get the boat going before you are able to drop the oars. One day, maybe today, as you move further and further away from the self into non-self, as you melt deeper into existence, bliss will come. It will not come if you are waiting for it, it always comes when you least expect it. It is this way because if you are expecting then you are searching and your attention is out there on the horizon looking for a distant shore that exists only within your mind; your attention is not here and now, right with you in the boat where reality is. So don't look for bliss, don't be impatient for it, don't long for it, just be open; then it will happen. The more you are open, the more it happens; it is always this way.

When you are no longer the 'meditator', when there is no motive behind your search, when the dreaming mind has stopped, when you have finally given up seeking, when you are totally Being without the discipline to 'be' and the self is no more, then the connection is made. You will feel it. The rush will flood into you, blissful and sweet! There is no need for anything; it arises in a deep gratitude for life. When the desiring mind is no more and when you are vulnerable and fragile like a dandelion clock, blown into existence by the wind – then it happens.

You cannot seize this illumination; it is soft and gentle, feminine and subtle. Reality is delicate, and your desires push her away. There is nothing to conquer, only surrender; nothing else is needed. Always reality waits for you, waiting for you to give in and this is possible at any and every moment in your life. Yet behind this gentleness and softness there is immense strength, an unfathomable strength that you cannot possibly comprehend. When it arrives, you will speak *the speech that is inexpressible*, not in your words but in your way of Being. Your luminosity and grace will be felt by others, they will feel it when you walk past; your power is internal but others will feel it. This way of Being is so vast and so connected to reality that you will feel joyous, connected, calm and unbounded. Look at the sutra above; it expresses this depth. Understand it and you understand The Way.

In the universe, nothing is personal. Reality is universal; it is where all personal dreams are no more. In reality, all is one. The universe holds trillions of personal dreams, trillions of personal life experiences. To meet with the universe you have to *be* universal, so your private dreams must go. When you awaken from your private dreams, ideas, hopes and beliefs – what you have known as your life – it is there. But to awaken from your personal dream requires a genuine interest to discover what is false. You may have to go to the end of the earth to realise that what you seek can never be found. You have to truly *know* this; it has to be a part of your Being. So search and search until there is no more searching left to do; listen to teachers, be conned by false teachers if this is what you need to do in order to learn, try out all the various techniques, put in all the effort that you can. No effort is ever wasted in the search for Truth if it brings you to realisation. It is when you realise that effort is no longer going to do anything for you, when you have come to the end and realised that there is nowhere left to go, that you finally understand the desiring mind and can transcend it into gratitude.

When you have travelled every corner of the earth looking for liberation only to find nothing there, when you have seen that your efforts to follow various systems and methods have all brought you to nothing, it is then that something remarkable happens. Your effort drops away with the realisation that all the years and years of searching were false. This dropping away is not an intellectual action; it is effortless non-doing. When there is no more effort within you, when your heart and mind have been spent, then you realise that effort is futile. When you realise that any future efforts would be wasted, the effort that you have been putting in for so long will drop of its own accord; not by you, by its own accord. Your effort becomes effortless. You have been everywhere and there is nowhere left to go but here; you have done everything and the only thing left to do is to 'not do'. Your not doing will be your undoing. We are used to associating 'undoing' as something negative, but it is most positive because it is the breakdown of your dream, which is only negative from the perspective of your ego. It is most positive for your freedom. This 'undoing' will break down the process that props up the 'I', allowing meditation to really happen. Meditation does not come from effort but is a happening of no effort. When you are not, when the mind is not of its own accord, when the mind can see that its own activities lead nowhere, then the mind ceases and meditation begins.

> "The doing of non-doing is the greatest doing, and the effort of effortlessness is the greatest effort."
>
> Osho

Meditation: The Art of Being

ARE YOU ABLE TO SWITCH off all the noise between the ears so that more subtle tones can be heard? For this there must be self-acceptance, not in the form of self-affirmation (as we have explained before) but so that we are free of conflict and the need to adjust, so that we can simply be ourselves and enjoy that Being. This is why there must be self-love; this is why meditation only happens in a state of freedom. Without love and freedom meditation is a waste of time. If there is no freedom to simply Be, then you must be doing meditation to reach some sort of goal. How then is it possible for you to just Be, and revel in that Being? If you cannot take joy in your own existence, then you are not meditating. These primary things must be understood.

In the West we hold a perception of meditation as being a rigid practice of concentration and single pointed focus. We imagine scenes of Buddhist monks chanting mantras whilst sitting in awkward positions. If this is your idea of meditation then you are mistaken. How many of us have found that if we sit still and try to meditate, it can last for only a few minutes before our thoughts wander off and start thinking about what to eat for supper, or what to do tomorrow? Minds are like an ocean of thoughts in the form of ideas, concepts and errands; it is never long before something new pops up in front of us. The question is, are we directing our thoughts, are they directing us or can we be free of direction altogether?[1] Meditation highlights the extent of our mental imprisonment; you will be amazed at just how erratic your mind is. To counter this, many of us try to concentrate our minds into a narrow, single-pointed focus of thought. Judging by the wide array of teachers, classes and guide books, it is interesting to observe the extent of misunderstanding worldwide about this, our most natural state of Being. There is no control. The controller can only ever be the controlled, and how is this freedom? Try the age old, simple trick of paying attention to the breath if you wish to break out of this cycle; soon you will forget about the breath altogether, soon you will completely forget yourself.

> "Look within – the rising and the falling. What happiness! How sweet it is to be free!"
>
> *Buddha*

Why do we find such a seemingly simple practice so difficult? The answer, of course, lies with the ego. The ego struggles to keep the mind occupied by grasping onto thoughts as they arise. Thoughts will always arise, but they will only fall if we do not engage with or bind ourselves to them. Rather than forcing thoughts away, yield completely as they arise. If you strive for silence, the ego is grasping and you are not silent. If it is complete silence that you seek, what purpose would this silence serve? Such silence may be just a mask for a whole

---

[1] Please put the book down and meditate for 10 minutes without thinking of the colour purple or of a pig... How did you get on?

host of issues which bubble underneath. Is the world silent? Can we carry our practice out into the world? Consider the purpose of silence in practice; is it just to follow the instructions of some guru, or is it to gain an awareness of our inner nature? If you are caught up in grasping silence, then your mind can never *be* silent. Silence is not the goal; awareness is the goal.

Pure awareness does not arise out of silence if that silence has been a goal, only an effortless silence will help your awareness to become clear. It is awareness that is meditation; meditation is awareness. Silence is not exclusive to meditation, it merely encourages clarity and it is this clarity that is meditative; clarity to ponder and be concerned about the danger of what is false, which is intelligence. It is the purity and clarity of awareness that is the step of freedom. Can there be clarity of total awareness in your mind as you walk through the busy streets of Mumbai? Can there be sensitivity to all that is happening in and around you without attraction or aversion, without preference or prejudice, without any direction at all, where there is total attention to everything within your highly alert and finely tuned sensitivity? Are you sensitive to everything – what you observe, what you hear, what you smell and how the mind perceives this information, without interpretations that distort recognition and thus create reactions? This sensitivity is the beginning of meditation; it is far from complete silence. Then you can meditate as you walk.

> "Silence cannot make a master out of a fool."
>
> *Buddha*

Sitting down to meditation is the practice of sitting still and doing nothing, just Being. Even the word 'practice' here is misleading, for how can you practise what you already are? Sitting next to a bubbling stream, lying down in a meadow basking in the sunshine, leaning up against a tree with your eyes closed just savouring the moment, not doing anything at all, completely chilled out and relaxed; this is meditation. Total relaxation is meditation – no thought, no reaction, just inaction; the birthplace of right action which draws from the intelligence of clarity and love. In this stillness there is joy and freedom; in the releasing of oneself to be more natural and more relaxed, not as an action but as a non-action, one comes to bliss. Just stop, be sensitive and bliss is there, always. Bliss is what existence is built upon. Tuning into existence happens in total relaxation and you can do it at any moment of the day. You can wash the car, you can go out on your roller skates and you can take this relaxation with you wherever you go. The world around you can be hectic, but inside there is this calm and deep relaxation. There is no centre; it comes from nowhere and yet everywhere. It may feel as though there is a centre, like the calm in the eye of a storm or a sense of stillness in your chest which is directly linked to the centre of the earth. This idea of a centre, which many teachers use, is purely metaphorical. Where there is a centre there is a boundary, a frontier and thus limited space, instead of an open, limitless, joyful sense of awareness that is free and truly unbounded.

In meditation there is no direction, there is no focus and attention is not even taken inward. Instead, attention and awareness are simply allowed to Be. This awareness may appear to be internal, but with sensitivity there is the discovery that it can reside outside of you. If you are delicate enough with your sensitivity, you can sit next to a tree and feel something of that tree. There can be a communion with the tree and other life around you – with the birds, the animals, the flowers, the hills and the streams. Suddenly everything feels precious to you, as though it is a part of you. You feel related with the world and where there is this relationship and awareness of interdependence, there is love. You are in love with existence, truly rich and finally free. This way of Being is incomparable; the idea of comparing anything to this is absurd!

A Typical Class

Look into the body and, just at the outset, bring all awareness into yourself, collect it and let it simply be. Fill up the room with love, a love that radiates from your heart centre, a love that appears to well up from within your Being. What is happening is that your heart centre is the first location in the body to whirl ever closer to the true vibration of (non-local) existence; the vibration of pure love. Other centres may give you strength, the ability to see, communicate and so forth, but it is the heart centre that is the master key. Unless the heart centre is open and there is already fulfilment and bliss within you, the spectacular openings of true divinity will remain elusive.

The way is, and has always been, the heart. This is why you feel centred at first, as you gather a sense of a glowing, whirring vortex in the centre of your Being. This idea of a centre is purely perceptual, it is just the beginning.

When attention is simply allowed to be – it is not taken inward or contained under direction, but instead allowed to be wherever it wishes to be – next you become alert to many tingling sensations in your toes, in your earlobes, from your fingertips; that little buzz at the very tips. If you do not feel this at first, in time you will and in time the sensations become ever more blissful as the buzz moves up into your arm, your shoulders and your torso. It ascends up past your legs and into the belly; it descends downwards from the top of your head in a similar manner to the sensation of dripping water from wet hair except the water is now the nectar of bliss and is unfathomably more delightful. Such rushes make the hairs on the back of your neck stand up. Something is beginning to happen, and you remember glimpsing something like this before. It was on that mountain top! It was looking at that sunset! It was at that gig in anticipation of watching your favourite band! Only now it is different, those moments in the past were just your first clues, now it is much more intense; something larger than you is happening. More and more your bliss can be; there is no boundary to that bliss, there is no limitation. In time you can zing in an orgasm that is so sweet, you no longer feel that you are in the body at all.

In the meantime be sensitive to all the subtle tones of sensation that arise and fall within the body. Fine-tune the attention within yourself, not through the effort of focus but through effortless surrender. Relax and be more gentle, open and sensitive to all sensations without identifying with those sensations. The more you do this, the more you will find your body's own equilibrium and inner harmony.

Watch your thoughts, be aware of their nature and understand their origins. Just as everything else in reality, thoughts will arise and fall away. There is nothing to be done but simply watch; watch all thought, feeling and emotion within. This observation will bring about balance, calming the distortions of your chaotic mind until, by and by, there will be accord within you. You will no longer be a slave to the multiple directions of thought going on inside you, pushing you one way and pulling you the other. There is observation, free from identification and all the travail that comes with that. Now you are free of all that activity and an inner calm and quality of stillness descends upon you.

Now you can see every activity within with clarity, you can go to the end of emotions and understand where they arise. What was once the observer of only outside objects and inner sensations has now become the observed. The observer has become the observed; there is just observation. Such a mind is a meditative mind, an awakened mind that has returned to its inherent state of clarity. What begins as a perceptual centring and funnelling exercise for your attention can now be set free as attention without direction, as awareness that is choiceless and without centre. Out of this awakening there is contact with Truth; there is freedom which brings with it joy, serenity and bliss.

With this quality of awareness the mind is meditative, no matter where you are or what you are doing. Once you get used to being in this stillness, to being highly sensitive to the suchness and quiddity of each and every moment, you take this sense of deep relaxation with you everywhere you go in daily life. Think of the tranquillity in the eye of a hurricane.

What is going on around you could be total chaos, it could be very hectic indeed, yet you remain unmoved and unshaken by any of it. You are still and calm inside, fully intelligent in your ability to respond. Everything within will be calm, as if reality is playing itself out in slow motion around you.

You are like a fly on the wall, just observing the theatre of life unravel itself in front of you. Understand that you cannot practise Being, you cannot practise relaxation, you can only have purer, *clearer observation and sentient awareness of this, your natural state. So meditation is not something that you do, it is something that you are. All that can be 'done' about meditation is to understand it. In this understanding you will find that when you can just Be without doing or thinking anything at all, there is nothing but elation and euphoria for this is your natural state. Reality is ecstatic; it is built upon the joy and euphoria of its own ISness, just as you are.*

It is the movements of your mind which separate you from this euphoria, and create time. They are like a canvas between you and existence, a distortion which clouds your awareness of the essence of existence. This distortion separates you from reality and so you feel cut off from your natural state of bliss. It is this disconnection that drives your desire to recapture bliss – through sex, drugs, food, God, addiction or whatever it is that you seek. Remember that the whole idea of fulfilment through something external is fundamentally driven by the desire to return to bliss. It is this disconnection from bliss – and your unawareness of this disconnection – that drives every aspect of all of your activity. The more wrapped up you are trying to recapture your missing bliss through chasing desires, the thicker are the clouds of distortion and distraction between you and reality, between you and your inner Being. Wrapped up in these clouds of distortion, you cannot notice the beauty and intrinsic quality of existence. When the mind is meditative and still, that connection between you and the bliss of existence – and the majesty of existence – is revealed in all its beauty.

Freedom without Practice

THERE IS NO SUCH THING AS HOW TO MEDITATE.

Was there the cessation of self when you were following 'a typical class'? Be honest. The above 'typical class' is both accurate and also inaccurate, disguised in flowery words and inserted to see if you have been paying attention. Dissect it sentence by sentence. Test it out for yourself. Find out what is real and what is not. The author is deliberately disturbing you now because the author is trying to show you something.

How enamoured are we by words? Notice how we each seek a system, a practice or a method to follow in our search for freedom. Do not be fooled by teachers. Do not be fooled by methods or techniques, they are all meaningless. The description is not the described. A technique will not bring one to freedom. A technique will not elicit a true state of love. It is only your understanding that is the intelligence of love, and no teacher has authority over that understanding. There is no such thing as personal salvation, in the sense of something to be achieved. There is no such thing as personal freedom if one is not concerned about humanity as a whole. We are only humanity; we are not, in spite of our thinking, individual. Individual means whole, not broken up into the idea of 'me'. You have been conditioned into believing that the 'me' is real and that the 'me' can be free through some technique, system, structure, dogma or doctrine. What is 'me' and what supports or purports the 'me' can never be free. Let us go into this one last time so we fully understand it, not verbally or intellectually but in our hearts.

Why does the mind fragment itself into parts? Why does the mind create one structure of thought – as ambition, anxiety, jealousy, frustration, antagonism, depression, loneliness and so on – and then create another structure of thought as the 'me', the 'I', the centre, that then sets about overcoming, denying, suppressing or controlling the first structure of thought? Why does the mind divide itself in this way, as the thinker and the thought, between thought and that which thought has created, when there is only thought? This is a question that we must each ask ourselves. If we cannot see why fragmentation occurs we will always be caught in this trap of psychological division and the ensuing conflict. Corruption means being broken up, fragmented, divided, and what is divided will inevitably produce conflict between the 'I' and its ideals, between 'me' and 'you', between 'we' and 'they'. It is because the human mind is so corrupt that there is identification with ideals, like the religious or the political ideal, resulting in the 'me' belonging to one group opposing another, and all the mischief and conflict that results from it.

If we can solve the problem of psychological conflict then all of the outward structures created by humanity can cease. All of our isms, dogmas, doctrines, methods and systems can be rejected. Never has this happened in the past, never has humanity been free of conflict. Surely this is the revolution of our time? Only when conflict has been understood is there love. When conflict and contradiction cease meditation truly begins.

Why does the mind create the psyche, the inner world with all of its characteristics and idiosyncrasies, and then a controller to act upon these elements? Both are thought, there is only thought, but thought is constantly dividing itself. Why? Thought, being impermanent in nature, seeks permanence and so sets about ascribing to itself the quality of permanence. It does this by creating an image, the idea of 'me' that is permanent, that is enduring, because everything else is seen to be transitory. And so the 'me', the 'I', the ego is created as something lasting; an unseen illusion of something fixed, something permanent. In creating the 'I' thought must divide itself. Fragmentation is therefore the mechanism for thought to find security. It is the seeking of security through whatever means – systems, patterns, structures, dogmas, doctrines – that is the very foundation of corruption. To remove the contradiction, to be free of the need for security, to understand that there is no such thing as permanence for the 'me' or the 'I', this is the foundation of meditation. Then there is observation without the word, without the image that thought creates; seeing without memory, without recording, without being caught in the ego trap of experience, knowledge, memory, thought, action, reaction; a cycle in which most of us are stuck. Then there is discovery that is free of the past. Then there is resurrection.

There cannot be preparation for meditation. There is no system, method or practice to undertake, no breathing exercises, postures or mind control techniques that must be followed. Systems, methods and practices are the creation of human thought. Some guru has meditated, reached a state that he considers to be free, and then invented a system to reach it. Can you see how absurd this is? How can a mind make such a claim, how can a mind ever know the state of freedom when the mind itself is not free, the mind being fragmentation and therefore conflict? The mind is the product of time, a product of the known. How can that which is the product of time ever know that which is timeless? A consciousness that is aware of its own freedom is never free. Remember, there is no such thing as how to meditate.

As soon as you ask 'How?', who is asking and who is implementing the imported technique? No practice, method, discipline, sacrifice, subjugation, sublimation or act of determination can ever reach freedom. Freedom is not something to be achieved, it is not a reward brought into being though control, suppression, compulsion or by repeating the practices of some guru. Virtue and discipline will not bring freedom into being. You cannot go to freedom; it doesn't come to you, as many have stated, since there is no 'you' there to receive it. You only receive it, or rather the 'I' – the observer – receives it, when there is partial perception of 'what is'. The 'I' itself is partial, built upon contradiction. But in total perception of 'what is' with all the senses, there is only 'what is'. There is only observation of whatsoever is happening both in you and around you; what is within and without are not separate. All the sensory responses are firing and fully illuminated. There is no recorder, no self-recognition. In complete perception there is no recording, no 'you' present to record. The observer is the observed. There is an integrated wholeness; an indivisibility in the art of observation. So meditation is a happening, it is not a thing that the mind can define, name or label. First the truth of this must be understood. Only in the complete abnegation, absolving and dissolving of all self-centred activity, which includes all of the techniques that humanity has invented, is there freedom. What we are discussing is the complete loosening and acquittal of all chains of thinking, something that is free of all bondage. For freedom to be you must cease and this is the only true meditation.

A system, method or practice, perhaps in the form of a chant or a mantra or a breathing exercise or that age old system of thought control, all of these are premeditated. Real meditation can only ever be unpremeditated, the unpremeditated art of Being. What is unpremeditated is free of time. Not only is this logic, but it can also be tested and proved by you, for yourself.

We have discussed the idea of control being abandoned; control in the form of identification with a word or a symbol and then an aspect of thought taking shape to concentrate on that, or perhaps thought fragmenting itself into contradictory parts as the controller and the controlled, with one part subjugating the other. We have discussed the futility of all this, the conflict that comes with psychological fragmentation; thought taking shape as the 'I' in order to control and subjugate that which thought thinks about (which is another structure of thought) as though they were separate from one another. We have also discussed the petty numbing of the mind through the repetition of a mantra or chant, a mere slogan created by thought. We have discussed the danger of being caught up in systems because they provide psychological pleasure, like in an Ashram where the residents end up swapping one attachment for another. If meditation is psychological satisfaction, then we have reduced meditation into a product of thought, to mere sensation, which it clearly cannot be. We go on meditation retreats because they provide quietude from daily life, a temporary escape from the stress of modern living. Is meditation an escape from daily living? Is meditation separate from life – your work, your family, your inner emotions – or can meditation be more than this? Surely meditation is the whole, undivided, non-fragmented, awareness of every aspect of living. Perhaps we meditate in the morning to find stillness to carry into our day, something that we have created to escape life or to be more efficient and effective. If this is so, then we are using meditation in a process of becoming, which is not meditation. So why should we meditate, at all? Is it part of your idea of what should be? If it is, then you have made meditation into a product of your conditioning.

Real meditation is to be free of all conditioning. It is the put aside all that has ever been said about meditation – silence, eternity, timelessness and so on (descriptions which are never the described and therefore utterly otiose and vain) – and discover the art of unpremeditated being for yourself. Can you throw away all human traditions, all traditions that require adherence to certain sets of rules or to a dogmatic structure? Remember the conflict and mischief that arises in our relations to such structures. Can you deny all of your Hindu and Buddhist practices, knowing that they are the creations of human thought? Can you deny the guru you have served for so long? Meditation is to be free of all dependency, to be free of all the knowledge that you have accumulated over time and also humanity's knowledge. One must not be psychologically dependent upon anything, for if you are psychologically dependent upon something – a system, a structure or a pattern – then of course there can be no freedom.

There is no meditation without freedom. You must be free of fear, have understood the nature of despair and desolation if freedom is to be. This cannot be enforced because the enforcer must either become hard, callous or self-determined, a process which is isolating in nature. Meditation is not isolation, it is very the opposite of isolation – it is love and freedom. Freedom must be absolute, for there is no such thing as partial freedom. This means to be free of everything that anyone has ever said about meditation. For whatever humanity has devised, or described, it is not the thing, it is not the actual. The word or description of meditation is not meditation. Only meditation is meditation, meditation being also discovery. And there is no meditation without love or compassion. You cannot shortcut your understanding of love with effort in the form of some silly technique, a trick created by the mind. If you are corrupt, if you lack integrity, if you are immoral then your meditation will become a self-projected illusion; it will become an attachment.

Meditation begins with love because meditation is love. Love is not a practice; it is a state of intelligence and deep understanding of one's consciousness and therefore the consciousness of humanity. The fallibilities of the human mind are then seen. To come to love you must be psychologically free of all conflict, all fragmentation, and there cannot be any dependency. Only when such a state of understanding exists will you be able to put aside all that you have ever heard and enter a whole new dimension of understanding. Practices, systems, methods, postures and so on, only exist because humans are greedy. We want to arrive at a state which the mind has decided is desirable, and it is because we desire that we have no humility. Only in humility is the brain truly quiet and able to see clearly. Humility is unbroken, whole, holy. Only when the hole in the heart, the hole that we seek to fill but never will if we desire or try to fill it with accumulated knowledge, only when this hole can close, when the heart is made whole and undivided in deep humility, can meditation truly begin.

It is because we lack humility that there is very little beauty in our lives, the beauty of clear discovery. Meditation is the discovery of 'what is' when 'what is' is seen so very clearly, away from our need to become or achieve. Humility does not create freedom, it is freedom; a wholeness and integrity that cannot be broken. Then there is beauty in life, a deep gratitude and appreciation for the world. Then life becomes a blessing, an everlasting beatitude, something deeply sacred and whole.